ALSO A FEATURE FILM

JOEL GILBERT

THE TRAYVON HOAX

Unmasking the Witness Fraud that Divided America

Published and Distributed by Highway 61 Distribution, LLC

ISBN: 978-1-64293-396-3

ISBN (eBook): 978-1-64293-397-0

The Trayvon Hoax

Unmasking the Witness Fraud that Divided America

Highway 61 Entertainment, LLC

Los Angeles

highway61ent.com

Published in the United States of America

thetrayvonhoax.com

CONTENTS

For The LORD hates a heart that devises wicked plans,
a false witness who
breathes out lies,
and who sows discord
among brothers.

— Proverbs 6:16-19

PROLOGUE

As a filmmaker, I did not set out to write a book. I set out to produce a documentary about the rise of Florida politico Andrew Gillum. Even after I thought a book would be useful, I certainly did not expect to write *this* book. But I have done so, along with a documentary feature film of the same name.

The more I looked into Gillum's success, however, the more need I saw to investigate the unanswered questions of the criminal case upon which Gillum built his career. I had followed the 2012 shooting death of seventeen-year-old Trayvon Martin and the subsequent trial of George Zimmerman from afar and, like many others, I had grave concerns about the lynch mob mentality that drove the case.

The shooting and trial took place in Sanford, Florida. I intended to visit Sanford, but this investigation took me places I never expected to go. From the back alleys of Little Haiti in Miami to the bucolic campus of Florida State University in Tallahassee, I got an earful and an eyeful. I met George Zimmerman as I had hoped to, but I ended up centering both the documentary and this book on a young woman I did not even know existed when I started the project.

In getting to know this woman–"Diamond"–I was introduced to Miami's urban youth culture, a culture that thrives on some mix of sex, drugs, gangs, texting, clubbing, shopping, and social media. Diamond's particular Haitian-American milieu featured its own unscrupulous subspecialty: identity switching. Only after I started the project did I realize I had stumbled into the most spectacular case of identity fraud in modern American judicial history. The fraud resulted in the seminal race hoax of the Obama years. I call it "The Trayvon Hoax." As shall become clear, no one has suffered more from this ongoing hoax than the black youth of America.

As shall become clear too, any number of interested parties profit from such hoaxes. The railroading of George Zimmerman, for instance, helped Trayvon Martin's biological parents shift the blame from their parenting deficiencies to a racial scapegoat. They extracted a huge settlement from a homeowners association and cashed in on book and movie deals. Their attorney, Benjamin Crump, got his slice of the insurance payout and forged a national identity as a civil rights champion. The old school race hustlers like Al Sharpton and Jesse Jackson reestablished their relevance and refreshed their cash flow. Of even greater significance, politicians like Gillum and President Barack Obama successfully exploited Trayvon Martin's death to harvest votes and win elections–power!

If there is a main culprit in this story, however, I would argue that it is the press. The Zimmerman case was ground zero for the explosion of fake news and the race hoaxes that have followed, one more preposterous than the next. Think "hands up don't shoot" or the beyond preposterous Jesse Smollett racial "attack" by Trump supporters, a hoax so phony only the media could fall for it.

We expect individuals to be greedy and exploitive, politicians especially. It is the nature of the beast. As their very mission, however, the media are charged with shining light on political schemes. Time and again, however, the media have betrayed their craft. On the subject of race, they do so routinely. It is appalling that six years after the Zimmerman trial so much information was left for me, an independent filmmaker, to discover.

If the media had wanted to find the truth, it was there for the plucking. I was able to uncover it simply by reading publicly available information from the legal proceedings and following up on what I read. How is it possible no one in the media chose to do what I did? The answer is simple. The media did not want to know. The truth would not have advanced their fear-fueled racial agenda.

The power of Investigative Journalism is the ability to set the record straight, to change history for the better by shedding light on facts and exposing lies and liars. Can anyone even remember the last major investigation broken by a major news organization? I can't. In an odd way, I suppose I should thank our lazy and disingenuous friends in the media for making it possible for an independent film maker like myself to tell this incredible story. My hope is to show how politicians and the media have pulled us apart, when our true aspirations have always been to come together as one nation.

So, sit back and stay calm, or at least try to. You are about to see how America got played by an epic race hoax that divided us for no reason and, alas, just keeps on killing.

Joel Gilbert
July 2019

1

TELL MAMA 'LICIA I'M SORRY

In Sanford, Florida, on the night of February 26, 2012, 28-year-old George Zimmerman shot and killed 17-year-old Trayvon Martin. This is the one fact on which everyone agrees.

With his dying breath, Trayvon Martin made a final, desperate request of the man who shot him, "Tell Mama 'Licia I'm sorry." I was the first person in the media with whom George Zimmerman shared Trayvon's last words. On hearing George reveal this, I had to rethink the direction of a documentary I was planning on the unexpected rise of Florida politico Andrew Gillum, the 2018 gubernatorial candidate who had repeatedly cited the Trayvon Martin case as the reason for his success. As with Citizen Kane's dying "Rosebud," I was convinced that if I could decipher the meaning of Trayvon's last request, I could find my way to the heart of the case, maybe even to the dynamic behind Gillum's rapid ascent.

In the way of background, a week before the Florida gubernatorial primary in August 2018, pollsters had Gillum coming in third behind two more moderate Democrats. But then again, what Democrats weren't more moderate than the openly radical socialist Tallahassee mayor? Then, lo and behold, Gillum surged past both opponents and won the Democrat primary. In the November election, he lost the race by only a hair to Republican Ron DeSantis.

Gillum intrigued me. The more closely I explored Gillum's history, the larger the Trayvon Martin story loomed. Indeed, a *City Lab* article published the day after his primary win began, "Last night Andrew Gillum became the first African-American candidate to win the Democratic Party nomination for Florida governor and it's not out of the question to say that he can thank Trayvon Martin for that."

Thank Trayvon Martin? What a cold-blooded way, I thought, to explain a politician's success. Cold-blooded or not, there was apparently some truth to it. Throughout the campaign, Gillum made provocative comments about race, such as "I've always been black, I was born black and as far as I know I will die black." Another doozy was, "I'm not saying Ron DeSantis is a racist, I'm just saying the racists think he's a racist." Gillum often spoke of the Trayvon Martin shooting, linking it to Florida's "Stand Your Ground" law.

I had followed the Zimmerman case closely enough to know that virtually everything Gillum said was wrong. Zimmerman's acquittal had nothing to do with Stand Your Ground which wasn't even used by his attorneys; rather it was a case of traditional self-defense. This wasn't even a matter of debate. Gillum knew this, yet he had been stoking racial paranoia among blacks since the trial. He wasn't about to stop when it could benefit him most. Trayvon's mother, Sybrina Fulton, endorsed Gillum and made frequent appearances at his campaign rallies for governor.

Maybe it was true that Gillum's improbable run all started with Trayvon Martin. So, I started thinking, who was Trayvon Martin really? What was Trayvon's true legacy? To understand Gillum's success, I needed to understand the Trayvon Martin case. That is why I spoke with George Zimmerman and how I learned about Trayvon's Mama 'Licia, whom I identified as his stepmother Alicia Stanley. In exploring Trayvon's relationship with her, I came to see Trayvon's life as a series of betrayals, one more crushing than the next. The media shielded the public from this information. It did not fit their agenda.

On the day of his death, Trayvon feared one more betrayal, this from the girl he knew as "Diamond," the girl who had stolen his fragile heart, the girl with whom he was on the phone up to the very minute he died, the girl who would emerge, in various forms, as the "star witness" in the case against George Zimmerman. Indeed, it was Diamond's recorded phone interview with Martin family attorney Benjamin Crump that prompted George Zimmerman's arrest and the subsequent 2013 trial. The massive racial turmoil stirred up by media coverage of the shooting followed.

In my quest to learn more about this mystery girl, Diamond, something unexpected happened. I found myself being pulled down a mysterious side road, a dark one. To understand Gillum, to understand Florida, to understand Trayvon, I would have to travel this road of many unexpected turns. At the end of it, I would discover, was hard evidence of an epic and ultimately lethal deception, a stunning witness fraud that divided America. For lack of a better name, I have come to think of this grand deception as "The Trayvon Hoax."

2

THE ZIMMERMAN DECEPTION

AT A HOTEL ON LAKE MARY, just south of Sanford, Florida, I watched carefully as a bearded man walked in. He was wearing shades, a US Marines cap, and an old camouflage jacket. He looked all the world like a grizzled Vietnam veteran. I approached him, held out my hand tentatively, and said, "George?"

I was the only one in the lobby who knew the man was George Zimmerman. He had warned me on the phone that he had to circulate in a disguise for his own safety, and this was it, fake beard and all. I never would have recognized him without the heads up.

More than six years after the shooting, George had reason to be cautious. Rap mogul Jay-Z's six-part TV series had aired just months earlier, amplifying the narratives spread in 2012 about Zimmerman as a "racist loose cannon." Scarier still, Jay-Z added a line to a recent release by the hip-hop artist Drake that amounted to something like a *fatwa*. It basically chastised Floridians for allowing Zimmerman to live.

On first meeting, George–I will call all the key characters by their first name–seems smaller than you might expect, 5' 6", maybe 5' 7", more than half-a-foot shorter than Trayvon Martin was at the time of his death. Yes, he looks Hispanic, whatever that means. He is soft spoken and unfailingly polite–'yes sir, no sir.' His father Bob Zimmerman, a career Army non-com and Vietnam veteran, taught George and his siblings not just manners but values. His mother Gladys, a strong-willed, educated and intelligent Peruvian immigrant, reinforced them.

Almost everyone heard something about George's life after the trial: the altercations with girlfriends, the threats against Jay-Z's investigator, the general disorder. However, other than one bar fight in his distant past, few know anything about George's life before the shooting. The media did not want anyone to know.

In attempting to explain the nature of his early life, George spoke of one memorable image that put his life in perspective. The image was of a naked toddler chasing a chicken across a dirt road. This was not something he saw in a magazine or witnessed in Peru, where his mother took him from time to time to learn about his roots.

No, this sighting was in Apopka, Florida. At the time, on alternate weekends, George was driving to Apopka to mentor "my two kids," Casey and Koko, African American siblings whose father was in prison for life. They were barely in their teens. In their neighborhood, a chicken-chasing naked toddler barely merited a second glance. For George, the image reinforced his desire to work with these needy minority kids.

Before the shooting of Trayvon Martin, George thought of himself as "something of a nerd." He had been working for Digital Risk as a forensic fraud auditor full time since July of 2009. In the evenings, he went to either the gym or school and sometimes both. George was working toward a degree in criminal justice, but never did get his degree. After the New Black Panthers called in a bomb threat, the school quietly "withdrew" him.

On Saturdays, George split his time between the gym and homework. On Sundays he did "God's work." Although not a regular churchgoer, he did the kinds of things he hoped God would approve of, mentoring the distressed kids in Apopka and tending to the homeless in Sanford. He was a liberal social activist, both walking the walk and talking the talk.

Back then George had a plan, and it was pretty simple: "I aspired to be a good Christian, a good citizen, a good neighbor, a good husband, and one day, a good father," said George. "God had plans for me, I knew. He would take care of me."

Given the image of George in the major media, I knew I had to speak to him in person to get a sense of who was telling the truth about who he was, his supporters or his critics. We spoke for about an hour that first evening at the hotel. Before launching a formal interview, I wanted to assess his reliability and make sure he was comfortable with me and I with him.

Early the next morning George met me and my camera crew at a public park on Lake Monroe in Sanford. We had scouted out the spot the afternoon before, and it appeared to be almost totally isolated. Given our security concerns, it seemed an ideal location. It wasn't. Although the morning was unusually cool for Florida even in December–about 45 degrees–the entire area now bustled with people. They were walking dogs, jogging, fishing, eating breakfast on the benches, and heading for work. Plus, there were many cars passing by, some repeatedly. Camera crews always attract attention, and attention was just what I was afraid of attracting.

Sure enough, during the interview, people started to stare, and they were zeroing in on George. One black woman in a Toyota drove by multiple times. Upon spotting her, George would turn his head away, but I think she recognized him. We were right there in Sanford where, among African Americans, the media-stoked rage still simmered. We agreed on an escape plan. If someone menacing approached, we would take off toward the back door of an adjacent retirement center. Barring that, we would soldier on. George said he was tired of living in the shadows.

In the interview, I hoped to get George's up close and personal take on several key issues. I had heard that George had been a Democrat before the incident. He shyly admitted this was true, and he had been an Obama supporter as well. "I'd been caught up in the promises of hope and change," he told me ruefully. He told me too about his planned life of service and confirmed just how seriously he took his mentoring work with the two black youngsters in Apopka. His time with them, he said, was mostly "to let them know they were important, that they mattered to me."

A social activist, George told me about his role in the Sherman Ware case. The media's failure to cover his role in standing up for the homeless Sherman Ware was more egregious than I imagined. In December 2010, a little more than a year before the Trayvon Martin shooting, George happened upon a local news report that showed a drunken man, the son of police lieutenant, sucker punching a black homeless guy. George had searched the Internet to see what the consequences were. There were none. Nothing happened. It was George who then made the case happen. "I felt it was wrong," he told me. "I decided I would take up my time, my resources to print up a flier I had written myself."

Sunday after Sunday he distributed the fliers, printed on yellow and pink fluorescent paper, placing them on windshields in the parking lots of Sanford's black churches. On a few occasions he stopped by the social gatherings after church services and talked to the congregants.

The color of the paper mattered. On the fliers George had asked people to attend the next town hall meeting and make their presence felt. When George got to the meeting, he was heartened to see many in the crowd waving his glowing pink flier in their hands. After George addressed the city commissioners indignantly about the lack of action in Sherman Ware case, several Ware supporters came up to him and patted him on the back. George's impassioned speech supporting Ware was captured on audio, but after the shooting no media outlet would play it. George's civil rights activism on behalf of a homeless black man and his mentoring of black kids belied the media's framing of him as a racist for their agenda.

In the weeks after the shooting, the media repeated the mindless mantra that George Zimmerman was a thuggish vigilante, an unhinged wannabe cop, or, as the Martin family lawyers insisted from their very first press release, "a loose cannon." If this characterization was false, I wanted to know from George what prompted him to join the neighborhood watch at the townhome community in which he lived, The Retreat at Twin Lakes.

Next, George told me of an incident involving a young neighbor couple that he particularly liked, Michael and Olivia Bertalan. They lived about five doors down from George and his wife, Shellie. The Bertalans had a baby boy, not yet one-year-old. A few months before George's world collapsed, Shellie called him at work, her voice trembling with fear.

"Something terrible happened," she told him. George asked her to elaborate. She was not sure what caused the police cars to flood the neighborhood, but they were now surrounding the Bertalan's townhouse. Still, that did not fully explain her anxiety. George inquired as to why was she so shaken, and Shellie told him, "I think they saw me."

George asked her, "Who saw you?"

She replied, "the bad guys."

Still confused, George wanted to know if she was okay.

"I think so," Shellie said, "but I don't want be home alone right now." She wanted George to come home, but she knew he could not afford to take the time off. And although not eager to drive given the state of her nerves, Shellie thought she could safely make it to her father's house.

Once the plan was settled, George asked Shellie to explain who these "bad guys" were. She told him she had been standing in front of the kitchen sink washing dishes with the blinds open when she saw two young black men run through their fenceless backyard carrying what appeared to be electronics equipment. She saw one of the pair drop something near her window. When he stopped to pick it up, he made eye contact with Shellie and stared at her for a brief moment before taking off. She feared these two men had something to do with the police activity at the Bertalan's home.

When George got home that evening, he stopped by Michael and Olivia's house to see if they were okay. Olivia explained she had been upstairs when she heard knocking at the front door. Not expecting visitors, she looked down from the nursery window and saw two unknown young black men at her front door. She chose not to respond and remained quiet inside her home with the baby. Suddenly, Olivia heard someone messing with the sliding glass door that led to her backyard. At this point Olivia decided to call the police.

While she was on the phone with the 911 dispatcher, the unthinkable happened. The men forced their way in through the sliding glass door and started rummaging through the first floor of the house. Olivia held her baby tightly in her arms and desperately pleaded with the dispatcher for help. The dispatcher instructed her to lock the bedroom door. When she heard the men storm up the stairs, Olivia clung to the phone as a lifeline and begged for advice.

The 911 dispatcher asked if she had a weapon handy. Olivia looked around in a panic. All she could find was a rusty pair of sewing scissors. The dispatcher told her to grab the scissors and prepare to resist even with the baby still in her arms. Just as the men reached her room and started wrestling with the doorknob, the doorbell rang. The dispatcher told her it was the police. At the sound of the doorbell, the men rushed down the stairs, out the back, and through The Retreat's shared backyards. That was when Shellie must have seen them, and they her.

Returning home, George told Shellie about Olivia's home invasion. He insisted she talk to the police and give them an accurate description of the suspects since she saw them more clearly than Olivia had. But Shellie was afraid. George couldn't blame her.

"What if they come back?" she pleaded. "What if I have to testify? They'll know it was me, and we would be next if they retaliate."

Shellie thought their best option was to move. There had been other burglaries in the community, other home invasions. Their "gated community" was not quite as "gated" as advertised. The developers never got around to building a wall on its North flank. George told Shellie moving was out of the question. Between work and school, he would not have the time to pack up and move. Besides, there was no guarantee their new home would be any different or better.

Shellie begged George to "do something." There was no clear solution. They lived in a "gated" community. They had an alarm system. They had a dog. A short time earlier, on the advice of an animal control officer and a cop, George had bought pistols for Shellie and himself to deal with a problem not usually associated with gated communities–unattended and uncontrolled pit bulls.

In reviewing options, George remembered that the entrance and exit of the neighborhood had clearly posted "Neighborhood Watch" signs. Hoping to put Shellie's mind at ease, George told her he would attend the next homeowners association (HOA) meeting and find out about the watch program.

A short time later, George's heart sank when he came home and saw a moving truck in front of the Bertalan's townhouse. Michael was packing up his family's belongings. In the way of explanation, he told George that Olivia felt violated by the incident and no longer felt safe.

At the next HOA meeting, when the time came for questions from the residents, George asked how to sign up for the neighborhood watch e-mail list. The HOA officers look puzzled. They explained there no longer was a neighborhood watch program. After some back-and-forth, the HOA president asked George if he wanted to coordinate the program. Having told Shellie he would do whatever he could to make her feel safe again, he could hardly turn the offer down. George wanted to be a good neighbor, a good citizen, a good Christian. As he had posted on the fliers for the black churchgoers after the Sherman Ware incident, George believed, "The only thing necessary for the triumph of evil is for good men to do nothing."

Said George of his wife Shellie, "I was willing to do anything to give her comfort." In retrospect, he regrets that he did not pick up and move, which was what Shellie really wanted. How different his life would have been had he done so.

3

INCIDENT REVISITED

IN THAT THE media had done a thorough job misleading the public about George Zimmermann and his neighborhood, I had no reason to believe they had done a more honest job reporting on the incident that made George infamous. For his part, George proved more than willing to correct some media disinformation. Prior to the home invasion, he had no interest in the Neighborhood Watch program. Nor was he driving on a patrol the night in question. He never did because there was no such thing as a patrol in the Neighborhood Watch program. George was driving to Target to buy lunch meat for the week ahead when he saw "a man skulking about in between the houses." He stopped his car and called the non-emergency police number as he had been instructed to do. If it had not been raining, he might have kept on driving. What troubled him was that the man, Trayvon Martin, was making no effort to get out of the rain.

As to why he got out of his vehicle, George explained that the dispatcher asked several times in which direction Trayvon had gone. Sitting in his vehicle, George had no idea and said he felt obligated to assist the dispatcher who wanted specifics on where the man was heading. Trying to be helpful, George said he exited his pickup truck and simply walked in the direction he had last seen Trayvon. "I never saw Trayvon at all during that time," George told me. In any case, he stopped walking in Trayvon's direction when the dispatcher suggested he not. There was no way George was going to catch up with him in any case.

Instead, George walked across the east-west cut-through between the streets to get an address on the far street where he could meet the police. When he saw car lights back by his vehicle, he walked back in that direction, thinking it was a police car. As George approached his truck, Trayvon surprised him at or near the intersection of the long north-south dog walk behind the townhouses and the cut-through between the streets. George had not seen Trayvon since before he had gotten out of his truck.

The details of what happened next are well known to the people who wanted the truth, and I will provide more detail later in the book, but to hear George tell the story is chilling. Approaching George from the rear, Trayvon called out to him, "Do you gotta problem?" When George replied no and reached down to grab his cell phone to call 911, Trayvon closed the space between them in a heartbeat and punched him hard in the nose, breaking it.

Disoriented by the sucker punch, his eyes watering from the broken nose, George had no chance to fight back. Trayvon quickly wrestled him to the ground. With George's body on the grass and his head on a concrete sidewalk, Trayvon knelt on top of him and started pummeling him mixed martial arts style, and slammed his head repeatedly against the concrete as well.

Hoping the police were nearby or that a neighbor might intervene, George yelled "help" repeatedly as loud as he could. It was his voice that 911 calls picked up. The prosecutors knew this from the beginning. The closest neighbor, Johnathan Good, heard the mayhem from his living room and slid open his patio door. From his patio, about 30 feet away, Good yelled, "Stop! I'm calling the police!"

Despite this, Trayvon did not stop raining blows. Good retreated back into his townhome. This is when George got really scared. The neighbor's threat to call the police did not dissuade the attacker at all. To silence George, Trayvon put one hand over his mouth and punched with the other. "I had blood going my throat and he was trying to smother me." With the blood from his broken nose running down his throat, George was having trouble breathing and thought he might choke to death.

Fearing he might go unconscious, George shimmied off the concrete sidewalk to protect his head from being further slammed against it. As he did, his coat rode up on his chest, exposing the gun in his belt holster. George had all but forgotten he had a gun. Otherwise defenseless, he had endured at least forty-seconds of head blows before reaching for it.

George fired one shot. "I was simply trying to stop the attack," he told me. He had no idea where the shot went. He feared the bullet might have pierced the wall of one of the townhouses. Then suddenly, Trayvon sat up and said something like, "You got it" or "You got me." George doubted he'd shot him, and felt Trayvon was simply stating he was giving up the onslaught because George had a gun. When George pushed him off to the left though, he knew the bullet had stuck him as Trayvon slumped face down, mumbling.

I asked George if Trayvon had said anything understandable in those final moments. "Yes," said George. "He said, 'Tell Mama 'Licia I'm sorry.'" It was not until much later that George learned about whom Trayvon was talking, namely his stepmother Alicia Stanley. Trayvon's final words told a story in themselves. George had not gone public with this information before, nor even told his attorneys.

I asked George how he felt about shooting someone, especially a seventeen-year-old. "I was absolutely devastated," he told me. Trayvon, he learned, was not unlike the two kids he was mentoring, just a little older and troubled in different ways. "He was the kind of kid I would have wanted to help," he said.

If anything, the aftermath of the shooting tested George more than did the shooting itself, but not at first. "I had a lot of faith in the justice system," said George, who studied criminal justice and at one time aspired to be a police officer. He appreciated the treatment he received at the hands of the Sanford Police, and he obliged them every way he could, including agreeing to multiple interviews, a voice stress test, and a reenactment of the incident on site–all without a lawyer present.

As the outside pressure grew, however, George began to wonder whether the justice system would hold up underneath it. It did not. When President Obama announced to the world, "If I had a son, he would look like Trayvon," George knew he was in trouble. George had voted for Obama. "I was disgusted and disheartened," he told me, "frankly, because I thought I was one of them."

From the beginning, George understood what was at stake in the game President Obama was playing: the State of Florida's twenty-nine electoral votes in the upcoming November 2012 election. George told me the whole drama turned on his name. His mother's intention was to name him the Spanish version of George, Jorgé, after her brother. But while his mother was still recovering from the birth, his father wrote "George" on the birth certificate. The media, George understood, would have wanted no part of an incident involving a "Trayvon" and a "Jorgé." Said George, "In my opinion if I had been named Jorgé, this would never have made the national radar." I could not disagree.

"Emotionally, the trial was very devastating on me," George told me. Although acquitted, he had little chance to enjoy his exoneration. From the President on down, the people who had been demanding "just an arrest" refused to accept the trial verdict of the justice system. Innocent or not, George would get no relief from their hatred. When he pulled a family of four from a burning vehicle on a Florida interstate not long after the trial, he was accused of staging the incident. In 2015, when a man tried to assassinate George and missed shooting him by inches, the media ignored the incident or blamed George.

His life in disarray, unable to get a job or even have a fixed address, George started acting out. "I kind of internalized all this negative attention," he admitted. "If people were going to label me as such a bad person and a jerk, I was going to show them just how bad I could be." A series of incidents followed, including a messy divorce and some inopportune rows with girlfriends, all publicized, all used to discredit the verdict. He told me, "it took me a few years to work through it and get back to being the person that I was." George used the occasion of our filmed conversation to apologize to his supporters "for being a knucklehead."

After the interview, my camera crew and I headed for The Retreat at Twin Lakes. We turned into a townhouse complex, well-maintained and upscale. The few people I saw seemed relaxed. Not seeing any street signs, I looked for the site of the shooting but without success. Then it dawned on us. We were in the wrong complex. I was glad this wasn't live TV. We exited what we now saw to be "Colonial Townhomes at Twin Lakes," hung a right, and drove into "The Retreat at Twin Lakes."

Right away, I could see we had crossed the metaphoric tracks and arrived on the proverbial "other side." The buildings at The Retreat were poorly maintained, even shabby. There were no road signs, thus no clear understanding of which small outlet road to take in a series of semi-circular roads where the townhomes were all identical. It was an endless maze. A few of the cars parked on the streets were beat-up or missing hubcaps. One side of The Retreat was missing a wall. This was not the "gated community" of the media's imagination.

Using a Google satellite map, we located the building behind which the incident took place and parked. Just before we could exit the car, two police cars and an unmarked police vehicle came roaring past us, sirens blazing. They slammed on their brakes and exited, banging on a townhouse door just across from us with weapons drawn.

This, I sensed, was *not* an eviction! An action junkie, my cameraman instinctively started to film, but I yelled, "No, stop!" I thought it inadvisable to lift up a large dark object and point it at armed police officers. We sat still until someone came to the townhouse door. The cops quickly cuffed the man, stuffed him into a vehicle, and hauled him away.

Once the police left, my film crew took footage of myself walking the area of the incident. I immediately noticed the gap between two groups of townhouses where Zimmerman spotted Trayvon as he drove by. There was no reason for anyone to stand there in the rain, and I'm sure that is what drew George's attention given the recent spate of burglaries and home invasions.

I walked George's walk along the cut-through that took me from the street where he had parked to the next street over where he looked for an address. The cut-through would have been completely dark and lonely and quiet. It would have taken George only a minute or two to walk to one end and back.

Intersecting the cut-through was a long, sheltered pathway that led toward Trayvon's temporary residence, the townhouse of Brandy Green, the girlfriend of Trayvon's father, Tracy Martin. The townhouses flanked the cut-through on either side. Walking up the pathway, looking only at back patios, I had a feeling of total isolation. On a rainy night, had someone been beaten and left for dead here, he would have gone unseen until dog walkers came out in the morning. No one on the streets would hear or notice anything. Even in broad daylight, it felt creepy.

From where I stood, I could only hear a few dogs barking. I had a feeling of great sadness to stand at the intersection of that long walkway and the cut-through between the streets. The incident seemed totally tragic and stupid and avoidable, the result of a compounding series of misjudgments by both Trayvon and George. There was no marker or monument of any kind at the site of the shooting. It was as if nothing of consequence had ever happened there. I was happy to leave that haunted spot, stash away our camera gear, and exit The Retreat.

Next, I drove to the 7-11 to which Trayvon had walked that night. From the 7-11, I could see a clear shortcut back to The Retreat at Twin Lakes that would have measured less than a mile, an easy 15-minute walk. The 7-11 store had been completely redesigned inside and looked more up to date than the interior I had seen on the security footage. Outside, the facade seemed modern and cheerful. The clerks working there likely had no idea of the role the store played in the case that reshaped America's racial landscape.

That same day I visited the police station where George had been taken after the shooting. Large and bustling, the station was located on Goldsboro Boulevard in the historic Goldsboro Community of Sanford. Apparently, the Freedmen's Bureau established the Goldsboro site during the Reconstruction period after the Civil War for blacks who worked nearby. In 1891, residents incorporated Goldsboro as a town, and Sanford annexed it in 1911.

It was here among the old historic homes and established churches that George went to mobilize the citizens in the Sherman Ware case less than a year before the Trayvon Martin shooting. As George learned the hard way, the residents responded much more eagerly to calls for a lynch mob for him in the Trayvon shooting than for justice in the Sherman Ware case. Those who knew of George's leadership in the Ware case kept silent to a person.

From the police station, I drove to the Seminole County courthouse, a newish, regal looking building on the outskirts of Sanford. During the trial, the ample parking spaces in front were filled with television trucks from all over the country, even the world. The extensive grounds had room for hundreds of protestors, maybe thousands. Walking through this chaos had to be intimidating. Inside, however, I felt relaxed. The grand scale of the foyer recalled the courthouses I had seen in countless movies in which common sense prevailed. In the summer of 2013, this institution offered George his one chance for justice.

Outside the courthouse, as George knew, any chance of a fair hearing evaporated because a young girl named Diamond had come forward and introduced a story line that contradicted all other witnesses and physical evidence collected by the police. The statements this young girl made on a recorded phone call with Martin family attorney Benjamin Crump led directly to George's arrest and subsequently to a racial firestorm that would divide America. Having watched the girl testify at the trial, I sensed something was wrong. I had no idea, however, just how wrong that "something" was.

4

LEFTISTS AND ANTI-RACISM

GEORGE ZIMMERMAN SURPRISED ME. He was clearly not the brute the media made him out to be. What was brutal, however, was the irony that shrouded this case from the beginning. George was a Democrat, an old-time liberal and a walk-the-walk civil rights activist. He devoted his free time to helping black youth. He inspired the black community to take up the cause of a homeless black man who had been knocked senseless by the son of a white police officer. George voted for Obama. He believed in "hope and change," although like most others, he had no idea what Obama was really talking about.

On top of that George was Hispanic, a real Hispanic, one who knew his roots and spoke the language as well as he spoke English. George was right. Had his parents named him Jorgé, we would never have heard of him nor of Trayvon Martin. But this was Florida, the ultimate battleground state in a presidential election year, and the man running to retain the White House depended on a highly motivated African American electorate to offset the continued flatlining of the U.S. economy. Jobs were scarce due to Obama's increasing taxation and regulations, and an influx of illegals was driving down wages in inner cities nationwide. Black voters were not motivated, not yet.

For political purposes, the media refused to acknowledge George

Zimmerman as Hispanic. As his father noted, "They had to make him white" and not just white but something of a white supremacist. If George went to jail or was murdered before he got there, *c'est la guerre*. This should have been a warning, I thought, to every well-meaning white person or light-colored Hispanic out there, liberal or conservative–you could be next.

Pitting one race or one ethnic group against another is a game the Left has been playing for a very long time. In my 2014 documentary *There's No Place Like Utopia,* I explored the rarely told history of Leftist exploitation of race and ethnicity, a practice that dates back to at least 1924. In January of that year, Vladimir Lenin died and was replaced by Josef Stalin as the leader of the nascent Soviet Union. More of a realist than Lenin, Stalin focused his American propaganda efforts not on fomenting a workers' revolution–unlikely given America's free market history–but on discrediting the very idea of America both to its own citizens and to the world.

For the COMINTERN (Communist International), the Soviet international arm, the "Sacco and Vanzetti" case was made to order. In 1920, local Massachusetts police arrested Nichola Sacco, a shoemaker, and Bartolomeo Vanzetti, a fish peddler, both Italian nationals with no love lost for their country of residence. They were charged with the murder of Alessandro Berardelli, a security guard killed in a South Braintree, Massachusetts payroll robbery.

The evidence against Sacco and Vanzetti was compelling. The alibis they offered quickly fell apart, and in September 1920, the two anarchists were both indicted for the murder. The case would have passed into history with little notice if the fledgling ACLU had not gotten involved. Seeing no other way to save the pair, the ACLU politicized the case, transforming Sacco and Vanzetti from a "couple of wops in a jam," as one liberal reporter phrased it, to a pair of political dissidents on trial for their ethnicity and unpopular opinions.

As the case moved through the appeals process, the ACLU's Fred Moore lost confidence in the pair's innocence. Sensing his attorney's unease, Sacco fired Moore, and the case sank back into obscurity. The COMINTERN had influence well beyond the ACLU's and had even less conscience. Its officials created a Chicago-based legal institution, the International Labor Defense, and assigned it the Sacco and Vanzetti case. Working through its agents worldwide, the COMINTERN turned the case into an international cause célèbre.

The Soviets had no intention of saving Sacco and Vanzetti from execution. That would do them no good. Rather, they hoped to exploit the men's deaths to turn the world against America. And at this, they succeeded marvelously. As would become Soviet practice, the COMINTERN recruited a wide range of media, literary and academic celebrities–"innocents"–the Soviets called them or, more accurately, "useful idiots"–to take up the cause of the doomed anarchists. To this day, the American Left insists on the pair's innocence despite all evidence to the contrary.

As something of a post-script, in 2005 a California collector stumbled upon a letter from popular socialist author Upton Sinclair to his attorney written nearly 80 years prior. As the letter revealed, Sinclair met with the ACLU's Fred Moore while still writing a novel about the recent executions. What the letter showed was that Sinclair learned of the pair's guilt while the novel was in progress.

"Alone in a hotel room with Fred, I begged him to tell me the full truth," wrote Sinclair. "He then told me that the men were guilty, and he told me in every detail how he had framed a set of alibis for them." Fearing for his life if he told what he knew, Sinclair finished the book under the pretense that the pair were innocent. No fool, Sinclair understood that telling the truth in Communist circles could get you killed.

Seeing how well the exploitation of Sacco and Vanzetti's ethnicity played, the Soviets soon turned their attention to America's Achilles heel–race. Julia Ioffe, writing in *Atlantic*, traces Soviet involvement in America's racial strife to a 1931 incident in which nine young African Americans were accused of raping two white women on a freight train in Alabama. By 1932, even before most Americans had heard of the so-called "Scottsboro Boys," the Soviet Union's most famous propaganda artist had created a poster "Freedom to the Prisoners of Scottsboro!"

As with Sacco and Vanzetti, the COMINTERN employed its legal arm, International Labor Defense, to push the NAACP aside and defend the young men. The Soviet goal in Alabama was not unlike its goal during the Civil War soon to erupt in Spain, namely, to advance the Stalinist agenda and suppress the forces of both the Left and Right that resisted it.

In his book *Black Bolshevik,* party regular Harry Haywood proudly owned up to the strong-arm Communist tactics in Alabama. "Scottsboro represented our first serious challenge to recognized Black reformist leadership," wrote Haygood. He continued, "The Party's strategy at the time was to wrest hegemony from the reformists and win leadership of Black workers in the Black Freedom front."

For the Soviets and their Leftist American allies, the Scottsboro boys provided a field of battle. If the Communists were to seize that field, liberal black reformers had to be eliminated just as surely as white traditionalists. "It was necessary to struggle on two fronts," Haywood wrote, "for both deviated from the line of proletarian internationalism."

Whether all or any of the Scottsboro boys were innocent is unknown, but what was clear is that they were not going to get a fair trial in Alabama. The case dragged on for years, and Communist Party USA exploited the young men at every turn. For the COMINTERN, the goal was not justice for the boys but revolutionary hegemony for its apparatchiks. "The case became a symbol of the injustices of the Jim Crow South," wrote Ioffe, "and the young Soviet state milked it for all the propagandistic value it could."

Although writing for a liberal publication, Ioffe offered a clear-eyed assessment of Soviet goals. That goal was never racial equality. It was disruption and revolution. Long before the Republican Party had a "Southern strategy," the Soviets did. "The point then, as it was in 2012, was to discredit the American system," wrote Ioffe, "to keep the Soviets (and, later, Russians) loyal to their own system instead of hungering for Western-style democracy. But it was also used in Soviet propaganda around the world for a similar purpose."

Hoping to embarrass the United States during the Depression, the Soviets lured many black Americans to the Soviet Union. They became known as "Black Bolsheviks." Prominent among them was a Communist activist named Lovett Fort-Whiteman. In fact, the then conservative *Time* magazine called Fort-Whiteman "the reddest of the blacks." A true believer in Communism by the mid-1920s and a willing propagandist, Fort-Whiteman proved to be a highly successful recruiter as well. Thousands of Americans, many of them black, flocked to the Soviet Union during the Depression, Fort-Whiteman among them.

Communists viewed American blacks as "the raw material for revolution" according to former KGB spy Konstantin Preobrazhensky. In this regards, Fort-Whiteman served as something of a prototype. The Left would use African Americans like Fort-Whiteman for their propaganda value and dispense with them when that value was exhausted.

In the Soviet Union, that value was short-lived. The Black Bolsheviks proved to be too Americanized to yield to the mindless brutality of the Soviet regime. In time, Stalin did with them what he did with other troublesome minorities. He eliminated them, Fort-Whiteman included. In 1938, Fort-Whiteman, the reddest of the blacks, was dispatched to the notorious Kolyma Gulag in Siberia, and he was dead within a year. No black American survived to tell the tale of the purge by the Communists that killed Fort-Whiteman and uncounted other "Black Bolsheviks".

The Russians continued to exploit black-white friction right up until the end of the Soviet era, perhaps even beyond. Vasili Mitrokhin, the senior archivist for the KGB, confirmed this in his 1985 book, co-authored with Christopher Andrew, *The Sword and the Shield.* For any number of years, Mitrokhin copied the more relevant KGB files in his possession. One recurring pattern he noticed was the KGB effort "to weaken the internal cohesion of the United States and undermine its international reputation by inciting race hatred."

According to Mitrokhin, in 1971 KGB Chairman Yuri Andropov initiated a series of "active measures" to "stir up racial tensions in the United States." One tactic was to send "forged letters" to prominent

African Americans and attribute them to the Ku Klux Klan or the John Birch Society or the Jewish Defense League. The outspoken Communist Jim Jones, of Jonestown notoriety, boasted of doing the same and for the same reason: to keep African Americans stirred up and angry, all the better to recruit and exploit them.

No one has better tracked the shifts in progressive thinking than Laird Wilcox. To this day, the Wilcox Collection of Contemporary Political Movements is housed at the University of Kansas's Spencer Research Library. A lifetime ACLU member, Wilcox has monitored extremist movements both Right and Left.

According to Wilcox, many of America's hard-core progressive groups made a conscious shift after the Berlin Wall fell and the Soviet dream died. "Rather than present socialism or Marxism-Leninism as their goal," Wilcox wrote, "they piggy-back it onto anti-racism which is far more popular."

Writing more than twenty years ago, Wilcox anticipated the future of the so-called civil rights movement in the Obama era and beyond. In their new role as anti-fascist watchdogs, various Leftist groups dealt with the objective decline of racism "by expanding the definition of racism to meet their needs, to include more and more behaviors, and to require more and more invasive remedies." Those remedies were always socialist, of course.

Although now cloaked in the garb of anti-racism and anti-fascism, these progressive groups adopted the "ritual defamation" used routinely by Stalin and his heirs, including Obama friend Bill Ayers and Obama's guru, Saul Alinsky. Said Wilcox, "The primary purpose of Watchdog organizations seems to be to call people names in the hope of defaming, discrediting, stigmatizing or neutralizing them."

No American in recent years has been defamed and stigmatized more ruthlessly than George Zimmerman. His case represented a dark turn in Leftist history. No longer content to declare the guilty "innocent" to push their political narratives, the Left was now prepared to declare the innocent "guilty."

5

THE TRAYVON DECEPTION

If the media were willing to deceive us about George, I had to ask myself whether they would deceive us about Trayvon Martin as well. The answer, of course, was yes. Trayvon, I would learn, was not a smallish boy with Skittles and iced tea, "just trying to get home." Not at all. If the media would not tell Trayvon's real story, Trayvon's own words would and did.

Save for the fact that Trayvon Martin was on foot, the encounter between him and George Zimmerman had all the characteristics of road rage. George apparently did something to set Trayvon off. One would have to imagine that George interrupted something important to Trayvon. Instead of easily walking back to the townhouse of Brandy Green, his father's girlfriend, Trayvon chose to intimidate Zimmerman by approaching his truck and circling it. If he had a gripe about being observed by Zimmerman, he could have knocked on George's window and said, "Yo, dude, what's up?"

For that matter, George could have rolled down his window and said, "Excuse me, but do you live in the neighborhood? We've had a lot of robberies." From the dispatcher's call, however, Trayvon had George worried. "Something's wrong with him," George told the dispatcher. "Yep, he's coming to check me out. He's got something in his hands. I don't know what his deal is." Seconds later George added anxiously, "See if you can get an officer over here."

After circling George's car, Trayvon took off quickly. In less than twenty seconds he could easily have made it back to Brandy's townhouse where her young son Chad was waiting for him. Instead, he seems to have circled back to look for George and found him walking *away* from him and toward his truck four minutes later.

Even then tragedy was still not inevitable. Trayvon could have cursed George out, flipped a middle finger, or even shoved him and walked away. Instead he sucker punched George much the way the police lieutenant's son had sucker punched Sherman Ware. That punch broke George's nose. Disoriented, George was no match for his much taller assailant who pushed him to the ground, straddled him with his knees, and started pounding away at George's head, "mixed martial arts-style" according to eye-witness Johnathan Good.

Trayvon had no history with George Zimmerman, and George did not deserve a beating this ferocious and reckless. Looking at the evidence, I felt strongly that Trayvon had issues that had nothing to do with George. I decided my next step was to get to know Trayvon in order to better understand what was going on in his head in the days, hours, and minutes leading to the moment of the attack.

The major media offered no clues. In their collective corruption of the story, they had the public believing Trayvon was a smallish teen boy in a hoodie, "just walking home" with candy for his little brother when profiled, stalked and attacked by the thuggish Zimmerman. Yet, as Trayvon indicated in his dying breath, "Tell Mama 'Licia I'm sorry," there was a lot more going on here. Though the media refused to hold Trayvon accountable for his actions, Trayvon knew he had something to be sorry about. I figured only he could tell me what that was, and the answer, I was convinced, could be found in his cell phone records.

Early on, Florida prosecutors told Zimmerman defense attorney Mark O'Mara that the rain had so badly damaged Trayvon's cell phone on the night of the shooting there was no point in trying to recover any data. On a subsequent visit to the police station, however,

O'Mara saw Trayvon's phone, a T-Mobile Huawei U8150 Comet, laid out on a table with other evidence. He asked that a charger be located, and the phone plugged in. A police officer obliged and *voila,* the cell phone lit up, "Welcome to T-Mobile!"

As was his right, O'Mara requested that the Florida Department of Law Enforcement (FDLE) extract the data from the phone. To accomplish this, the FDLE used a computer program sold only to police departments called "Cellebrite." Apparently, the FDLE had only limited success and sent the phone to Los Angeles where the LAPD had more advanced capability and were able to extract even more data.

O'Mara soon learned about the results through a whistleblower named Wesley White, an attorney who had worked as a prosecutor in the State Attorney's office in Duval County, Florida. "It came to my attention through a client that there existed certain materials generated by my client, a report, that relates to this case that may have not been turned over to the defense," White would later tell the court. Prosecutors objected to White's claim about the phone, dismissing it as hearsay, but White surprised them by naming his source, Ben Kruidbos, the IT director for the Fourth Judicial Circuit.

Prosecutors were not keen on sharing the information contained in Trayvon's cell phone. O'Mara told me that to avoid doing so during the discovery process, prosecutors mailed the defense a disk containing a binary computer file of Trayvon's cell phone records, rather than a printout. To open the file, the *pro bono* defense team would have to purchase the $8,000 Cellebrite computer program and get training on how to use it. The defense attorneys successfully protested to the court, and the prosecutors were compelled to hand over a printed copy. Testifying before the trial, Kruidbos claimed the cell records contained 2.5 gigabytes of data but that only 2.1 gigabytes were turned over to the defense. This was only one of the many items of evidence kept from the defense as long as possible. Kruidbos's whistleblowing got him fired. He later sued Florida State Attorney Angela Corey for wrongful termination.

From reviewing the trial video, I knew Trayvon's complete phone records existed. Knowing the lengths the prosecutors went to keep those records out of court, I felt they must have been explosive. I decided to do a deep dive on Trayvon's cell phone records as no one had done before.

Florida is an open records state. That means virtually every public document is available upon request, including every document that was used in a court case. I put in a public records request online for all cell phone records in the George Zimmerman case with the Florida Department of Law Enforcement (FDLE). The texts and other phone records, I believed, held the key to Trayvon's soul. Who were his friends? How did he relate to his peers? What kind of temptations did he face? How did he treat others? Was he a good kid? What was he really into?

Soon enough, the Cellebrite report arrived. The size of it overwhelmed me. It was 750-pages long. The report began with an index listing what it contained, dating back to summer 2011:

- 3,000 text messages
- 3,000 photos
- 1,500 contacts, many with nicknames, photos, email addresses and phone numbers
- 300 bookmarks of web pages
- 300 chats
- 300 emails
- 1,200 applications
- Hundreds of GPS coordinates fixing Trayvon's locations

Although massive, I knew I had to read the entire document slowly. The report would tell me more about Trayvon than even his friends and family knew. My first challenge, though, was to decode the "Urban English" in which many texts were written, a task made more difficult because the language was compressed to make texting quicker. On several occasions I had to read the texts multiple times before I could fully grasp the digital patois.

The *Urban Dictionary* was indispensable in interpreting Trayvon's texts. The first word I checked was "Nigga." Used repeatedly, the word carried no real stigma and simply meant "dude," usually a male. Some others:

Jit – a child
Deuces – get lost
Slid – very tired
Gshit – keeping it real
Face – marijuana
Kush – marijuana
Bru – brother
Bae – babe
Boo – sweetheart
Green – lame
Og – old girl or Mom
Ob – old boy or Dad

No one used the possessive. "Can I go Mario house?" translated to "Can I go to Mario's house?" There was also urban text shorthand to learn:

ion – I don't
finna – about to
imma – I'm going to
wya – where you at
gud – good
dis – this
dat - that
wat – what
pose – supposed to
cuz – cousin or because
fne – phone
da – the
wit – with
aigh – alright

ppl – people
na – now
m – me or my
n – and

So for example, "Im on da fne na. M n Zach finna go Mario crib" translated to: "I am on the phone now. Me and Zach are about to go to Mario's house."

Among the things I learned about in decoding Trayvon's texts was his relationship with his mother, Sybrina Fulton. I had followed the case just enough to recognize Sybrina from her frequent television appearances as well as her attendance at the 2016 Democrat National Convention. At the latter event she joined other "mothers of the movement" who were demanding changes to gun laws.

Like most people, I had tremendous sympathy for Sybrina and gave her a great deal of latitude for her actions after the shooting. Given what happened to her son, I did not blame her for opposing Florida's Stand Your Ground law, even though it had nothing to do with her son's death nor Zimmerman's defense. One can imagine her desire to find something, anything, that might in her mind give some meaning to her son's death.

In her text messages with Trayvon, Sybrina dutifully planned family get-togethers and routinely asked Trayvon to attend. Often, I noticed Trayvon's cell phone would spit out GPS coordinates, followed by Sybrina texting him "Wh r ru?" or just "call me." This was a little too coincidental. I looked through the applications list and found one called "DM Tracker." This program shoots out GPS coordinates on demand to another cell phone.

Sybrina communicated typical 'mom' things like ordering Trayvon to clean up his room and waking him up with affectionate text messages such as, "Azz up soldier, rise & shine." Trayvon would dutifully respond, "Im up captain."

The exchanges between Trayvon and Sybrina mirrored those of millions of other mothers and sons across America. Texted Sybrina, "And ur still in trouble. What did I tell u to do!!!!" Trayvon texted meekly in return, "Ima do it wen i cum home 2day." And Sybrina, "Then get ur azz home. And clean up." To smooth over their relationship, Sybrina, who had a good government job, would usually agree to Trayvon's requests for small amounts of cash.

I sensed that Sybrina was communicating with Trayvon as though everything were normal–parents do this with troubled kids. On Christmas Eve 2011, Sybrina texted, "I'm concerned about u but I'm praying for u and I want u to pray for yourself EVERYDAY, ok." Two days earlier, she had texted him, "Pack up ur clothes now." She was throwing Trayvon, not yet seventeen, out of the house. She added, "I love u but I think u being w/ur Dad is best."

Sybrina loved Trayvon, and he loved her. She knew he was getting into problems she could not handle, but, like many parents, she blinded herself to the depths of the issues. The school system helped keep her in the dark. For the sake of racial balance, the Miami-Dade Schools were downgrading crimes into school rules violations as a matter of policy. As a result, even Trayvon's parents did not know how far he had gone astray. Trayvon's father, Tracy Martin, would later describe his son to Sanford Police as a "well-mannered, non-violent child." In his deposition, he told defense lawyers "to my knowledge, his act wasn't bad." Unfortunately, this disconnect was not unusual in black America.

In fact, Tracy was as unmoored as his son. In November 2011, when Trayvon was sixteen, Tracy split with Alicia Stanley, the stepmother who had largely raised Trayvon for the last fourteen years. Tracy himself was now drifting from home to home–his sister's, his brother's, and girlfriend Brandy Green's.

When Trayvon was suspended from school in February 2012–the third time that school year–he was again exiled by Sybrina from Miami to Sanford, near Orlando, where Brandy lived. At the time, Tracy worked as a delivery driver for Sysco. According to his March 2013 deposition, Tracy had fathered six children with five different women, including one with Brandy after Trayvon's death, but none with Alicia Stanley.

As I researched Trayvon's background, a portrait began to emerge of a good kid, a loving kid, one with many friends and family members who cared for him. "R u comfortable on the bus??" Sybrina texted him on his final trip to Sanford. "Go to sleep n u will be there soon." She continued, "And listen to chickenhead." This was a reference to Brandy Green and her hair style. Trayvon responded, "ok she nice." Sybrina replied, "She better be or I'll come crack her wig."

According to his cell phone records, until mid-2011 Trayvon's activities seemed to revolve around school, church youth groups, and going to the movies with female friends. But then in late 2011, Trayvon's behavior took a sudden, dark turn. This likely had a lot to do with Tracy Martin leaving Alicia Stanley, or "Mama 'Licia," and Trayvon losing his stepmother and being sent to live with Sybrina. Trayvon's pastimes now included street fighting, drugs, sex, and dealing guns. He texted often about these pursuits with his friends.

This exchange between Trayvon and a female friend on November 21, 2011, three months before his death, spoke to where his life was heading. After he told her he was "tired and sore" from a fight, she asked him why he fought.

TRAYVON: Cause man dat nigga snitched on me
FRIEND: Y you always fightinqq man, you got suspended?
TRAYVON: Naw we thumped afta skool in a duckd off spot. I lost da 1st round :(but won da 2nd nd 3rd)
FRIEND: Ohhh So It Wass 3 Rounds? Damn well at least yu wonn lol but yuu needa stop fighting bae Forreal
TRAYVON: Nay im not done with fool..... he gone hav 2 see me again
FRIEND: Nooo... Stop, yuu aint gonn bee satisfied till yuh suspended again, huh?
TRAYVON: Naw but he aint bleed nuff 4 me, only his nosez

What is shocking here is that in November 2011 Trayvon was boasting about beating up a snitch. Worse, he felt that busting his opponent's nose had not drawn enough blood. The snitch needed to bleed more. This sounded eerily reminiscent of Trayvon's attack on

George. The *Urban Dictionary* defines snitches as "motherfuckers who gets they ass beat up." In Ferguson, after the Michael Brown shooting, the phrase "snitches get stitches" was painted on a burnt out QuikTrip wall among other places. I had to wonder if when Trayvon observed George pull over and make a cell phone call, he thought George was "snitching" on him for smoking pot. If anything could provoke Trayvon to fight, snitching could, especially since he had an audience of one very important person on the phone with him at the time.

Trayvon often texted with his friends about fighting. On November 22, 2012, Trayvon told his friend Michael French that his opponent "got mo hits cause in da 1st round he had me on da ground nd I couldn't do ntn."

On January 6, 2012, in an exchange with an old girlfriend, Ashley Burch, whose contact name was "Sunshine," Trayvon told her he had gotten in trouble in school. When Sunshine asked why, Trayvon responded, "Caus i was watcn a fight nd a teacher say i hit em." Sunshine found that amusing. "Lmao," she replied.

On February 12, 2012, Trayvon had a text conversation with Brenda, who bragged about the fights *she* had been in. On February 14, in a three-way conversation with two girls, Trayvon told them how he had been suspended from school for fighting. This suspension provoked his mother to kick him out. He texted, "my ol g say she dont want me home caus she think ima get in mo trouble." On February 21, cousin Stephen "Boobie" Martin tweeted to Trayvon, "Yu aint tell me you swung on a bus driver." If Boobie's information was accurate, Trayvon's fighting was escalating dangerously, he had attacked an adult who was someone of authority no less. Trayvon's best friend I was able to identify as Romario Carridice, known as "Mario." Mario could not have been a good influence. His social media displayed photos of himself flashing gang signs, holding wads of cash, and a video of himself firing pistols at targets of people at a shooting range.

Guns were coming into play as well for Trayvon. On February 18, Trayvon texted friends Fruit and Dario, asking each, "U got heat??" and "I got a bill right n 4 some fie." A bill was a hundred dollars and fie meant "firearms" in Urban English. Later that day, Trayvon's cousin Ronquavious Fulton texted him, "You want a 22 revolver." Trayvon responded, "Wat shoota??," meaning what model? Two days later, he texted Ronquavious, "Tell fool i got 80 4 him right na." It appears that Trayvon was prepared to pay $80 for the gun, possibly as a down payment.

On February 21, five days before his death, Trayvon was brokering a gun deal, this time with friend Zachary Witherspoon, known as "Spoonhead Zack," and another friend who went by "Jay Black." Trayvon asked Jay if he wanted to "share a 380" with Zack. Although Jay was game, Zack was already taken care of. He informed Trayvon he was finally going to "cop a 38." Trayvon may have been trying to show off, but he sounded like a knowledgeable broker. The next day, February 22, Zack asked him if he wanted $150 for the .38. Trayvon begged off, saying it was "2 late."

Boobie tried to warn Trayvon not to deal drugs, but Trayvon wouldn't listen:

BOOBIE: I ain't ya parent but gshit thro it away
TRAYVON: Y u gotta knock my hustle??

Trayvon was also doing drugs, but that hardly set him apart from his peers in Miami. A video posted on Facebook by another close friend, Stephan Bramble, showed Trayvon puffing away, smoking marijuana, something he did often, perhaps daily. Stephan Bramble, whose contact name was "Steve-O," proudly displays on his Facebook page dozens of photos of himself holding handguns, bags of marijuana, wads of cash, a codeine bottle, and the codeine infused "purple lean" beverage that Trayvon was expert in concocting to get high. Most disturbing of all is a video where Steve-O is dancing to rap music with a machine gun when a small child appears suddenly in the frame. Steve-O was tight with Trayvon.

At the time of his death, Trayvon had the active ingredient of marijuana, THC, in his blood, at a level considered in most states high enough to impair driving. A June 2011 Facebook exchange with a character known as "Mackenzie DumbRyte Baksh" showed Trayvon's strong knowledge of the urban concoction known as "purple lean" or "purple drank":

> *TRAYVON: unow a connect for codine?*
> *MACKENZIE: why nigga*
> *TRAYVON: to make some more*
> *MACKENZIE: u tawkin bout the pill codeine*
> *TRAYVON: no the liquid its meds. I had it b4*
> *MACKENZIE: hell naw u could just use some robitussin nd soda to make some fire ass lean*
> *TRAYVON: codine is a higher dose of dxm*
> *MACKENZIE: I feel u but need a prescription to get it*

On February 21, when he arrived in Sanford, Trayvon's friend "Lonel" texted him, "Got some fire ass sour og kush on deck fuck with me." In the days leading up to his death, "lean" was very much on Trayvon's mind. Other than Robitussin, the two other ingredients that went into "fire ass lean" were a sweet drink along the lines of an Arizona Watermelon Fruit Juice Cocktail, and any candy, with Skittles being something of a standard. Trayvon was carrying both when he encountered George Zimmerman.

6

LOVING DIAMOND

ONE THING that jumped out of Trayvon's massive phone records was that he liked girls. A lot. His cell phone photo gallery was filled with images of girls–girls blowing kisses, girls showing a little skin, girls making overtures. To find out who was who, I cross-referenced their phone numbers, email addresses, texts, and searched for twitter and Facebook accounts. I also used an online background database called Instant Checkmate, which helped me identify Trayvon's friends with a phone number or email address.

Most of the girls Trayvon communicated with were nice, church-going girls who exchanged friendly texts without any sexual innuendoes or street talk. Several of them were former girlfriends. They genuinely seemed to care about Trayvon and reached out to him almost daily with amiable, everyday banter. "Sunshine" Ashley Burch, for example, would greet Trayvon in the morning with "Good-morning Sunshine!" She and Trayvon appear to have dated at one time and maintained a friendly relationship, sometimes going to movies together with other girls.

Trayvon would typically respond to Ashley in similarly agreeable fashion, but more and more he projected his newfound bad boy image and often asked the girls to pray for him as well. "Iyanni," Ayanna Flemming, knew Trayvon from Miami Carol City High School, which he attended prior to transferring to Michael Krop. She and Trayvon were very friendly. One exchange in particular from November 22, 2011, stands out as ominous though:

TRAYVON: My mom just told me i gotta mov wit my dad.... She just kickd me out :(
IYANNI: What did you do now?
TRAYVON: Da police caught me outta skool
IYANNI: So you just turning into a lil hoodlum
TRAYVON: Naw I'm a gangsta
IYANNI: Boy don't get one planted in ya chest
TRAYVON: Lol im scared
IYANNI: You should be

Here, Iyanni made one hell of a prophetic warning: "Boy don't get one planted in ya chest." Trayvon wasn't listening. By this time, he self-identified as a "gangsta" and was using the twitter handle "No Limit Nigga," the name of a Miami-based street gang.

Daisha Mitchell, or simply "Daisha," appears to have been Trayvon's sweetheart in junior high and was now just a good friend. She attended Miramar High School. She would often text Trayvon, "hi bestfriend."

As late as February 2012, Faith Miller thought of herself as Trayvon's girlfriend. Faith was literally the "preacher's daughter." Her father, Glenn Miller, was an attorney but also moonlighted as the minister of his own church, Bright Star Missionary Baptist Church. Faith and Trayvon exchanged texts and several phone calls each day.

From her messages, Faith seemed like a sweet girl. She did not wear much in the way of makeup, and her texts to Trayvon were kind and loving. Of all the girls in his life, Faith may have most reminded him of his mother. The relationship, however, seemed to start fading in early February 2012.

It could not have helped that Trayvon texted Faith an inappropriate photo on Valentine's Day 2012. As a result, Faith's parents confiscated her phone. They were no doubt monitoring it. The loss of her phone led Faith to reach out to Trayvon through Facebook and through the phones of friends and siblings. By this time, though, Trayvon was hooked on a much more provocative girl and could barely spare Faith the time.

The girl who stole Trayvon's heart was different than the others. He started texting and calling her on February 2, 2012. On February 10, 2012–sixteen days before his death–he initiated a conversation with the girl with one word, "Diamond." That is the name she wanted him to know her by. Towards the end, her texts with Trayvon numbered in the hundreds daily, and sometimes their phone calls consumed as much as eight hours per day, including at least five hours on the last day of his life.

Diamond's text messages with Trayvon ranged from highly sexual and graphic to kiss-offs like "leave me den." If Trayvon complained about her not responding, she felt no need to explain or apologize. As I combed through the texts between Diamond and Trayvon, I came to see that the two were indeed in a romantic relationship–crude, combative, and sexual. I also saw that Trayvon's constant insecurity about that relationship added to the many pressures he felt in the days and hours leading up to his death.

As the texts showed, Diamond was a "bad ass," boastful, confident and overtly sexual, while claiming to be gun-savvy as well. At this stage I did not know if "Diamond" was her real name. Several other girls in Trayvon's world used the name "Diamond" too, given its commonly understood meaning in street culture. According to the *Urban Dictionary*, "Diamond" is a "an awesome, smart, random, crazy, sexy fun-loving girl." The definition continues, "She can make you laugh all the time and can pull off any outfit any day. She's the sweetest and nicest person you'll ever meet but don't piss her off or you'll end up in the Nevada Desert." As the texts showed, this definition fit Trayvon's "Diamond" like a pair of super skinny jeans.

When Diamond responded "wat" to his initial greeting, Trayvon reassured her he would not say anything about her to anybody. Although she seemingly wanted Trayvon to keep their relationship on the down low, in reality she was not averse to Trayvon discreetly spreading the word about her charms. At sixteen, she was that vain. "Oh course you have to say something about me," she texted Trayvon. "I am gorgeous fabulous sexy and hoe will always hate on dis diamond Cuz they want wat I got." In this world, "hoe," as in "whore," was a generic word for any post-pubescent girl.

On February 12, a Sunday, Diamond initiated an early hours text conversation with the single word "sweetheart." Later that day, she texted Trayvon saying she was in church. Many of the girls in Trayvon's circle were churchgoers. None was as casual about her faith as was Diamond. "I'm a child of God on Sunday," she texted Trayvon, "but Mon - sat I'm a pimpin." In this context, "pimpin" meant being cool, dressing well, having fun.

On a more serious note, Trayvon asked her while she said she was at church to "say a prayer 4 me." It was hard to tell from Diamond's response whether she is being sarcastic or sincere–"LOL u crazy yea I'm going pray for u"–but Trayvon knew he needed intervention. His mother recognized the need as well.

On February 13, the relationship seemed to be tenuous. Diamond texted Trayvon he was "acting like a ass lst night." He explained why, "Cuz u b confusn me." Trayvon response showed he sensed that he was being played with.

"Smh u think i only fuck nd show off u pretty," he texted her that evening, "ion even tell nobody bout yo green ass caus u ask me not 2..... im happy dats how u fuckn feel." The shorthand "smh" meant "shaking my head," in this case out of disappointment. Diamond would make Trayvon shake his head a lot in the days to come. The "fuck" reference may or may not have been literal. In either case, Diamond then asked Trayvon, "do u want to be my ride to die nigga." This is Urban English for going steady. You and I are a couple. We "ride" together and we "die" together. Whatever happens to me also happens to you, because we are together. Trayvon texted back a smile in acceptance to the proposal. Later that night when he asked Diamond what she was doing, she answered "taking a hot bath." Said Trayvon, "I wanna join." Diamond responded, "I bet u do."

The State of Florida had access to all these texts. Prosecutors knew, as I know, that the girl Trayvon wanted to join in the bathtub was the same girl who was on the phone with Trayvon when he died. This is not speculation. This is fact.

February 14 was Valentine's Day. Diamond implied that she and Trayvon may have engaged in some phone sex while she was bathing the night before. "Last night me u have a good time I like making u mad now I like the make up sex."

Although Trayvon was frustrated with Diamond's elusiveness, he had little cause to complain. Something of a player himself, Trayvon texted at least four girls the equivalent of "Happy Valentine's Day" that day. On February 15, Trayvon's frustration with Diamond seethed to the surface. After a day of contentious texts, he sent Diamond a series of increasingly hostile messages, sixteen in all, spaced several minutes apart as if to allow Diamond time to respond. She would not text him back for more than an hour.

"Man stop playn w/ m emotions," Trayvon told her at one point. He followed that seven minutes later with, "Uggghhhhh i hate yo fuck ass i hope u choke." Eight minutes later, he told her, "Die." Ten minutes after wishing Diamond dead, Trayvon sent a long and despairing text that spoke to a deeply felt anxiety. He was not playing here:

> *Kno wat if it was dat easy 4 u 2 quit mayb u aint da right 1 4 me..... u made me like u nd u wasted my time if u neva liked me.... u makn me hate u.....nd i guess we dont feel da same..... wen u askd me 2 drop u i sayd naw..... but u quick 2 drop m..... i so fuckn angry at yo fuck ass u dumb hoe i hope u choke on a fat 1 whicho dirty ass..... i swear if u was by m right na ill fuck yo shit up stupid bitch.*

The millions of people worldwide exposed to the innocent candy toting child "Trayvon" after his death had no idea just how disordered his teenage life had become. Whatever Trayvon once was, the Trayvon sending this text was distressed, potentially violent, and misogynistic in the extreme. The prosecutors knew this. They had an obligation to share this information with the defense. They did so only under pressure.

7

THE DIAMOND DECEPTION

I TAKE a certain pride in being halfway fluent in six different languages. After obsessively reading and rereading the text messages between Diamond and Trayvon, I am prepared to claim a seventh. Let's call it BFLAT, black Florida adolescent text. BFLAT is kind of like Latin: no one speaks it, few people write it, but it's not that hard to understand if you put your mind to it.

To supplement the *Urban Dictionary* and a glossary of standard text shorthand, I recruited a young black friend to help me through the more difficult passages. After twenty or so reviews of the text dialogue between Diamond and Trayvon, I felt like I had a grasp of it all.

Knowing the language, though I had set out to get to know Trayvon, now I had unintentionally gotten to know Diamond as well, almost personally–her vibe, her jive, her attitude. I began to feel increasingly that Rachel Jeantel, the plus-sized girl who claimed to be "Diamond" when testifying at George Zimmerman's trial, was NOT the same person as Trayvon's "Diamond." Reviewing video of Rachel at the trial, I was unable to imagine her wearing sexy clothes, dancing at clubs, getting hit on by boys and putting nasty "hoes" in their place who were jealous of her.

Looking for leads, I turned to the "contacts" section of Trayvon's phone records in the massive 750-page Cellebrite document. Incredible as it might seem to those who have not explored this scene, Trayvon had fifteen hundred contacts. I have no reason to believe that number exceptional for a socially active black teen in South Florida. These kids do not have much experience in the larger world, but what experience they do have, they love to share.

In reviewing Trayvon's contacts, I was able to identify almost all of the girls with whom Trayvon interacted frequently. Their photos were adjacent to their nicknames and phone numbers. As for "Diamond," there was a contact entry under that name with Diamond's phone number, 786-419-3726, but no photo. To help me identify her, I created a spreadsheet listing the people who had communicated frequently with Trayvon. Although Diamond had the most interactions–about fifteen hundred texts and phone calls–identifying her was going to take some work.

Other girls proved easier to find. Faith Miller, the preacher's daughter, had exchanged roughly twelve hundred texts and calls with Trayvon. Her contact name was "Really ??". Then, by cross checking the timing of Faith's messages, I was able to determine she was not Diamond. Unlike our mystery girl, Faith came across as modest and thoughtful, and she wrote in standard English.

I next assessed the possibility that "Sunshine" was Diamond. Sunshine appeared on the contact list and had exchanged some eight hundred messages with Trayvon. Cross checking her against my other lists and Facebook, I was able to identify her as "Ashley Burch" and eliminate her as well. Then there was Samii, Samantha Mason, another girl with whom Trayvon interacted frequently. Frequently perhaps, but not frequently enough–their four hundred exchanges did not measure up to Diamond's output nor her attitude.

Daisha, Trayvon's girlfriend from junior high, was an easy one, no nickname, and there was an entry right next to it with her full name, Daisha Mitchell. Trayvon reached out to her often. Initially, I suspected Daisha of being "Diamond" because she used the name "Dee Dee" as a twitter handle. That was one of the nicknames Rachel

Jeantel claimed as her own. In addition, Daisha had tweeted about Trayvon's death. Back when the story was in the news, however, Daisha's mother, Adrienne Choates Johnson, had written a scathing post to one of the conservative websites saying Daisha was only a friend of Trayvon's, not "the girlfriend". Johnson demanded that activists leave her daughter alone. At first glance I could not rule Daisha out, but I was not about to speculate without hard evidence.

Rachel Jeantel was proving impossible to find in the phone records. I looked in Trayvon's contacts under "Rachel" and "Jeantel" and found no entries. I reviewed all fifteen hundred contacts and three thousand photos in the photo gallery in search of the easily identifiable Rachel, and there was no photo of her. In the text messages, Trayvon had constantly implored Diamond to text photos of herself, and I knew she obliged him at least six times. If Rachel Jeantel were "Diamond," surely there would be photos of Rachel among the three thousand or so stored in Trayvon's photo gallery for my review. Again, there were none. No Rachel Jeantel.

Exhausting the possibilities, I decided to see if there was a listing under "Bae," short for "Babe," Trayvon's pet name for Diamond, the girl with whom he was so infatuated. I looked alphabetically through the contacts, and sure enough, there it was! The contact entry for "Bae" was right next to a photo of a thin, shapely young girl and the same phone number used by Diamond to call and text with Trayvon, 786-419-3726.

I knew for sure "Bae" was not Rachel Jeantel. Rachel was taller and hefty with a wide head. This girl was slim and short. Despite a nose larger than she liked, Bae wore a long hair piece, a ton of light makeup, and an expression that said, "too hot to handle." No sighted person could plausibly confuse her with Rachel.

"Bae" was "Diamond." I was almost sure of it. I quickly scanned the three thousand gallery photos to find other images of "Bae." This proved even harder than it sounds. In her contact photo, Bae was heavily made up and wearing a weave or a wig. Given the poor quality of most of these photos, I was unable to confirm another match.

That said, "Bae" fit a pattern. All of Trayvon's female friends appeared to be short, slender, and a year or two younger. This made sense. Until he shot up in the last year or two of his life, Trayvon had not been very tall himself. Then too, one of his Twitter handles was the altogether appropriate "Slimm."

I started thinking. Would Trayvon really be over the moon for Rachel, a girl who was a year older and roughly a hundred pounds heavier? As per the text messages, would he really be eager to jump into a bathtub with Rachel Jeantel even if he could find the room? The answer to both questions was surely *no*. Rachel, I was sure, had her virtues, but there was nothing confident or boastful about her as an adolescent. She was not likely to define herself as a "sexy hoe." Nor did she have a shapely "duck ass" as Diamond bragged. Nor did she wear long weaves.

When defense attorney Don West asked Rachel at the July 2013 trial, "Were you Trayvon's girlfriend?" she answered, "No. He had a girlfriend. We were just friends." If they were "just friends," as she claimed, prosecutors should have looked for "the girlfriend," the one with whom Trayvon spent several hours a day speaking and exchanging sexually explicit texts. No, Rachel was not sexy. She was not sixteen. She was not in love. She was not "Bae." She was not Diamond. Most critically, she was not the girl on the phone with Trayvon just before his death, and not the girl who provided Benjamin Crump with a made-to-order storyline over the phone that instigated George Zimmerman's arrest.

Rachel, I suspected, was a counterfeit witness. What I did not know was whether the sixteen-year-old girl who spoke on the phone with Martin family attorney Benjamin Crump was counterfeit as well. "Phone girl" clearly served a role, namely to help move the case forward. My instincts told me "Diamond" was that girl. For some reason she must have bailed out, and Rachel was substituted to take her place. To solve the Diamond enigma, I turned to the most tangible evidence of phone girl's identity.

8

THE SYBRINA LETTER

To EXPLAIN the witness fraud that I was beginning to unravel, I think it might be useful to provide a list of the players, their ages in February 2012 if relevant, the names I will use to describe them, and some minimal background:

- *Trayvon Martin*, "Trayvon," 17, the alleged victim.
- *George Zimmerman*, "George," 28, the alleged perpetrator.
- *Diamond,* "Diamond," 16, Trayvon's girlfriend, real name at this stage of my investigation still unknown.
- *Rachel Jeantel*, "Rachel," 18, the girl who testified at trial that she was "Diamond."
- *Tracy Martin*, "Tracy," Trayvon's father.
- *Sybrina Fulton*, "Sybrina," Trayvon's biological mother.
- *Alicia Stanley*, "Alicia," Trayvon's stepmother, also known as "Mama 'Licia."
- *Benjamin Crump*, "Crump," the lead Martin family attorney.
- *Bernie de la Rionda*, "de la Rionda," the lead prosecutor.
- *Felicia Cineas*, "Felicia," 16, Diamond's best friend.

- *Francine Serve*, "Francine," 21, Felicia's older sister and caregiver for Sybrina's brother.
- *Stephen Martin*, "Boobie," 20, Trayvon's cousin.
- *Brandy Green*, "Brandy," Tracy's girlfriend, who lived in the Sanford townhouse where Trayvon stayed.
- *Romario Carridice*, "Mario," 17, Trayvon's best friend
- *Stephan Bramble*, "Steve-O," 16, close friend of Trayvon.
- *Chad Joseph*, "Chad," 13, Brandy's son.
- *Team Trayvon*, advocates for the arrest of George Zimmerman that included Crump, Crump's law firm, Tracy, Sybrina, Mario, Steve-O and several others

In the way of background, the media and various protest groups began demanding George's arrest as soon as the details of the case became public in early March 2012. On March 12, just over two weeks after the February 26 shooting, the Sanford police declared that the evidence and witnesses supported George's claim of self-defense, and there were no grounds for his arrest. On March 16, the *Orlando Sentinel* quoted lead detective Chris Serino as saying, "The best evidence we have is the testimony of George Zimmerman, and he says the decedent was the primary aggressor in the whole event. Everything I have is adding up to what he says."

During these weeks, Trayvon's parents and their attorneys–I call them "Team Trayvon"–were desperately trying to secure anything or anyone they could find to contradict the evidence and eye witness statements gathered by the Sanford police department, and to have George arrested. For Martin attorneys Benjamin Crump and Daryl Parks the immediate motive was simple: if there was an arrest, they would be able to sue the homeowners association at The Retreat at Twin Lakes for wrongful death.

On Saturday, March 17, a day after the *Sentinel* article, Tracy Martin called Diamond on the phone. Crump later claimed that Tracy discovered her existence and her number only the next day by reviewing his phone bill that included Trayvon's phone number. Tracy and Diamond talked briefly on both Saturday and Sunday evenings. On Monday, March 19, Sybrina *texted* Diamond at 5:13 a.m. Diamond promptly texted her best friend, Felicia Cineas. Diamond then texted Sybrina back at 5:22 a.m. After a quick flurry of texts with Sybrina, Diamond exchanged forty more texts with Felicia before 6 a.m. A plan was clearly taking shape. This same morning the Sanford PD released the 911 tapes and Zimmerman's call to the dispatcher.

At 12:44 p.m. Diamond received another text from Sybrina. Diamond called her at 3:39 p.m. after school was out, and Sybrina called Diamond back one minute later. Diamond quickly returned that call. This exchange appears to indicate that Diamond and her friends, likely Felicia and her older sister Francine, were on their way to Sybrina's house. Francine, who had worked at that house taking care of Sybrina's paralyzed brother, Ronald Fulton, knew the way and was driving.

At about 4 p.m. Diamond was dropped off and met with Sybrina at Sybrina's house. Although no official account puts Crump at the meeting, his future statements suggest he participated as well. The various accounts of Diamond's visit–as told by Sybrina, Tracy, and Rachel Jeantel–are all at odds with one another. The only constant in all accounts is that Diamond and Sybrina met in person and that Diamond was pitched on the idea of returning later that evening for an on-camera interview with ABC-TV. According to many accounts, Diamond gave Sybrina a letter telling what she knew about what happened just before the shooting.

As I will explain later, I believe the letter delivery actually occurred five days later, but I am confident Diamond was dropped off at Sybrina's house on March 19 at around 4 p.m. as claimed. Best evidence is that Sybrina drove Diamond home after the meeting. Sybrina, in fact, told the authorities she drove Diamond home and spoke to her mother. This information would prove significant, but more on this later.

Diamond's letter to Sybrina, whenever it was delivered, piqued my interest for a number of reasons. Firstly, the stories were wildly divergent as to how the letter came into existence. Most importantly, the information contained in the letter and in the related phone interview by "Diamond" led to George Zimmerman's arrest. Fortunately, I was able to download a copy of the letter as written.

What follows are the nature and dates of sources available to me and the name by which I will identify each going forward.

- *The Sybrina letter*, the letter Diamond submitted to Sybrina, dated March 19, 2012.
- *The Crump tape*, Benjamin Crump's phone interview with Diamond on March 19, 2012.
- *The 2012 interviews*, the de la Rionda interviews with Rachel, Sybrina, and Tracy on April 2, 2012.
- *The 2013 depositions*, the depositions taken of Tracy, Sybrina, Rachel, Brandy, Chad, and Boobie in March and April 2013
- *The trial testimony*, the testimony at the June-July 2013 trial by Rachel, Sybrina, and Tracy.
- *Rest in Power*, the account in the book Rest in Power, alternately written by Tracy and Sybrina, 2017

According to Sybrina's March 2013 deposition, no one else at Sybrina's house, including Tracy, saw Diamond during her visit on March 19. Diamond remained in the car, and Sybrina met her there. Sybrina said it was an emotional meeting that lasted only about fifteen minutes. Sybrina at first claimed they did not discuss the details of the fatal encounter. Diamond delivered the letter, said Sybrina, as a way of "verifying" she had been on the phone with Trayvon. Sybrina described the letter to defense attorney Mark O'Mara as "sentimental" and "a personal letter that [Diamond] wrote to me... I guess it was just more of her feelings and, you know, what happened."

Although Sybrina refused to surrender the original letter, given its "personal" nature, the copy I downloaded showed that everything Sybrina said in regard to the letter was wrong, starting with the fact that there was nothing personal about it, no feelings, no "I loved

Trayvon," and not even a "Dear Sybrina." The letter reads like a witness affidavit, not a message to a grieving mom.

I immediately sensed this letter must have some great significance in what I now believed to be a switch in witnesses from Diamond to Rachel. The fact that Sybrina kept even the prosecutors unaware of the letter for a full year made me even more suspicious. The letter reads as follows:

> *March 19, 2012*
>
> *I was on the phone when Trevon decided to go to the Cornerstore. It started to rain so he decided to walk through another complex because it was raining to hard. He started walking then noticed someone was following him. Then he decided to find a shortcut cause the man wouldn't follow him. Then he said the man didn't follow him again. Then he looked back and saw the man again. The man started getting closer. Then Trevon turned around and said why are you following me!! Then I heard him fall, then the phone hung up. I called back and text. No response. In my mind I thought it was just a fight. Then I found out this tragic story.*
>
> *Thank you,*
> *Diamond Eugene*

I had strong suspicions that Diamond had been coached to create this narrative incriminating Zimmerman. With years of experience in examining documents and graphics, I started by reviewing the letter in Photoshop. The first thing that stood out was that letter did not start with "Dear Sybrina." There was no salutation whatsoever, just two paragraphs of narrative with a "Thank you" and a signature at the bottom and a date on top. The handwriting seemed very distinctive and deliberate, with exaggerated stylized capital letters everywhere.

Next I noticed that the signature made no sense. The letter was written in cursive, but the author signed "Diamond Eugene" in stylized block letter signature. The signature was an intriguing riddle in itself. The two words had a large space between that was unnatural for someone signing their first and last name. Also the first name, "Diamond," was slanted to the left, while the last name, "Eugene," was straight. The capital letter "D" in "Diamond" was much larger than the rest of the letters in the word, while the capital "E" in "Eugene" was the same height as the rest of the letters in "Eugene". It was as though a different person had signed each word, which seemed nuts. If the letter was not authentic though, wouldn't the forgers have had Rachel sign it "Rachel Jeantel" to avoid any questions? Maybe the name was authentic? But then, I wondered, where in the hell was Miss Diamond Eugene?

As far as the body of the letter, it was clear to me that a young, poorly educated girl was the author. The syntax is basic and the grammar rough. Sentences like, "Then he decided to find a shortcut cause the man wouldn't follow him," sound as if they were written by someone used to writing Twitter-style. In addition, the name Trayvon was misspelled as "Trevon," the more common spelling of the name. I concluded the person who wrote the letter did not know Trayvon Martin well or for very long.

Upon viewing the video of Sybrina's 2013 deposition, I saw her display the original letter on camera. Its jagged edges suggested that it was written in a spiral school notebook and roughly detached. Ironically, in that she was about to be faced with whether or not to bear false witness, Sybrina had removed the letter from her ever-present copy of the Christian Life Bible. Why did Sybrina feel a need to cloak the letter within the pages of holy scripture?

9

THE CRUMP TAPE

On March 19, 2012 at around 4 p.m., Diamond was dropped off at Sybrina's house. In an interview with state prosecutors only two weeks later, Sybrina told them she drove Diamond home after the meeting and spoke with her mother. I believe the goal of this initial in-person meeting at Sybrina's house had been to convince Diamond to return that evening for an on-camera TV interview with ABC's Matt Gutman. Diamond would not consent to the proposal.

Instead, she did agree to a recorded over-the-phone interview with attorney Benjamin Crump later that evening. It should be noted that Crump referred to her as "Diamond" on the phone recordings. Matt Gutman of ABC was present at Crump's end to record the phone interview as well. Despite his insider role, Gutman is not mentioned by name in the *Rest in Power* book. It is always just "ABC News."

I began to wonder whether any of the witnesses in this case could be trusted, including Diamond herself. In listening to the Crump tape, it was apparent that Crump was leading the witness.

"Let me do this here," said Crump at one point. "Let me have you start over and just saying that there, and say it loud and slow for me

OK? 1, 2, 3." Diamond promptly responded, "In this situation, in this kind of case, to me it's a racial. It is a racial. And at the end of the day, it is a innocent boy, just because he had a hoodie on." It was clear she was just repeating back to Crump the narrative he had been feeding the news and that he certainly wanted to hear.

"Say it in your words and say it loud and slow," said Crump after a pause. "He ain't do nothing," repeated Diamond dutifully. "He was just like going to get his little brother a little Skittle and a Arizona Ice tea. That's it." This was more channeling Crump. Even worse, whatever question Crump asked, Diamond simply responded in the affirmative.

"Did Trayvon sound scared?" Crump asked.

"Yeah," said Diamond as expected.

"Did Trayvon sound normal throughout the whole day since you had talked to him from that morning?" asked Crump.

"Yeah!" answered Diamond even more enthusiastically, adding, "Yeah he sound real happy!"

I had to laugh. From the texts, I knew Trayvon was *not* happy that day. Diamond knew that too, and she had been the one making him unhappy! Trayvon had texted her that day, "u makn m feel lik uon want m [you don't want me]" and again, "u sayd ima waste of yo time."

"it wat it is," responded Diamond.

"u really hurt a nigga feelns."

"It whatever."

"u done wit m??" Trayvon pleaded.

Texted Diamond coldly in return, "nigga go fuck a hoe."

Not being under oath, Diamond told Crump what he expected to hear. Diamond's willingness to misidentify the brand of drink Trayvon was carrying as "Arizona Iced Tea" was more indication she was on board with Team Trayvon's media narrative. In fact, Trayvon was carrying Arizona Watermelon Fruit Juice Cocktail.

Diamond also made numerous statements that suggested George hunted Trayvon down, such as, "The man started getting closer."

These comments flew in the face of all evidence. Prodded repeatedly by Crump about the effect of this incident on her health, Diamond claimed, "I was in shock, I was just really in shock." When Crump asked why she didn't attend Trayvon's wake five days after the shooting, Diamond replied, "I was just sick. I didn't go to school that day."

With Crump steering her, Diamond claimed she "was home all day" the Friday of the wake and that she "went to the hospital the next day." Crump then asked, "So you had to spend the night in the hospital?" Diamond answered hesitantly, "Yes." Crump repeatedly tried to get Diamond to affirm that she was taken ill only upon learning the news from her doctor that she was "the last person to talk to him." Oh the drama! This was all total rubbish.

At the end of the March 19 phone interview, Crump asked Diamond again if she would consider coming on camera "like we talked about earlier." Here, Crump gave away the game. The "earlier" referred to the apparent afternoon meeting with Sybrina that he also attended, either in person or on the phone.

Crump slipped up again later when his ego got the best of him during a Court TV interview. Crump took credit for Diamond's emerging out of nowhere three weeks after the shooting to make the phone recording contradicting all evidence. Crump told Court TV, "This interview happened, Jane, because we pushed her making a statement." Here Crump admitted there was a team effort that took time, the "pushing" was not Tracy's two minute phone call. Also, the "we" from "we pushed her" included Diamond's peers and Trayvon's close friends. Diamond's phone records, which I had also obtained, showed that for three weeks she was hammered day and night by calls and texts from Trayvon's two best friends, Mario and Steve-O. Felicia occasionally joined them in three-way calls. Unlike Trayvon's phone records, however, Diamond's did not include the content of the text messages. I was wishing they did.

At a noon press conference the next day, on March 20, Crump broadcast excerpts of his phone call with Diamond. Crump told the media, "They were dating." He also recounted how, as a sign of "puppy love," Diamond and Trayvon had spent hours on the phone that final day. "She couldn't even go to his wake she was so sick," he claimed. "Her mother had to take her to the hospital. She spent the night in the hospital."

For some reason, Crump shut off the tape with Diamond in mid-sentence when she was saying, "I thought it was a fight and then the next day..." He did not need to hear any more. "She connects the dots," Crump exclaimed to the media audience. "She completely blows Zimmerman absurd self-defense claim out of the water!" Crump asked the media repeatedly to respect her privacy, "She is a minor child."

Crump concluded his presentation, demanding, "Arrest George Zimmerman for the killing of Trayvon Martin in cold blood, today!" Matt Gutman might as well have been Crump's press agent. ABC.com headlined his article, "Trayvon Martin's Last Phone Call Triggers Demand for Arrest Right Now."

Crump also said he would give the tape of the Diamond interview only to the FBI, meaning officials under President Obama's control, and not to the local police. By the next day, the FBI and the U.S. Justice Department were announcing their intent to send agents of the Community Relations Service (CRS) to Sanford. When they did arrive, the CRS helped to organize protests and "actively worked to foment unrest" according to information later secured by Judicial Watch.

There was still much more for me to learn. I quickly downloaded Crump's entire twenty-minute March 19 phone interview with Diamond and brought it into my audio editing program. I also found an audio recording of Rachel Jeantel's April 2 interview with prosecutor Bernie de la Rionda, recorded two weeks later. I selected similar word sequences from each to compare their voices word for word, phrase for phrase. I listened over and over. It didn't take long.

Although both girls grew up in the same Miami Haitian-American community, their voices shared little. The tone, inflection, syntax, rhythm and accents varied conspicuously between the two girls.

Diamond spoke more rapidly and confidently than Rachel, and at a notably higher pitch and with much greater range. The variation in accents was almost as distinctive. Diamond, for instance, said, "Trayvon was walkin' out-da-STO" in a thick urban Miami accent. Rachel spoke slowly and with almost no accent. "He was leaving the store," she said. Diamond said, "Trayvon he was like walk." Rachel said, "Trayvon started walking." The terminology was different too. Rachel talked about her "mother," Diamond about her "mama." Diamond had a distinctive verbal tic, namely the repetition of the word "ahhh-ite" (alright) to answer in the affirmative. Rachel never used the word. Even the stories were different. Diamond told Crump, "It was raining hard," while Rachel told de la Rionda, "It was not raining."

Clearing my head after days of often numbing research, I realized I had all but confirmed the existence of a conspiracy to corrupt justice. In the era of increasingly fake news, I believed a fake witness had testified, that some people had to have known about it, and they got away with it. This sleight of hand had clearly encouraged other activists. If fake witnesses could go unchallenged, and nonsense slogans like "Skittles and iced tea" were accepted uncritically as fact, why should radical provocateurs *not* use false slogans like, "Hands up, don't shoot?" Social justice warriors now understood that the media had no incentive to look for the truth when the lie advanced their own radical agenda.

If my analysis so far was right, I had just uncovered perhaps the most flagrant witness fraud in modern times. Had The Trayvon Hoax been exposed at trial, the whole course of recent history would have been different. The Black Lives Matter movement might not have coalesced. The city of Ferguson might not have blown up. Colin Kaepernick might still be playing for the 49ers. And, Barack Obama might not have won reelection.

My plans for a film about the Trayvon Martin shooting and politics had suddenly and dramatically changed. I was about to shift from political analysis to investigative journalism. To help flesh out The Trayvon Hoax, I decided to write a companion book as well. There was too much at stake, and a book could cover many details that were too complex for a film.

I had not, however, abandoned political analysis. When all was said and done, I hoped to discover whether the individuals who exploited Trayvon's death–Andrew Gillum, Barack Obama, Obama's "wing man" Eric Holder, Florida State prosecutors and others–knew about the fraud at the heart of the case. The political implications went even deeper than the judicial ones.

So who really was "Diamond?" Even with all the phone records, I still could not identify her. Maybe that was by design. There were more than one hundred texts between Diamond and Trayvon that were missing from the Cellebrite phone records document. That said, the George Zimmerman case had helped launch the modern era of fake news and race hoaxes, it was ground zero. Diamond appeared to be at the center of it all. I had to find her. Knowing she was not Rachel Jeantel, I felt compelled to scour the 750 pages of Trayvon's cell phone report for clues again and again. The task was daunting. There were thousands of contacts and photos. Diamond was in there I knew, but searching for her real name and identity seemed an endless task.

In the contact list, for instance, there were five girls with "Diamond" as a first name. Although their phone numbers were different from that of Trayvon's Diamond, it was possible she had simply gotten a new phone number and Trayvon hadn't yet assigned it to her contact entry. Diamond also had a second phone number that she used to text Trayvon on at least a few occasions with the contact name, "RIDE OR DIE."

I decided a good starting point would be to find the five "Diamonds." If I could identify them and locate their photos, maybe I could find the "Diamond" at the heart of the story. Complicating the issue was the fact that "Diamond" was a common self-designation. "Diamond" might have been our girl's alias, the name she gave to people she did not want to get too close to her, a nickname or even a middle name.

To identify this girl I realized I first needed to know more about her back story. I needed to understand the culture, the street life, even the geography of the Miami area in order to sort out the hundreds of girls in Trayvon's cell phone records. To do this project right, I had to put filming on hold and do a little anthropology. For my fieldwork, there was only one place to go–Miami.

10

MISSION MIAMI

ARRIVING IN MIAMI ON A COOL, overcast December day, my film crew and I headed for the side of town that is on no known tourist route, the East side. This is where most of the characters in our drama lived: Rachel Jeantel, Mario, Stephan Bramble, Felicia Cineas, Francine Serve, Alicia Stanley, Ashley Burch, Faith Miller, very likely Diamond herself, and, when he was alive, Trayvon Martin. The streets were flat, linear and easy to follow: 100th Street, 99th Street and on down. It would be hard to get lost.

The main streets were lined with strip malls, the side streets with old Florida houses: detached, small, single level, no basement. These homes were clustered in a roughly four square mile patch of the Miami Gardens, Miramar, Opa Locka area. I managed to locate almost all their homes, including the very nice house in which Sybrina lived. I wanted to get a sense of the geography and also the life style. The only house I could not locate was Diamond's. I still did not know her real name, and her address was redacted in the summary of the State's April 2012 interviews with Sybrina and Tracy.

For the most part, these girls lived among their extended families with some combination of siblings, half-siblings, cousins, aunts, uncles, mother's boyfriends, and a grandma or two. Although the homes were small by suburban standards, they all had yards, front and back, and sat on their own lots. Most were well preserved. Faith Miller was the rare teen in this world with parents who were married to each other. She lived in a slightly larger home with two Baptist church vans in the driveway, one of which had a boat attached.

Although more than a month after the November 2018 election, I saw a large banner sign on a Miami Gardens street corner featuring a beaming picture of Andrew Gillum. With a disarming, aww-shucks smile and slightly bulbous nose, he reminded me of none other than Gomer Pyle, a name I am sure would not be recognizable at Michael Krop High School. Shazaam!

Leftists learned long ago that in America the man carrying the radical message has a much better chance of success if he looks and speaks like the people he is selling to. When a super friendly black guy says, "Anybody who works a full time job ought to earn a wage they can live on," or "We have to treat health care as a right not a privilege," he has a much better chance of winning votes than if a screaming old white man says what the end game really is: termination of the free market constitutional republic and the implementation of socialism in a one-party state. Progressives "progress" toward socialism. That is the nature of the beast.

In my research on Andrew Gillum, I soon saw he was not just selling pie-in-the-sky hope. He was selling fear. On June 9, 2018, Gillum tweeted, "We need look no further than the death of Trayvon Martin..." Two days later, during a Democratic primary debate in Pinellas County, Gillum focused his attention on the man who shot Trayvon, "George Zimmerman was able to interpret the very presence of Trayvon Martin to be a threat. And because of Stand Your Ground laws, which have no place in civilized society, was able to engage him, snuff out his life and get away with it." The following month he tweeted, "Stand Your Ground has created a state of emergency in Florida."

I now understood these comments to be false in every detail. That did not much matter. In a Democrat debate no one was about to correct Gillum. If there were a litmus test among Democrat candidates in Florida, it was the belief that Trayvon Martin was an innocent child, "just trying to get home to deliver candy," whose life was wantonly terminated by a racist white man.

In truth, the "very presence" of Trayvon did not disturb the Hispanic Retreat at Twin Lakes resident. What disturbed George Zimmerman was that Trayvon was wandering around in the rain, in a townhouse community that had been plagued by break-ins and home invasions. In no sense did George "engage" Trayvon. It was Trayvon who tried to intimidate George while he was in his car, and soon thereafter Trayvon confronted and surprise-attacked Zimmerman from behind, a man nearly half-a-foot shorter. As shall be seen too, and as Gillum surely knew, Florida's Stand Your Ground law was not used in Zimmerman's legal defense.

It would be wrong, however, to presume ignorance on Gillum's part. He knew what he was saying, and he knew he could get away with it. Gillum is a knowing participant in a long tradition. A self-identified "Democratic Socialist," Gillum showed no more commitment to the truth than Marxists of yore. The Bernie Sanders-inspired "Our Revolution" saw Gillum as one of its own and endorsed him. For its mission, this organization proudly aspires to "reclaim democracy for the working people of our country by harnessing the transformative energy of the 'political revolution.'"

The radical leftist group "Dream Defenders" did more than endorse Gillum. They worked to get him elected. In August 2013, this group came together to protest the justice system and Zimmerman's acquittal. When Gillum won the Democrat nomination for Florida governor in 2018, Brentin Mock wrote in *City Lab*, "It's not out of the question to say that he can thank Trayvon Martin for that." Mock was right. Gillum and the Dream Defenders worked the Trayvon angle often and shamelessly.

As a signal of his support for the Dream Defenders during the 2018 campaign, Gillum signed their incoherently Marxist "Freedom Pledge." Florida was "a for-profit police state," according to the Dream Defenders' manifesto. The group's rhetoric was inflammatory and anti-cop. "We can live in a state where parents and teachers are given everything they need to support the raising of our children," reads the pledge. "We don't have to let another parent lose their child to a bullet, a badge or a dollar sign." The "child" at the heart of this pledge was, of course, Trayvon Martin. To win, Gillum ran a shockingly race-based campaign that accused his opponent of being a racist at every turn. He knew the socialist playbook called for making black voters angry and fearful.

I shot some video of the Andrew Gillum campaign sign and continued with my camera crew toward Michael Krop High, the school that suspended Trayvon three times in his final school year and was considering expelling him. I needed to obtain old high school yearbooks to help me identify more of Trayvon's contacts in my search to find the girl he knew as "Diamond."

I drove to the four nearby high schools that I thought Diamond might have attended. The schools were all modern and well-maintained. It dawned on me that the adolescents at the center of this drama all lived in respectable single-family homes, attended decent schools and had all they could want in terms of food, fun, fashion, phones, and other pastimes–licit and illicit both. Few of Trayvon's friends worked to pay for their pleasures, and most would go on to college, including Diamond herself. Yet, to hear Andrew Gillum tell it, you would think they were all marginalized and oppressed. In fact, this was the message they had been beaten into their heads since they were old enough to absorb the Leftist propaganda.

All the high schools I visited had security screening at the front door. That is the way of the world today. At each school, I asked for the administrative offices with a goal of purchasing yearbooks from 2011-2014, the time Trayvon and his friends would have been attending. Officials at Miami Norland High and Carol City High were happy to make a sale. Someone I met at Norland proved to be particularly helpful. This was Rachel Jeantel's school. This person told me Rachel Jeantel was an *18-year-old* ninth grader in 2012. I was also told that Rachel was enrolled in the Exceptional Student Education (ESE) program, a program designed for students with intellectual disabilities, autism, and language impairment among other problems. This made sense because Rachel had told Zimmerman defense attorney Don West in a 2103 deposition that she had failed twice and was held back two school years. I recalled that Rachel often demanded of West that he repeat questions over and over and would often mumble incoherently in response. Rachel also struggled to understand common words. When Don West asked if she had dictated the Sybrina letter to someone, Rachel looked puzzled and asked, "What is dictate? Explain dictate." West obliged, "It's when another person writes down what's being said." This confused Rachel even more. Later she said, "I don't even know what I remember," and, "I will get confuse."

After learning about Rachel and the ESE program, I began to wonder whether Rachel Jeantel's disabilities made her an easy target for being cruelly exploited by those who knew of her limitations. I learned a hell of a lot in my brief visit to Miami Norland High School!

At Miramar High and Michael Krop High, administrators were more suspicious of me. They questioned who I was and why I wanted to buy old yearbooks, even though there were public records. I did look a little out of place, being white in an almost exclusively black school and wearing a western shirt. Not wanting to reveal the nature of my investigation, I bluffed that my niece's best friend had attended school there and lost her yearbooks during a hurricane. I thought it was creative enough, and it worked both times.

Back in my hotel, I flipped through the yearbooks. There were thousands of students whose names and photos I would need to cross check with Trayvon's phone records.

Back on the hunt, I could not resist stopping at Diamond Girl Beauty Supply in Miramar. The "Diamond" imagery seemed to be everywhere. This store, I could see, had more kinds of wigs and weaves than my local Home Depot had of screws and nails. I figured the more I knew about the many varieties of hair pieces, the more easily I could identify Diamond. I quickly came to realize though, that in addition to being fashion choices, the wigs and weaves served as disguises. Hair mattered a great deal to the girls in this world even if much of it was harvested from other people's heads in far-off lands.

Next, I visited Antioch Missionary Baptist Church. The deeply Christ-centered church, located in Miami Gardens on the border of Miramar, was the one Trayvon and his mother attended. It was also the church where the funeral service for Trayvon was held. Despite the shabby neighborhood around it, the church was doing well enough to afford a major construction project that would triple its size and include an elementary school. However, in a nod to the teachers unions, Andrew Gillum was insisting that public dollars be spent only on public education. I wondered if the educators at Antioch who supported Gillum because of his skin color knew that?

11

LITTLE HAITI

I KNEW from Diamond's references in her text messages to Trayvon that she was of Haitian descent. "We Zoe", she texted Trayvon referring to her family. "Zoe" was a nickname for Haitian, though not derogatory, more like a "Yank" for an American or "Brit" for someone from the UK. In addition, Diamond's last name on the letter to Sybrina Fulton was "Eugene." If the letter were legit, this was more proof that Diamond was Haitian, given that Eugene is a Haitian last name.

I made my way to Little Haiti in downtown Miami, a rundown area just over the bridge from luxurious Miami Beach. In addition to tourist traps that sold Haitian crafts, the area did have some authentic Haitian stores and markets that catered to the large Haitian community in Miami. I walked around Little Haiti to get a feel of the place and the people. What I noticed right away was that there were no tourists at all, at least not at the time I visited. It was just my cameraman, Haitians, and me. I did not exactly blend. There were beautiful murals painted on most buildings, including one that said, "Welcome to Little Haiti" with a painting of a woman dressed as a priestess. She was surrounded on either side by giant diamonds. Needless to say, I felt this was a good sign!

I visited some of the stores and bought some tchotchkes including a Haitian spice grinder, a Haitian flag, and a bottle of "good luck" water. The storekeepers were all of Haitian origin, dressed in what I took to be traditional Haitian clothes. The females wore traditional head wraps with long flowing dresses and colorful robes. I spoke to them in French and they spoke back to me in French-based Creole. They appreciated the Frenchish chit-chat.

Hoping for some dumb luck, I asked one shopkeeper, "Je cherche Diamond Eugene. Est-ce que tu la connais?" She good-naturedly repeated the name but said, no, she didn't know Diamond and did not know where to find her. I suspect if Diamond had been working in the back room, I would have gotten the same answer. I also asked if they knew a "Voodoo priestess" who might give me some advice. The first four women I talked with said pretty much the same thing, no Diamond, no priestess. The fifth woman offered a little more help after I purchased a Haitian blanket and a hat from her. She suggested I go to a Haitian bookstore accessible only from a back alley on 59th Street. Intrigued, I ducked down the alleyway with my cameraman, and we entered a store filled from floor to ceiling with statues of deities, paintings, religious texts and just about every handicraft ever made in Haiti. A Haitian man, dressed in western clothing, greeted us. I asked him in French to see the Voodoo priestess. He answered in Creole, 'I am the Voodoo priest.' He looked more like an accountant, but I was in no position to argue.

When I told him I was looking for someone in particular, he advised that for fifty dollars, he could help me find her by arranging for me to ask "the spirit." I requested to film the session and he simply said, "Pay more," and I added fifty dollars. He told me to take the camera and motioned me into a back room behind the cash register. Statues of deities stood on the floor and hung from the wall. Mixed in among them were all kinds of exotic plants. He may not have looked authentic, but this room sure did.

For an additional eleven dollars, he offered a candle to be lit, which I paid, and then, without charge, put on a cassette that played Haitian music. He picked up a Bible and a bottle of whiskey. He read from the former and drank from the latter. I took a swig when he offered it. Crossing his arms, he shook both my hands one by one. He then poured whiskey on a large rock on the floor and lit it on fire. The flames shot up until he spit on them with holy water. With the fire extinguished, the priest began to gyrate, his whole body now convulsing as he motioned for the spirit to overtake his physical being. The spirit settled in with a sudden jolt and a massive inhale by the priest. He then chanted in Creole.

Then he asked what I wanted, and I explained I was looking for someone named Diamond Eugene. "When did you last see her?" he asked. "I've never met her," I answered. This seemed to disappoint him. He then asked me why I wanted to find her. Without giving too much away, I told him, "Someone was killed six years ago, and she knows what happened. I need to find her."

The Voodoo priest ordered me to cut a beat up, seventy-eight-card deck of Tarot Cards. That done, he began dealing. The first card he held high and said, "This is the Hermit. It means I can't help you. I don't know where she is." I began to think I had just been fleeced out of what was now one hundred and eleven dollars by a Haitian con artist.

"You don't know where she is? No idea at all?" I asked the spirit.

"She is out of town. She's out of town."

I felt the spirit should know more! "Will I find her one day?" I asked, hoping to get some return on my investment. He dealt another card and held it up. "It is positive you will find her one day," he said.

"I will?"

"Yes."

"When will I find her?" I asked, now feeling more encouraged about my investment. He dealt another card and held it up. It was the World.

"I don't know," he said.

"You don't know?"

"No. I don't know." What kind of spirit was this anyway?

"Okay," I said, giving it one more shot, "you say I will find Diamond one day, right?"

"Yes."

"When I do find her, will it be good or bad? Is Diamond a good person?"

The priest then dealt another card. It had a black background. It was the Devil. "It's black. Diamond is no good. She has a bad heart."

"So you mean I'll meet her and be disappointed. She's bad?"

"Definitely," he answered. "She's no good. Diamond is no good. When you meet her, you'll say that. She has a bad heart. Look again, its black.

I believed him, and with that I felt I got my money's worth. The priest began to gyrate as the spirit exited his body with another jolt. He acted like his old self had taken his body over again. He said a few prayers and the session was over. As far as one hundred and eleven-dollar experiences go, this was, if nothing else, a memorable one. I made my way out of Little Haiti with the Voodoo priest's prophecy heavy on my mind, "Diamond was no good. I would find her, but she would have a bad heart." I had been warned.

From Little Haiti, I headed to the Dade Memorial Park in Opa Locka where Trayvon was buried. More than just curious, I wanted to pay my respects. I felt as if I had gotten to know Trayvon and understood the betrayals that marked the last two years of his life. On the way, I stopped to purchase a bouquet of flowers.

The cemetery was large and well-maintained. The day was fittingly overcast. I drove inside and quickly found Trayvon's name engraved on the lowest block of a tall granite mausoleum. Seeing his name saddened me. It reminded me how short was his life and avoidable was his death. On the pink granite block were written the words, "Rest My Son," followed by "Job Well Done."

Above his name was a small photo of young Trayvon in a round frame. This was the photo that Team Trayvon used to establish their media narrative of a small child with candy who was stalked and murdered while just trying to get home. Wearing a red "Hollister" shirt, the eternally-smiling boy appears to be about twelve in the photo. This was Trayvon seemingly at his best, his happiest, his most cheerful before his life took a dark turn. I wondered if the family put this in place strategically after Trayvon became a household name or because in all the photos in his last few years Trayvon is scowling. I placed the bouquet of flowers and said a prayer in his memory.

Having accomplished what I came to Miami to do, I flew back to Los Angeles. I had learned a lot. I had driven by the homes of Trayvon's girlfriends, been to his high schools, gotten the yearbooks I needed, traversed his neighborhood, visited his church, learned all about Rachel, seen the vestiges of the Gillum campaign, and paid my respects at Trayvon's grave. The trip gave me a much clearer sense of the world Trayvon inhabited. Thanks to the Voodoo priest, I now had a glimpse, real or imagined, into the soul of the elusive Diamond.

12

UNMASKING DIAMOND

UPON RETURNING FROM MIAMI, I took all the high school yearbooks I had collected to my LA studio and spread them out–four schools, four years' worth from each school, sixteen yearbooks in all. I knew Diamond had to be in there somewhere.

The years ranged from 2011, Trayvon's sophomore year, to 2014, the year after he would have graduated. The high schools were all those in Trayvon's orbit: Norland, Miramar, Carol City, and Michael Krop. I first searched the yearbooks for photos of Trayvon's friends and girlfriends whose names or nicknames I had already gleaned from Trayvon's phone as documented in the massive 750-page Cellebrite report. I located many of them.

Since Facebook and Twitter are both public and searchable, I attempted to align the information from those sources with the yearbooks and the Cellebrite data from Trayvon's phone. Often, I had to look through an entire high school class to find a match with a single photo from Trayvon's cell phone photo gallery. Typically, I would pick out five or six likely suspects from the yearbook and try to match up the data from the other sources. It was a massive undertaking, but I could not afford to be wrong.

As I perused the personal information these girls posted on the various social media sites–Facebook, Twitter, Instagram and more–it occurred to me this generation put *way* too much info out in the public sphere. Without it though, I realized I would never be able to find Diamond or "Bae" as Trayvon sometimes called her.

One phone number I identified in Diamond's phone records was that of her friend Ariana. From reading Trayvon's texts, I knew that Ariana belonged to "da crew" and that she and Diamond went clubbing together. Having found her in the Miami Norland yearbook, I called Ariana and asked if she had a friend in high school named "Diamond."

"Yes," she said, "Diamond Dixon at Norland." I thanked her and excitedly hung up. With five "Diamonds" among Trayvon's contacts, I was convinced Ariana had just shortened my search considerably. Norland, as it happened, was the same high school Rachel Jeantel had attended. Although there was no photo of Rachel in the Norland yearbook for the critical year of 2012, there were photos of Diamond Dixon in 2011, 2012 and 2013. She looked like she could be a match for the photo of "Bae!"

I then looked for videos on Diamond Dixon's Facebook page. My goal was to match her voice in a video with that of Benjamin Crump's "phone girl." There were no videos. Complicating my search was that Diamond Dixon, like many adolescent girls, frequently changed her appearance, often dramatically. Smile, no smile. Weave, no weave. Makeup, no makeup. When I compared the photos of Diamond Dixon to the picture of "Bae" in Trayvon's cell records again and again, she looked similar enough that I judged the possibility of match at about 85 percent, but 85 percent was not good enough.

I began to focus on features that could not change over time, starting with the teeth. I also looked carefully at facial structure: the distance between eyes, from nose to lips, and lips to chin. I did a background check to find Diamond Dixon's phone number, but the numbers listed did not lead to Ms. Dixon. Was she trying to hide, I wondered? Could this Diamond be "Bae"?

After an anxious day comparing photos of Diamond Dixon to Bae, I decided she was not the one. Diamond Dixon had a large gap between her two front teeth. Bae did not, and Bae's nose was not as broad as Diamond Dixon's. Chagrined, I called Ariana back and asked her whether she knew any other girls named Diamond that she maybe went clubbing with during her high school days.

"There were several girls named Diamond," she told me, "but none I was close with other than Diamond Dixon." This floored me. Diamond told Trayvon more than once she went clubbing with Ariana but Ariana had no memory of a "Diamond" other than Diamond Dixon? I thanked her and got back to work.

Having learned a good deal about how I would need to approach this search, I moved on to the next Diamond in Trayvon's cell records, Diamond Johnson. I quickly found her photos in the Miramar High School yearbooks. This was the same high school attended by Daisha Mitchell, Trayvon's junior high girlfriend. Diamond Johnson's Facebook page had loads of information. She was now an accomplished author who had written a dozen romantic novels based on the urban Miami youth scene. Good for her.

I jumped to Diamond Johnson's Facebook page video section and was rewarded with twenty videos, many in which she was addressing her fans. I listened to her voice and felt it was well within the range of "phone girl" in terms of the tone and urban inflections. However, I realized that the voice of sixteen-year-old Diamond on a 2012 iPhone 4 speaker phone to speaker phone recording would sound somewhat different from that of a twenty-two year old young woman on a recent video recording even if they belonged to the same person. As much as I wanted Diamond Johnson to be "the" Diamond, I knew "Johnson" was not exactly a Haitian name. Hoping that perhaps Diamond's mother was Haitian, I found Diamond Johnson's phone number and called to inquire.

"This is Diamond," she said. This was a welcoming thing to hear.

"Hello, Diamond, my niece is a big fan of your books," I bluffed. "I just wanted to see if I could purchase some autographed copies." I thought if I could get an inscription from Diamond, I could see if her handwriting matched that on the Sybrina letter.

"Sure, which book did you want?"

I explained that I'd like her entire series and offered to pay an extra $100 for her time and trouble if she would inscribe and sign them too. She readily agreed, telling me she was nine months pregnant, but would try to ship them out the next day. I sent her the money by PayPal. Within a few days the books arrived with long inscriptions. I was able to compare her signature "Diamond Johnson" to the "Diamond Eugene" signature on the Sybrina letter. They did not match.

Further, although her books detailed the "fucked up situation" in which many of Johnson's friends must have lived, Johnson came from a much more stable background than "Bae." In the acknowledgement section of her novel *Little Miami Girl*, Johnson thanked her "amazing parents...for believing in me." In that same section, she thanked God, quoting Philippians 4:13, "I can do all things through Christ Jesus who strengthens me." Her faith struck me as much more sincere than Trayvon's Diamond, and I could not see that girl ever writing a novel. I was on to the next Diamond.

A similar pattern emerged as I continued to check out the rest of Trayvon's female friends. They all attended one of the four high schools within the four square-mile area. They all wore tons of make-up and different weaves. They all changed their looks dramatically from year to year, and even day to day, as documented on Facebook and Twitter. They all spoke in the urban Miami dialect. They all had, "We miss you, Trayvon," and, "Throw Zimmerman's fat ass in jail," Facebook and Twitter posts in 2012. And, they all seemed to know each other.

Many of these girls were Facebook friends. Daisha Mitchell was a friend of Diamond Johnson's. Diamond Johnson was a friend of Diamond Dixon's, and on and on. The connections seemed endless. Superficially, each girl I investigated had much in common with "the" Diamond. To prove or disprove that a given Diamond was the phone girl in question, I used all sorts of strategies to gather biographical data and voice and handwriting samples. I could only eliminate a girl after she failed to match on a critical variable: the phone voice, the handwriting, the photo of Bae, the family or ethnic background.

On one occasion, I convinced myself that Diamond Jones of Norland High School was "the" Diamond, only to find a piece of information that eliminated her. On more than a few nights I went to sleep depressed, forcing myself the next morning to plow ahead. Will the real Diamond please stand up, pretty please? After weeks of stumbling into investigative cul-de-sacs, I had to wonder how police detectives maintained their sanity.

After my "Diamond hunt" proved fruitless, I decided to make a list of all the girls from all the yearbooks with the last name of "Eugene," a Haitian name. I did not know for sure if the "Diamond Eugene" signature on the letter to Sybrina was legitimate, but it was a lead worth pursuing.

I had figured if someone had forged the letter given to Sybrina, they would have had Rachel sign it "Rachel Jeantel" to avoid suspicion. The possibility remained strong that Diamond's last name was "Eugene," and the name "Diamond" was a nickname or middle name. Drawing from the high school yearbooks, I put the names of eight girls with the last name "Eugene" on a spreadsheet. Given that Rachel's mother's name was Marie Eugene, one theory I had was that Rachel might be covering for someone who was a close relative. Unfortunately, I could not find any familial link between my list of "Eugenes" to Rachel Jeantel or her mother. Given that Rachel's mother, Marie Eugene, was from Haiti, I could find no family tree for her in my online database searches whatsoever.

They say that 3 a.m. is the worst time of the day, too late or too early to do anything. For some reason that was the time I would wake up and mentally review the evidence, occasionally in a sweat. On one unhappy night at 3 a.m., I found myself wondering whether Crump's "phone girl" was a total imposter. What if the real Diamond had refused to come forward for some reason and "phone girl" was only the first of two counterfeit witnesses?

I imagined a scenario in which the real Diamond had urged Trayvon to attack Zimmerman and felt guilty about it. If she then resisted coming forward, what if someone who wanted Zimmerman arrested found a random female to make the recorded phone call to

Crump? Of course, this would have meant a switch to a second fake witness in Rachel when a live body witness was needed for prosecutors, but I was running out of ideas.

As a possible candidate for "fake phone girl" I considered Shawnika Carridice, the sister of Trayvon's best friend Mario. Shawnika was Trayvon's age and in his contact list. She traveled in the same circles. If she wasn't the real Diamond–and I could not rule that out–maybe she served as the first fake Diamond? If my thinking sounds a little desperate, it was.

I checked out Shawnika's Facebook page. She had posted videos. Her voice had all the Miami urban inflections, but by now I knew Diamond's vocal range well enough to sense the difference between her voice and Shawnika's. To prove or disprove the Shawnika theory, I obtained handwriting samples of Shawnika's. They came, unfortunately, from the Miami Courts. Shawnika had charges for grand theft auto and juvenile delinquency. She had also taken out a restraining order against her "baby daddy." Her handwriting, as I quickly realized, did not match Sybrina's letter for the Diamond Eugene signature. I was emotionally exhausted. Diamond baby, where are you?

Next, I decided to turn to Diamond's cell phone records. Like Tracy Martin, Diamond had refused to provide them to authorities. As with Tracy, the FDLE had to subpoena Diamond's cell records from her carrier, Simple Mobile. The subpoena yielded details of calls and texts from February 26, 2012, starting at 7:08 a.m., all the way through to April 2, 2012, at 8:58 a.m.

The report accompanying Diamond's phone records explained that Simple Mobile was a "prepaid cell phone provider." The phone Diamond used was essentially a "burner" phone. According to the report, "no first or last name information was present" on the account. "Our subscribers are not required to enter name, address, or contact information," the report continued. Diamond had a $40 per month prepaid plan that offered unlimited talk and text.

In her April 2012 interview with prosecutors, in what seemed like a risky move, Rachel Jeantel answered in the affirmative when asked by Bernie de la Rionda if her cell phone number was 786-419-3726.

This, I knew for a fact, was Diamond's number. Then de la Rionda asked her, "Is that phone number under your name or under somebody else's name?" Rachel answered, "It should now, it should be now under my name."

In her short answer Rachel used the word "now" twice. That word mattered. As of April 2, 786-419-3726 was *now* Rachel's phone number. This was, of course, the number to which Trayvon sent his hundreds of texts, many of them sexually explicit. This was the number from which Trayvon received his final phone call. It seems highly likely that the real Diamond gave up her burner phone number to Rachel, and Rachel had the number transferred to a new T-Mobile account in her own name, perhaps that very day. There is much about the world these girls did not know, but they did know their phones.

In buying Rachel's story, the prosecutors accepted that she was the hottie of Trayvon's dreams. Although Rachel told de la Rionda she had a T-Mobile account, and he knew Diamond's account was a Simple Mobile, he let the discrepancy pass. If de la Rionda had wanted to, he could have blown the whistle on the witness switch right there.

In retrospect, I probably should have started with Diamond's phone records. There was a wealth of information within, including the times, dates, and phone numbers of the calls she made and the calls she received in a period that stretched from February 26 to April 2, 2012. Text message times and dates were included as well.

I had no idea of the work involved when I undertook this project, but by now I was hooked. I decided to identify all the phone numbers in Diamond's phone records too, and, by cross checking Diamond's contacts, deduce her identity. This task was complicated by the fact that Diamond had another phone. This I knew from Trayvon's cell phone records. That phone number, RIDE OR DIE 786-537-3121, was registered to Daniel Eugene, Rachel Jeantel's half-brother on her mother's side, who was born in Haiti. Diamond's phone records were a place to start, and I dove in.

I did Instant Checkmate background searches for every phone number on Diamond's cell records. I quickly identified Diamond's most frequent caller on the day of and in the weeks after Trayvon's death as sixteen-year-old Felicia Cineas. Felicia, I figured out in reviewing her social media accounts, was the younger sister of Francine Serve. What a small world! Francine Serve was the woman Rachel Jeantel claimed she had asked to pen the letter to Trayvon's mother, Sybrina Fulton. And, Francine Serve had worked at Sybrina's house as a caregiver for her brother who lived with her. Well, well, well–this was getting interesting!

Felicia Cineas was a classmate of Trayvon's at Michael Krop. She had exchanged a few text messages with Trayvon in September 2011 on a Sunday. The texts likely revolved around church youth group activities. Background research revealed that Felicia had Haitian roots. Her mother had recently died but not before giving birth to seven or so children by at least three different fathers.

Two days after Attorney Benjamin Crump's press conference starring Felicia's BFF Diamond, Felicia was featured in an Associated Press photo sporting a Trayvon T-shirt. The occasion was a series of impromptu school walkouts across South Florida. They began on March 22 at Miami's Carol City High School, which Trayvon had attended for two years. The school principal had approved an on-campus demonstration, but students seized the moment and kept on walking.

On Friday, March 23, students from a dozen more Miami-Dade high schools and a couple of middle schools joined the walkouts. Students in neighboring Broward County walked out as well. If adults were unable to check the movement, they had the power to fuel it. At Southridge High in Miami-Dade County students formed giant initials "T" and "M" on the school football field, and in an obviously pre-arranged fly-over, the local media shot the formation from the air.

In Broward County, school staff helped lead the protests. "For the most part they are being organized and are being supported by the school family as an outpouring show of support," said a spokeswoman. "I think the reaction is similar to the national reaction. I don't think our students are any different than others."

Felicia's Facebook page showed her participating in many Trayvon protests. In reviewing her social media account, I got the impression that she was tight with two cousins of similar age, Chassidy McClenney and Sabrina Bellefleur. Given their closeness to Felicia, I had to check them out as potential Diamonds too. Like many other girls, they had much in common with Diamond, but when their voice and handwriting samples did not match up, I moved on.

In addition to friends like Felicia, Diamond's phone records revealed her calling many business numbers. Some calls seemed routine, such as those to Pizza Hut and Chinese take-out restaurants on the food front, and Proactiv and RX Brown Skin on the cosmetics front. What seemed a little odd were calls to Chase Bank, Capitol One, and Shell Oil Credit Cards. The fact that a sixteen-year-old girl with no car, no job, and no driver's license was calling financial institutions on an untraceable cell phone struck me as a wee bit suspicious.

Beginning on March 1, only four days after Trayvon's death, his best friend Mario began calling Diamond regularly. His calls soon increased in frequency and often included three-way calls with Diamond and Felicia. Mario was tight with Trayvon's family. In fact, he traveled with the entourage to Orlando for an early press conference. Sybrina Fulton mentioned Mario in her deposition. It seemed likely that given his closeness to the family and his constant communication with Diamond and Felicia, Mario was prodding Diamond to come forward on behalf of Team Trayvon.

Mario certainly knew about Diamond's relationship with Trayvon. When Diamond texted her teen "marriage proposal" to Trayvon on February 13–"do u want be my ride to die nigga"–Trayvon promptly forwarded the text to his closest friends. One of them, Michael French, one-upped Trayvon's boast, "I see u my nigga, but still ain't got nothing on me."

I was coming to believe that Mario, Felicia, and Diamond talked about Diamond's phone calls with Trayvon leading up to his death. Given his closeness to the Martin family, Mario surely must have shared this information with Tracy Martin in early March. Trayvon's good friend, Stephan "Steve-O" Bramble, was likely pressuring Diamond as well. He called and texted her often too. This was the same Steve-O who posted a video on his Facebook page of Trayvon and friends smoking weed. That video is still on Steve-O's Facebook page today.

There was a lot to absorb from Diamond's phone records. For me, it would be one new revelation per hour until I learned what I needed to learn. Among the more interesting of those leads were the seventy-nine communications, both phone calls and texts, between Diamond and ABC News correspondent Matt Gutman. I wondered about the ethical considerations of a TV news reporter calling a sixteen-year old, often late at night, but one thing these messages did was establish beyond any doubt that the "Diamond" whose records I had secured was indeed the girl on the phone with both Gutman and Crump.

Tracy Martin had called Diamond's number twice. The first one came in the evening of Saturday, March 17, just after Diamond received several calls from Mario. The second short call came on Sunday night, March 18, again just after Mario had called. From that time on, Sybrina Fulton, Trayvon's mother, was the one person on Team Trayvon with whom Diamond communicated. Later prosecutor Bernie de la Rionda admitted to HLN that his office's only means of communication with Diamond was through Sybrina Fulton. That was a shocking revelation. For state prosecutors to allow a victim's mother to be in charge of a mysterious witness who emerged out of thin air seemed to be opening the door for corruption of the case. Between early morning Monday, March 19, until the phone records expired on April 2, Sybrina and Diamond exchanged twenty-seven texts and had seven phone calls between them.

Diamond spoke with Crump only twice. The rationale for the first call I understood. It came in on March 19. This was for the actual recorded phone interview with Crump. The second call was suspicious. Diamond called Crump in the morning of Saturday, March 31. I had to wonder whether this meant Crump knew about the witness switch that followed two days later.

During the month of March 2012, Rachel Jeantel and Diamond called and/or texted just about every day, but never in the morning. As Rachel said in her deposition, she was not an early riser. In fact, she said she may have led the Miami-Dade Public Schools in "tardies," telling Don West, "When I like feel like wakin' up, I wake up."

As much as I was learning about Diamond and her world, there was even more that still eluded me. For starters, I still did not know her real identity. Then too, every time I identified another friend through Trayvon's phone records, I understood there was still much more to learn. I had to force myself to read Trayvon's 750-page phone records over and over, and slowly. Information that I once brushed by now seemed more and more relevant. It was like reading and rereading a massive novel, the ending of which still mystified me.

This was a journey of discovery, but the jewel of my Port-au-Prince, Diamond, resisted being found. On too many nights, I would wake in a sweat from one of those classic frustration dreams. Mine, however, wasn't about being late for class or missing a flight. It was about finding and then losing Diamond. I knew Diamond was "Bae," and I must have seen her photo many times while searching Trayvon's photo gallery, but this chameleon of a girl still defied my best efforts to identify her.

The answer just had to be there though! I reminded myself that Trayvon had often begged Diamond to send photos of herself, and she regularly obliged him, texting, "just sent it," and, "did you get it?" One early morning, I awoke with an idea. If I could cross check the times Diamond texted Trayvon that she had just sent him a photo against the times the photos arrived in the photo gallery, which should be almost simultaneous, I could solve the problem. True, there were three thousand photos in Trayvon's photo gallery to sort through, but they were all time stamped.

I shot out of bed, pulled out the 750-page Cellebrite report, and quickly made a spreadsheet list of all the times Diamond had sent Trayvon photos. I had to kick myself upon realizing how doable this task was. I should have figured this out sooner! I found a run where

Diamond had texted Trayvon four photo images in succession, each accompanied with an explanatory text exchange with Trayvon. These transmissions took place on February 19, one week before Trayvon's death. Each text gave a clue to what was in each photo:

- Diamond and Trayvon had been discussing setting up her cousin, "Lil Cuz JJ," with one of Trayvon's friends. She texted her cousin's photo.
- Diamond sent the same photo of "Lil Cuz JJ" again, two seconds later.
- Diamond sent a photo of herself, but Trayvon thought the photo was another of "Lil Cuz JJ." Diamond schooled him on the difference: "dat me u ass u dnt know how ur chick look."
- Diamond sent a photo of what I presumed featured her breasts. She texted, "just for my bae Cuz he had a bad day hahaha my two little friends will make smile :-) :-) I hope."

All I had to do was cross-reference the times these texts were sent against the "created" times the photos materialized in Trayvon's photo gallery, and I had my Diamond! Then it dawned on me that there was an even easier way to find her. Diamond had sent the same photo of her cousin twice in succession. I just needed to locate two back-to-back pictures of the same young girl. If I found those, the rest would fall into place, including the distinctive boob photo. There could not possibly be any similar photo run in the photo gallery.

I flipped forward five hundred pages to the photo gallery, and lo and behold, there were the photos all in a row: the cousin, the cousin again, Diamond, and Diamond offering up her chest. My excitement warred with my dismay at not having figured this out sooner. It was just too easy. But here she was at last, my Diamond–well dressed, well composed, and genuinely pretty. It was no wonder she mesmerized Trayvon. She was a heart stopper and a heart breaker. Just from looking at her, I knew she knew it.

My journey of discovery, however, was not yet over. Comparing the photos of Diamond to "Bae" was no slam dunk. This girl altered her appearance so much with weaves, makeup, and lighting I still could not be sure she and Bae were one and the same. More problematically, I still did not know her real name. Oy vey! I felt like I was starting all over again. I needed a name!

I went back to the yearbooks. I had long ago scanned them, so I put them up on the computer screen next to the new photos of Diamond. But before attempting the daunting task of looking through the photos of thousands of girls from four high schools, I decided to see if I could get lucky by revisiting the girls whose backgrounds I already knew. I started with Trayvon's old girlfriends and female friends. No, Diamond was not Faith, not Ashley, not Daisha, not Samantha, not Ayanna. Then I decided to revisit the girls named Diamond and compared them. No. No. No. No. No. All No. Then I decided to revisit those with the last name "Eugene." No. No. No. No. No. Yessssssssss! I found her! Diamond was Brittany Eugene, a sophomore at Miramar High School! In her 2012 yearbook photo she was even sporting the same Chinese weave with bangs as in one photo she sent Trayvon in February 2012!

I quickly did an online background check on Brittany Eugene and discovered her full legal name was "Brittany Diamond Eugene." Voila! There was the name "Diamond." It was her middle name! Born on January 2, 1996, she was the sixteen-year-old "minor child" that Crump implored the media not to contact. I had found my girl! All the puzzle pieces were falling into place.

Not quite all. At the very end of my investigation, I discovered one more shocking bit of information. Before revealing what that information is, let me preface all discussion of Diamond's relatives with the caveat that these are the people Diamond grew up thinking were her blood relatives. The DNA evidence, however, strongly suggests that if Diamond is related to these people, the nature of these relationships is not as direct as Instant Checkmate had indicated.

I quickly identified Diamond's mother, the woman who raised her, as Eliana Eugene and found her Facebook page. I then found Diamond's "Lil Cuz JJ" and visited her Twitter and Facebook pages.

Her real name was "Alexis Jacquet," a close cousin of Brittany Diamond Eugene who also went to Miramar High School.

There was more. I searched the name "Brittany Diamond Eugene" in Broward Country court records online. I found a traffic citation from 2015 and downloaded it. Diamond had signed the citation "Brittany Eugene". I quickly brought the signature into Photoshop and compared it to the "Diamond Eugene" signature on the Sybrina letter. The handwriting of the last name "Eugene" matched! I planned on seeking a court certified handwriting expert to confirm this, but I had little doubt Brittany Diamond Eugene had signed the letter at the center of this case, not Rachel. CSI Miami baby!

I then recalled Benjamin Crump's March 20, 2012 press conference, the one in which he presented three barely decipherable thirty-second audio clips from his phone interview with Diamond. After playing the third clip for the gullible press, he held up printouts of Trayvon's phone records and made a bombastic declaration. Alone in my office, and feeling exhilarated, I picked up the Miramar High School 2012 yearbook in one hand and the Cellebrite phone records in the other and raised them high. Mimicking Crump word for word, I shouted out, "We have ALL the evidence now!"

13

FAKE NEWS

As I IMMERSED myself into all things "Diamond" and followed the leads wherever they took me, I found myself wondering how it was that no one in the major media thought to do what I was doing. The answer was really simple. American journalists did not want to know anything that might disturb the evidence-free scenario they had imagined in those first few weeks after the shooting.

In 2012, the term "fake news" had yet to become a catchword. Just as well. In this case, the phrase would have quickly become redundant. The news was fake, dangerously so, more often than not. It did not have to be this way. Seventeen years earlier, the media covered the O.J. Simpson trial, another highly public and racially fraught case, with something close to objectivity. Then again California was not a battleground state, 1995 was not an election year, and the feminist lobby had a stake in the outcome. What follows are some of the more egregious distortions of the news about the Zimmerman case.

Erasing Sherman Ware

In December 2010, as reported earlier, a police lieutenant's son named Justin Collison sucker punched a black homeless man named Sherman Ware. The attack was caught on video, but nothing was done about it. George Zimmerman took action, printing up fliers and distributing them to black churches. He spoke out about the incident at a town meeting. As a result of George's actions, Collison was arrested and the police chief resigned. CNN quietly admitted in May 2012 to having obtained an audio copy of George's heartfelt speech in support of Ware at the meeting, but the media uniformly refused to share this information in any meaningful way. Indeed, NBC's Lisa Bloom wrote an entire book on the Zimmerman case, *Suspicion Nation*, without a single word about the incident.

Infantilizing Trayvon

As measured by the medical examiner, seventeen-year-old Trayvon Martin stood 5' 11" tall and weighed 158 pounds, although from viewing photos and videos I believe he was closer to 6' 3". Team Trayvon, however, manipulated the imagery from day one, flooding newsrooms with photos of a cherubic pre-teen. The journalistic standard is to use the most recent photo, but the national media had no interest in playing by the rules. A month after Trayvon's death, *People* magazine earned special honors in the propaganda hall of fame by putting on its cover a childlike picture of Trayvon, age about twelve. The "small child" nonsense persisted into the trial. Prosecutor John Guy repeatedly referred to Trayvon as a "boy" and a "child," even though he was half a foot taller than George Zimmerman. Worse, the state asked the jury to consider, in addition to murder and manslaughter, a "non-enumerated felony" based on "child abuse."

Branding Zimmerman a white racist

George Zimmerman was as Hispanic as Barack Obama was black, actually more so in that he grew up with his Hispanic mother and grandmother speaking Spanish. Incredibly, Bloom did not mention that heritage in her book. In a March 22 article, the *New York Times* famously characterized George as a "white Hispanic," a designation uniquely his own. George's father Bob would comment, "George MUST be kept white, somehow."

Having established George as white, the media had to prove he was a racist. The vilification campaign was launched at WJTV in Miami, an NBC affiliate. On March 19, 2012, the day the Sanford PD released the 911 tapes, the producers did their "fake news" editing magic. The actual recording went as follows:

GZ: This guy looks like he's up to no good. Or he's on drugs or something. It's raining and he's just walking around, looking about.
SPD: OK, and this guy - is he black, white or Hispanic?
GZ: He looks black.

The producers condensed this to, "This guy looks like he's up to no good. He looks black." Trayvon's blackness would seem to have made him a target. It would get worse. On March 20, Lilia Luciano, reporting for national NBC News, aired a segment on the *Today Show*. To set the mood, Luciano described Trayvon as the "the teen gunned down by Neighborhood Watchman George Zimmerman last month as he walked through this gated community wearing a hoodie." The edited exchange went as follows:

GZ: This guy looks like he's up to no good. He looks black.
SPD: Did you see what he was wearing?
GZ: Yeah, a dark hoodie.

When George was asked what Trayvon was wearing, he actually answered, "Yeah, a dark hoodie like a gray hoodie. He wore jeans or sweat pants and white tennis shoes." NBC presented George as focusing exclusively on Trayvon's race and hoodie. In time, NBC quietly fired a few people because of this incendiary distortion.

In the race to defame George, CNN came in a close second. The mischief began on the Current TV show, *The Young Turks,* On the night of March 19, 2012, the day the dispatch tape was released, host Cenk Uygur played the unedited Zimmerman tape, including the section where George says, "It's fucking c...." Although the third word is absolutely unintelligible, Uygur concluded, "It certainly sounds like 'coons.'"

This interpretation excited the media because it turned the shooting into a hate crime. On March 21, CNN reporter Gary Tuchman, working with an audio design specialist, concluded, "It certainly sounds like that word to me." In its haste to slander George, no one at CNN thought to ask why George would begin a sentence with "It's" if he were to complete it with the plural "coons," as in, "It's fucking coons." A rare voice of sanity, liberal comedian Jon Stewart said on playing the tape, "That doesn't sound like a word at all!" He was right. It didn't. "Coons" never made it to trial. George was most likely saying, "It's fucking cold," the same thing I found myself saying when I got off the plane in Florida in December.

Branding Zimmerman a profiler

Although technically gated, The Retreat at Twin Lakes in 2012 was no homeowner's idea of a "gated community." Following the Florida real estate collapse, prices plummeted, many of the units sat vacant, some were converted to Section 8 (government subsidized) housing, and more than half were rentals, including the one where Trayvon was staying. As witness Johnathan Good noted in his e-book on the case, house burglaries and home invasions "had the entire community at The Retreat at Twin Lakes on alert."

George and his wife had bought guns three years before the shooting to protect themselves against a pit bull that ran loose in the neighborhood. George volunteered to join the neighborhood watch only after two men broke into a neighbor's house while the young woman was at home with her baby. When George called the dispatcher on the night of February 26, he was following the repeated advice of the police, "Better to be safe than sorry."

Branding Zimmerman a stalker

NBC planted the thought that Zimmerman stalked Trayvon with one simple diabolical edit, an edit that was repeated routinely by broadcasters throughout out the world. Here is what the NBC audience heard:

SPD: Are you following him? [2:24]
GZ: Yeah.
SPD: Okay. We don't need you to do that. [2:26]

NBC edited out Zimmerman's one-word response to the dispatcher's request, "Okay." In reality, Zimmerman took the dispatcher's advice, though as he told me, he oversimplified his "yeah" response. George never saw Trayvon after he had circled his truck. Zimmerman meant he was walking in the direction he had last seen him, not actually following him.

Pushing the Skittles and iced tea con

Yes, Trayvon was carrying Skittles when he died, but he was not carrying iced tea. He was carrying Arizona Watermelon Fruit Juice Cocktail. The Sanford PD innocently misidentified the drink as "Arizona brand name tea," but the prosecutors continued to say "iced tea" during the trial even when showing images of the watermelon juice cocktail.

The media also continued to say "iced tea" even though they knew better. In part, this was due to racial sensitivity about the word "watermelon," but the more knowing in the media stuck to iced tea to preserve Trayvon's reputation. Trayvon was a connoisseur of a druggy concoction known by various street names including "purple lean" or "purple drank." The *Urban Dictionary* describes purple drank as "a mixture of Promethazine/Codeine cough syrup and sprite, with a few jolly ranchers and/or skittles thrown in." In fact, the Skittles were easy to procure and any fruity soft drink would do. The tough part to procure was the Codeine, about which Trayvon was consulting with his friend through Facebook.

Thanks to the skilled work of Team Trayvon publicist Ryan Julison, the very first national story on Trayvon's death by Reuters pushed the Skittles and iced tea angle, an angle that spoke to his presumed innocence. The iconography persisted up until the trial. Wrote the *Washington Post's* Jonathan Capehart on explaining why Zimmerman would not testify in his own behalf, "Zimmerman could be his own worst enemy in explaining how he killed a teenager armed with only a bag of Skittles and iced tea."

Misidentifying the cries for help

In the background of a 911 call, one can hear more than forty seconds of a man crying out for help. From day one, Sanford PD *knew* the voice was George Zimmerman's. George told the police he yelled for help even before he knew the cries had been picked up on the 911 call. Neighbor Johnathan Good confirmed the same. When Tracy Martin heard the tape two days later, he conceded it was *not* his son's voice. An April 5, 2012 FBI report noted, "Martin left the police station understanding why charges against ZIMMERMAN had not been filed."

Needing some evidence to get George arrested, Team Trayvon decided the voice had to be Trayvon's. The media refused to contradict them. In her book, *Suspicion Nation*, NBC's Lisa Bloom insisted the cries were Trayvon's. Her logic was perverse.

According to Bloom, George stalked Trayvon, confronted him, grabbed and shoved him until a "frightened" Trayvon punched George. A "tussle" ensued. For Bloom, it was "not particularly significant" who was on top. George pulled the gun, pointed it at Trayvon, and continued his "profane insulting rant" for forty seconds while Trayvon screamed "aaah" in fear. Angry and panicking, George then shot Trayvon.

As journalism goes, this is pure malpractice. Contrast Bloom's account of the screams with the written account of eyewitness neighbor Johnathan Good:

> *I heard yelling out back in the grass area of my home not sure at first but after second "help" yell I opened blinds, and saw clothing but everything dark outside. I opened door and saw a guy on the ground getting hit by another man on top of him in a strattle (sic) position hitting a guy in a red sweatshirt or on the bottom getting hit was yelling out help .*

Portraying Trayvon as an excellent student

On March 17, 2012, as the national media began to take an interest in the case, the *Orlando Sentinel* decided to reinforce Trayvon's scholastic reputation. Trayvon's English teacher Michelle Kypriss told the *Sentinel* that Trayvon was "an A and B student who majored in cheerfulness." The *Sentinel* added that he had an interest in aviation and was studying to be an engineer.

Unfortunately, at this stage of his life, if Trayvon had particular interests, they were drugs, guns, sex, and street fighting. He had been suspended from school on three occasions that school year and skipped class as often as he attended. To his mother's expressed regret, Trayvon failed to pass the FCAT, Florida's major standardized test. He could not graduate if he did not pass. Expulsion was being proposed by the school district following multiple suspensions.

Accepting the "grieving family" ruse

Trayvon's mother, Sybrina Fulton, and his father, Tracy Martin, were surely grieving, but they were not *family*. Tracy had abandoned Sybrina fourteen years earlier, and each had a child with other partners before they had Trayvon in 1995. By 1998, Tracy was living with Alicia Stanley. Just before Trayvon's death, Tracy's main squeeze was Brandy Green. Team Trayvon edited Trayvon's rock, stepmother "Mama 'Licia," fully out of the picture, even forcing her out of the front row of Trayvon's funeral, and the media obliged. Alicia told Anderson Cooper in tears, "I can't believe these people did this to me. He's not my son just because he passed?"

Deleting Johnathan Good

There was only one serious eyewitness to Trayvon's attack on George. Minutes after the shooting, Johnathan Good told the Sanford PD, "So I open my door. It was a black man with a black hoodie on top of the other, either a white guy or now I found out I think it was a Hispanic guy with a red sweatshirt on the ground yelling out help! And I tried to tell them, get out of here, you know, stop or whatever, and then one guy on top in the black hoodie was pretty much just throwing down blows on the guy kind of MMA-style."

Good spoke to a local TV station the day after the shooting and told the same story. He spoke to Tracy Martin as well. After that, fearing for his and his wife's life, he avoided all public exposure until he reluctantly testified at the trial. Although his testimony all but assured Zimmerman's acquittal, Lisa Bloom mentioned it only in passing and got everything wrong.

At some future date perhaps, they will be teaching the Zimmerman case in journalism classes as an example of how horribly wrong the media can go. In this case, America's journalists, virtually all of them, were willing to help send an innocent man, a Hispanic Democrat and social activist no less, to prison to advance a political agenda.

Without this kind of media support, Andrew Gillum could not have ridden the Trayvon Martin shooting anywhere useful. Although Gillum had allies throughout the media, none was more useful or more powerful Sean "Jay-Z" Carter, the rap mogul and film producer. Carter and co-producer Harvey Weinstein bought the rights to Bloom's *Suspicion Nation* and *Rest in Power* by Sybrina Fulton and Tracy Martin. For obvious reasons Weinstein had to drop out, but Carter went on to produce a six-part series, "Rest in Power: The Trayvon Martin Story." The premier aired conveniently on Monday, July 30, 2018, four weeks before the Florida Democratic primary.

Each episode centered on a theme fully rooted in a conspicuous falsehood. The first episode dealt with the voice heard screaming on the 911 call. To heighten viewer anger, the producers played parts of the tape multiple times and even repeated the sound of the gunshot multiple times to give the illusion of several shots fired. The Sanford Police, however, knew from the beginning that the voice was Zimmerman's. *All* evidence made this fact inarguable.

In the second episode, the producers told the sad tale of Sherman Ware, using this episode to show the implicit racism of central Florida. In making this point, the producers made one astonishing and unforgivable omission, namely that it was George Zimmerman who led the public outcry on Ware's behalf.

In the third episode, the viewers meet a young white couple who were Zimmerman's neighbors, the Bertalans. Left on the cutting room floor was any talk of the home invasion that prompted the young mother and her husband to move and George to join the neighborhood watch.

In the fourth episode, which aired on the eve of the Democrat primary in Florida, the prosecutors are criticized because "they didn't show who Trayvon was." In reality, the prosecutors blocked the defense attorneys from showing the jury Trayvon's deeply troubled teen life. The information captured in his cell phone records illustrated the downward spiral–the drugs, the promiscuity, the suspensions, the gang aspirations, the fighting, the gun dealing. Although the jury never knew about this side of Trayvon, the media did. They just chose not to report it.

The fifth episode showed the highlights of George Zimmerman's trial. Sort of. Predictably, the producers left out entirely the two most compelling bits of evidence in Zimmerman's defense, most importantly the testimony of Johnathan Good. None of it made the final cut of "Rest in Power." Nor did defense attorney O'Mara's dramatic illustration of just how long four minutes last. Trayvon had four minutes to walk away from George's truck and go home. He did not even try.

The sixth episode is the most egregious of all. It celebrates the rise of the Black Lives Matter movement and condemns the emergence of the "alt-right," both of which it ties to the Zimmerman case. Like the previous episodes, this one was dishonest, divisive, and downright incendiary. I had a hard time watching.

If his goal was to report the truth, then Sean "Jay-Z" Carter betrayed the concept. If his goal was to sow the seeds of discontent, control the black vote, and advance the revolution through whatever means necessary, Carter did not betray his craft at all. He proved himself a master propagandist. In the process, he came damned close to getting Andrew Gillum elected governor.

14

ALL ABOUT DIAMOND

For hundreds of years, up through the twentieth century, people exchanged letters and often saved them. For historians, these letters were a gold mine. They could comb through exchanges between, say, a man and a woman or among family members or political rivals and come to a pretty good understanding of how people felt and thought. When people ceased to write letters on any kind of regular basis, historians wondered how their profession could maintain its standards.

I wondered too, at least before I began my investigation. As I discovered though, young people, even those of limited means, do know how to communicate. They have devised among themselves a kind of written pidgin that, when mastered, has an admirable economy and precision. This truncated language is not that hard to understand. Once understood, it opens up to the researcher a world of information that has escaped not just the media but largely law enforcement as well.

Trayvon Martin and Brittany Diamond Eugene left behind a sketch of their relationship as revealing, if not quite as eloquent, as Robert and Elizabeth Barrett Browning's. Trayvon's phone proved to be the Rosetta Stone of my investigation. It allowed me to decode his language, to find Diamond, and to understand their relationship. More to the point, their phone and text record told me what Diamond and Trayvon had to say to each other during the last days of Trayvon's life.

What is surprising, disappointing really, is that no one in the media thought to do what I was doing, namely examine the record Trayvon and Diamond created of that life. The Florida state prosecutors either feared what they would find and avoided looking or, much more likely, simply kept silent once they learned the truth. I believe it was the latter. The media had no more interest in the truth than the prosecutors. By failing to explore this record, however, media and prosecutors both painted an image of Trayvon that was fully at odds with the Trayvon Martin whom Zimmerman encountered on that rainy night in Sanford.

As I was learning, the seventeen-year-old Trayvon was not the sainted child victim the media made him out to be. Nor was he the thug his critics thought him to be either. Unlike, say, a suburban teen, Trayvon inhabited a universe where the margin of error was perilously small. If he were to fall off the relatively straight and narrow path he once tried hard to walk, he would descend into an underworld more harrowing than any teen anywhere should have to face.

Like too many young black teens in inner city America, Trayvon was asked to explore this environment without a father in his house. In his texts and other messages, Trayvon bled insecurity, uncertainty, and fear. He showed moments of real vulnerability, tenderness even, moments when you can sense his longing for the little boy's life he had left behind.

But then he met Diamond. Ah, Diamond. To understand Trayvon's death and the ensuing investigation, I knew I would have to deep dive into her social media. Unlike texting, social media messages are, for the most part, knowingly released into the public sphere. I figured that once I penetrated any one of her social media accounts–Facebook, Twitter, Instagram for starters–linking from one to another would prove relatively easy.

There was a catch. Diamond never used her real name with Trayvon. He might not even have known it. After some effort I found my way to Diamond's Instagram account and that linked to her Twitter page, where she tweeted under the nicely narcissistic handle, "Shesbombb." As I started scrolling back from the present I took great heart in discovering that Diamond was a prolific tweeter. Twenty or so tweets a day was the norm, and fifty not uncommon. Typically the tweets were not about world affairs or sports or entertainment. Typically, they were about her. The box in the upper left corner indicated she joined Twitter in 2011 and had sent over twenty-eight thousand tweets! That was good! I scrolled quickly back through the years imagining what a treasure trove of information I would find when I got to 2012.

Then, bam! I ran smack into a wall. The Twitter feed ended at December 14, 2016. Now, I needed to figure out how to go around or burrow under the wall and hope that she had not deleted her earlier tweets.

I was not optimistic. In past research projects I had come to the occasional Twitter wall and found nothing beyond them but the ghosts of deleted tweets. I consoled myself with the thought that even tweets from the years after 2016 might tell me a good deal about Diamond given her willingness to share almost every thought and action. As I dove in, however, I found myself regretting what I might never see, namely Diamond's day-to-day, hour-by-hour activities in those first few critical months of 2012.

Although blocked from discovering Diamond's past, there was much to learn from Diamond's present life. In his text messages, Trayvon called Brittany Diamond Eugene "Diamond." I wanted to learn everything I could about her. I wanted to understand who she was and why she had for several weeks resisted coming forward and refused to speak with the police about what she heard the night of the shooting.

More importantly, I needed to know why Diamond exited the

scene as she did and why she allowed or possibly even arranged for the unlikely Rachel Jeantel to pretend to be her. I suspected that at the time of the switch she did not understand the consequences of her actions. That substitution led to Zimmerman's arrest and, in time, would subvert the most significant racial and political trial since O.J. Simpson's, and rock America to its core. Stranger still, the witness switch went seemingly unnoticed, as in "they got away with it". I wanted to know how that happened too.

As early as 2012, young people were giving away their privacy to anyone who cared to look. I worked under the assumption that if I could understand what Diamond had to tell the world, I could better understand how a tragedy like the Trayvon Martin shooting could take place and what role, if any, Diamond played in his death.

Diamond, I learned, was a born showgirl. On her Instagram account, I found her modeling clothes in hundreds posts dating back to 2014 when she was just eighteen. From her Instagram, I learned that Diamond had attended Broward College for her associate degree and had then gone on to Florida State University in Tallahassee, Florida. At FSU–irony alert–Diamond was studying criminal justice, a subject George Zimmerman had to abandon when the witness fraud denied him the ability to sit in a college classroom.

As of 2019, Diamond had thousands of Instagram followers. Just about every message Diamond posted on Instagram began with a tribute to her royal self. Some of the posts were combative, some contentious, and just about all were splendidly self-absorbed:

Always me, never you.
Remember this face cause I'm that girl you gonna lose to.
I'm the one killing shit, hands down.
Betting on me is the right risk.
I'm addicted to winning.
Top two, and I'm not two.
Maybe I'm not your speed, maybe I'm out of your league.

There were hundreds of comments on each post. The comments

mostly exclaimed how amazing and beautiful she was, like "Ohhh yessss honeyyyy" and "the baddest fc [fire crotch] in the game." Diamond was absorbing a constant flow of ego gratification through these comments. For a narcissist, this was mother's milk. From what I knew about this particular personality disorder, however, no amount of gratification would ever be enough to satisfy the need.

Most interesting to me was Diamond's Instagram post on January 3, 2017, the day after her twenty-first birthday. There was a photo of Diamond wearing a diamond necklace and diamond embroidered white dress. The post said, "On January 2nd God created Diamond," the diamond being in the form of a diamond emoji. There it was! This was first time I had seen her use her middle name, Diamond, other than with Trayvon.

The photo next to the following post was also from January 3, 2017, with the caption, "Because a picture does no justice... This is how you shine Diamond (emoji)." In the photo area was a video of Diamond wearing the same diamond dress and dancing.

The Instagram account had a link to a surprisingly sophisticated online boutique through which Diamond was marketing sexy outfits, including lingerie. "I will be selling clothes that are handpicked by me," she wrote on the introductory page, "to make every girl feel and look bomb." Diamond modeled all the clothing herself, striking provocative poses and sporting different hairstyles. Her make-up was as elaborate as her outfits. Unless I missed my guess, she appeared to have had a nose job some time along the way. "Self-confidence is the best outfit," she insisted. "When you look good, you feel good! We want every woman to look and feel BOMB when shopping with @shesbombboutique!"

In reviewing a sexualized rap video of Diamond modeling her outfits, she seemed to enjoy selling clothes that showed off every view imaginable of her gorgeous self. Outfits bore such come hither names as "Ready for War" and "Class and a Little Sass."

There was little of Diamond the viewer did not see. She seemed to have a particular affection for her protruding butt. "I love my duck ass," she once texted Trayvon. That she did. Trayvon liked it too. This affection may explain her fondness for Kim Kardashian, the queen of duck ass. "I wanna be a kardashian so bad," she once tweeted.

Although seemingly elegant, her outfits were selling for only fifty dollars. The buyer could have them shipped or could pick them up in "Tally." Perhaps the best way for me to meet Diamond would be to make a large order and pick it up in Tallahassee.

15

TALLAHASSEE BOUND

NOTHING, I realized, prevented me from meeting Diamond in person. I wanted to get to know her a little, but more tangibly I wanted to get her on camera and, if possible, secure some handwriting samples. If I were to confirm her role in The Trayvon Hoax, physical evidence was essential. In 2018, she was twenty-two and no longer a minor. There was nothing inappropriate about making contact with her now, unlike the way ABC's Matt Gutman had engaged at all hours with the sixteen-year-old Diamond in 2012.

My plan was to take Diamond's handwriting samples to a forensic document examiner to determine whether she was the writer–or signer–of the letter delivered to Sybrina Fulton and signed "Diamond Eugene." This is the letter Rachel Jeantel claimed to have signed after having dictated the letter to Francine Serve. Francine, if you recall, worked at Sybrina's home as a caregiver for the brother. Francine was also the older sister of Felicia Cineas, Diamond's best friend.

To establish contact, I found my way to Diamond's "She's Bomb" cyber boutique, the website through which Diamond exhibited her clothing line. I put in an order for one outfit, "Ready for War," and requested by email to speak with someone about a larger order.

Sure enough, Diamond called within twenty minutes. Immediately, I could tell her voice matched that of "phone girl" whom Crump had recorded. After speaking with so many girls searching for her, Diamond's voice was a sweet sound indeed. I told her I wanted to order outfits for a high school dance group and needed some help deciding on sizes.

Diamond walked me through the various available outfits, and I put in an order for ten of them. I told her I would be in Tallahassee in about a week and would like to pick the order up in person. "No problem" she said. I made some small talk to hear more of her voice.

"Why are you in Tallahassee?" I asked, "Do you have a storefront?"

"No," she told me. "I'm a student at Florida State University."

I asked her what she studied, and she said, "criminal justice." I already knew this from her Instagram page, but to hear her say it amplified the irony. I spent the day making travel arrangements and searching online for a suitable public meeting spot in Tallahassee. I decided the Holiday Inn would work well. From the hotel photos on Yelp, the lobby seemed an ideal meeting place. I also knew that hotels typically had security cameras in their public areas and signage announcing video and audio taping at the entrances, which would make my video recording completely legal. I also read that Florida law allowed for recording in public places where there was no expectation of privacy.

I texted Diamond that I would be arriving late the following Monday and sleeping over at the Holiday Inn. I asked if she could meet me at 9 a.m. in the lobby the day after I arrived. She agreed, and the meeting was on. Given her status as a criminal justice student and her role in the Zimmerman case, I decided to pile on the irony by bringing Diamond an appropriate Christmas gift. I chose a sixteen-inch bronze statue of Lady Justice, blind as she could be.

A week later, I landed in Tallahassee with my film crew at around 3 p.m. The temperature that afternoon registered an un-Florida like forty-five degrees. As George Zimmerman might have said, "It was fucking cold!" Florida can be that way. I picked up a rental car and with my camera crew headed to the downtown area. I just wanted to walk around a little and get a sense of the place. Located on Florida's panhandle, Tallahassee has the look and feel of the small-town South. Driving in, I was reminded of East Tennessee where I grew up. There was nothing sophisticated about the city, nothing really "Florida." In Tallahassee, no fast food or hotel franchise goes unrepresented. I am not sure there were anything but franchises.

What distinguishes Tallahassee from other such cities, of course, is that it is the capitol city of Florida and home to the institutions that govern the third most populous state in America. Once downtown, I parked next to the Florida State Capitol building, a classy older complex dwarfed by a massive office tower right behind it. Two squat buildings flanked the tall office tower. The arrangement of the three newer buildings has lent the ensemble the unfortunate but understandable nickname, "cock and balls." What were they thinking?

Across the street sits the Florida Supreme Court, a building that has the gravitas you'd expect given its mission. The security guards that met me at the entrance looked bored enough to welcome my visit. They asked for ID and were excited to discover I was a filmmaker, from California no less. They invited me in with my cameraman and turned us loose inside the building as no court was in session.

In the center of the lobby was a six-foot-tall statue of Lady Justice, a blindfold across her eyes, the scales of justice in her hand. I had to laugh. The statue looked exactly like the replica I planned to give Diamond as a Christmas present the next morning. Unchallenged, I walked into the Supreme Court chambers. I had learned in high school civics class that the courts were the great equalizer. If there were excesses by the police or prosecutors, the courts would allow a fair hearing and deliver justice. I still believe that. You could all but smell the whiff of righteousness in the air, the history and depth of it. The old walls, the sixty-foot-high ceilings, and the dark wooden benches had the capacity to inspire citizens the way medieval cathedrals once did and still do. We rolled some tape on it and headed back out into the cold.

My next stop was the Florida State University campus. Although

Tallahassee was a dud, the campus had energy to it. Students were bustling around as though they actually had some place to go that mattered. To get in the school spirit, I walked to the bookstore and bought a "Noles" hat, short for Seminoles. From there I headed for the main quad, a graceful site redolent of the Old South and thick with Spanish moss on weeping willows.

Among the larger buildings on campus was Eppes Hall, which housed the College of Criminology and Criminal Justice, Diamond's field of study. In the lobby, I found yet more scales of justice. Justice was just about everywhere in Florida, I figured, except at the state attorney's office in Jacksonville where the decision was made to sacrifice justice in order to appease the mob.

The next morning at the Holiday Inn, I was up at 6 a.m. with my film crew. After some grits and waffles–this was the South after all–we set up the camera in plain sight about an hour in advance of the planned 9 a.m. rendezvous with Diamond.

At 9 a.m. Diamond had yet to make her entrance. I knew from her Twitter feeds she had trouble getting anywhere on time. The mandatory shower, the various weaves, the makeup, the choosing of an outfit, and all the other early morning rituals that slowed this highly self-conscious young woman down.

My film crew and I started to take bets on when Diamond would show up, with whom, and how well put together she would be. The crew bet on casual dress and alone. From what I knew of Diamond, I bet on her arriving at 9:15 a.m. and dressed to kill with a boyfriend in tow. At 9:13 a.m. she texted she was around the corner. I confess to being a little excited. Diamond was about to transform from a cyber ghost into a real, live girl.

And not just any girl, but the girl I had been seeking and studying for several months, the girl at the center of Trayvon Martin's world, the girl who knew exactly what had happened in the minutes leading up to his fatal encounter. Diamond had the power to do the right thing. She could have come forward, told everything she knew, and spared the nation both trial and a trauma. Instead, she participated on several levels in a hoax whose toxic residue spread like the Ebola virus. I was a little angry with her, but at this point I was more curious than angry.

And suddenly, there she was, resplendent in an all-black, high-fashion, loose-fitting ensemble. The Voodoo priest told me Diamond had a black heart. If so, the matched the outfit. Flowing from her head was a lengthy weave with full bangs, her "signature look." These twenty inches of some poor Malaysian woman's hair fell with a splash of red dye almost to the floor on this petite, well-shaped, dark-skinned girl.

Dutifully walking behind Diamond was a light skinned, African American male carrying my clothing order in a cardboard box. I stood up and waved to Diamond who smiled and walked over. I greeted her with a handshake and half-hearted hug and introduced a woman in the crew sitting next to me. Diamond introduced me to "Richard." I invited Diamond to sit next to me in the empty chair at which the camera was pointing. She agreed, and it was on. She looked right into the camera, said nothing, and then we started with some chit-chat.

I asked her why she was studying criminal justice. Did she want to study law? Were her parents lawyers?

"No," she told me. "Fashion is my first love, and criminal justice is my second interest. That's all." I immediately followed up with a similar question and got a different answer.

"Well then, is anyone in your family in law enforcement?" I asked.

"Yes," she answered, "my dad. My father is a police officer."

I had identified Diamond's father from her extended family's Facebook friends and Instant Checkmate address searches as likely to be a Haitian man named "Bodler Norelus." While I suspected her interest in criminal justice was inspired by the George Zimmerman case, I knew all about Norelus. He was involved in law enforcement only to the degree that he kept the cops busy. According to police records, Norelus was arrested in the Miami area in 1994, 1996, and 1998. The recurring charge was auto theft or attempted auto theft. When arrested in 1998 at age twenty-three for grand theft auto,

Norelus was sporting a tattoo that read, according to the police report, "Zoe-4-Life."

"Zoe" was shorthand for "Haitian," but the presence of the tattoo suggests an affiliation with the "Zoe Pound," a violent Haitian gang that was terrorizing Miami during Norelus' criminal days. After serving a year in prison, Norelus either fled or was deported back to his native Haiti. I found it somehow predictive that Norelus was also charged with possession of an altered vehicle identification number. Changing identities seemed to run in the family. The maternal side of Diamond's family included aunts and uncles with credit card and identify fraud convictions as well as prison time.

To verify additional information, I asked Diamond, given her allure, if she had even been a cheerleader or a member of a dance group. She said no. She was never in a group of any kind in high school. This confirmed what I knew from her tweets.

Next, I told her that I'd gotten her a Christmas present. She smiled widely in anticipation. I pulled out a gift-wrapped red bag and handed it to her. She smiled her wide magical smile once again and exclaimed, "Oh my God!" I told her to open it, and she reached in and pulled the heavy bronze object upwards. Upon seeing the statue, she couldn't even fake excitement. She just looked puzzled.

"This is Lady Justice," I said, thinking she would immediately smile in recognition. But she continued to look puzzled, even more than before. I explained the relevance of the statue for a criminal justice major: "The scales mean that decisions will be made by weighing the evidence, and the blindfold suggests the weighing will be done fairly with no bias." None of this registered. "You can put it on your desk," I offered, hoping for some reaction. After some awkward silence, she offered, "It's so cute," with a sing-song delivery. Then the light bulb went off. She smiled proudly, exclaiming, "Oh yeah! We got one like this in the lobby of the criminal justice building at FSU!" She may have finally recognized the statue, but the concept behind it seemed lost on her.

I asked Diamond if she was a full-time student or if she had a job on the side? She replied, "I am a student, but I also work at Pandora at the Governor's Square Mall."

"Pandora?" I asked, unfamiliar with the store.

My crew member chimed in, "That's a chain jewelry store that sells fake diamonds." Diamond nodded in confirmation. The irony just would not stop. Next, I pulled out something Diamond did understand, an envelope filled with cash for my purchase. I asked her to count it lest she feel embarrassed to count it in front of me. As she was counting, I told her I had added an extra one hundred dollars for her kindness in personalizing some Christmas cards. She was more than okay with that. I handed her eight blank cards and a print out with eight names on it that I had made up. To make it easier on a handwriting expert, each name incorporated one of the words on the letter Diamond gave to Sybrina:

Blessing Turner (turn)
Willow Conner (corner)
Melanie Walker (walk)
Katherina Mecided (decided)
Theresa Closerman (the man getting closer)
Tracey Rainier (rain)
Constance Trelock (Trevon, word ending in k)
Isabella Augastory (story)

Diamond personalized and signed each card with a flair, her weave flowing back and forth as she wrote. For my stylish young friend, this was a rock star turn, the kind, I suspect, she envisioned in her future. After dedicating a card to "Constance Trelock," she paused to exclaim, "These are some unique names!"

I could feel the entire crew cringe, but I did not let my concern show. I papered over the moment with some small talk, and Diamond went back to writing. She then made a remark about "Blessing Turner" sounding awfully weird, but I reassured her, "the family are religious people." When she finished, after some more small talk, I thanked her, and we exchanged hugs. She and Richard walked back through the lobby, Diamond's rock star self in full swagger mode, her twenty-inch Malaysian weave swinging as she walked.

This real-life Diamond brought the tweets and texts to life. I recalled the first text she sent to Trayvon, "all the hoes want wat I got," and a tweet, "My only competition is the mirror." That was the Diamond I met. She had the presence and the charisma her tweets promised. On the surface at least, she projected the confidence of a super model.

The swagger, however, struck me as a cover. The voodoo priest promised a bad heart. I sensed a heart that been hardened by anguish. Narcissists tend to project confidence. They often have personalities at least superficially attractive and engaging. I could see how Trayvon was easily so drawn to her. She was sexy and well put together, not a "home girl." The hair was perfect, the clothes just right, the smile electric.

More important than my impression of Diamond, however, was the hard evidence I had gathered in Tallahassee. I managed to obtain handwriting samples from Diamond, and, if proof were needed, we filmed her putting those samples on paper. All in all, it was money well and, if I must say so, cleverly spent. Mission accomplished, I flew home with some nice new clothes that the folks at Goodwill in Los Angeles would surely appreciate.

16

TWITTER TELLS ALL

DAYS BEFORE, on the plane flying to Tallahassee, I had hours to think about how I might get access to Diamond's tweets from the years 2011 and 2012. On other projects I had used Twitter's advance search tool to look for older tweets, but the result had always been the same. If the older tweets were not present in the live Twitter feed, it meant they had been deleted. I had also learned, however, that Twitter searches were not always predictable, nor even reliable. On any research project, little is certain. It is always best to check and double check until all hope is exhausted.

In the way of example, I had once requested from KDKA-TV in Pittsburgh a video of an interview with Bob Dylan during his 1979 "Gospel Tour" that no one was even sure existed. The KDKA archivist told me in no uncertain terms that if the video ever existed it would have been destroyed in a 2005 flood of the Alleghany River that inundated the station's tape library.

Taken aback, I asked the researcher spontaneously, "Well, would you mind taking a look anyhow?" Irked by my request after she thought she had dimmed my interest, she quickly ended the call but not before taking my address and lamenting my *chutzpah*. One week later, the video showed up in my mailbox. I featured it prominently in my 2010 film, *Inside Bob Dylan's Jesus Years.*

With this experience in mind and while on the plane to Tallahassee, I had pulled up the Twitter advance search tool and did a search for all the tweets from Diamond's account going back to 2011, expecting the usual disappointment. Kaboom! I was amazed. It worked! There they were, twenty-eight thousand tweets dating back to September 2011 in all their narcissistic splendor. Now back in Los Angeles, I really dove in!

Diamond's Twitter account, not surprisingly, proved to be the informational mother lode. Continuing to use the Twitter advance search tool, I was able to read just about every thought that passed through Diamond's mind since she was sixteen, with date and time attached! She often tweeted fifty times per day, an average of one tweet per every twenty minutes she was awake. At the time Trayvon stumbled into her life, Diamond had some five hundred followers on Twitter.

By mining the tweets, I sensed I would be able to get a much better handle on the death of Trayvon Martin and the prosecution of George Zimmerman. The key to understanding both was clearly Brittany Diamond Eugene. I decided to read all her tweets, three times as it turned out. Despite Diamond's use of what she called "Miami slang," she was fully capable of writing proper English, especially as she got older. "I cannot sit through long boring lectures or read boring class material with full focus," Diamond tweeted as a 20-year-old college student.

First things first though, I wanted to confirm beyond all possible doubt that this Diamond was the same girl who was on the phone with Trayvon in the moments before his death. The first thing I did was to look for similar speech patterns and events to see if the tweets matched the text messages she sent to Trayvon. I found a myriad of matches. For instance, Diamond texted Trayvon in February 2012 telling him about a classmate who had bruised her arm. Sure enough, on February 21, 2012, she tweeted, "@tycoppin5 Put A Bruise on My Arm." Diamond had texted Trayvon about how much she liked "make up sex" and had tweeted, "I Remember the Love Right After the Fights." She texted Trayvon she was eating at Denny's and would tweet in the same time frame "Denny's" or "At Denny's." Word of warning to IHOP: Diamond preferred Denny's. On March 5, 2012, Diamond tweeted, "my teeth hurt," while her phone records showed a call to the dentist that day. The matches seemed endless.

I also searched Diamond's Twitter account to see if the words and phrases she used in her letter to Sybrina appeared in her tweets. I hit several matches: "around here," "from the back," "raining hard," "shut off," "that man," "cornerstore" and more.

In my initial perusal of her tweets, the first thing I noticed was that many of them dealt with a major crush on her boyfriend, but that beau was not Trayvon. His name was Van Jefferson Watler, who went by "Jeff." On February 2, 2012, when she first started communicating regularly with Trayvon, she had already been hot and heavy with Jeff for six or so months.

Two other tweets grabbed my attention. They were dated April 2, 2012, five weeks after Trayvon's death and the day of Rachel Jeantel's first interview with state prosecutors. "Trayvon Martin Mom Just Called Me," she tweeted, following that up with, "She Thought I Was Trayvon Girlfriend , Asking me Hella Questions O_o." For me, this was pure gold. The significance would soon become clear.

In January 2013, as the case against Zimmerman moved inexorably towards trial, Diamond tweeted cryptically, "Everything you do in the dark will eventually come to light." A month later, she added, "Karma's a bitch." Diamond had a secret, an epic one, one that would have made national news if it ever got out. The deception had to be eating at her conscience.

I plowed on making notes. Another potential doozy was posted on March 20, 2016. Diamond shared with her followers not only a Q&A relationship survey, but also her very personal answers. The question and answer that jumped out most was number four–"Ever Cheated? Do You Regret Doing so?" Diamond answered, "Yes & yes." The significance of this too would soon become clear.

It crossed my mind that Diamond had from the beginning made

major efforts to erase her connection to Trayvon. From her social media postings I gathered she did not use her middle name "Diamond" with her friends, only with Trayvon. This was likely how she hoped to keep her relationship with Trayvon secret from her boyfriend Jeff Watler. Even her clubbing friend Ariana did not know her as "Diamond," which explains why Ariana could only name "Diamond Dixon" as a friend named "Diamond."

In Diamond's Haitian American circles, changing names and identities was not uncommon. If to me it seems mad to allow someone to assume my identity, it must not have struck Diamond as terribly unusual to ask Rachel Jeantel to assume hers. Having allowed that to happen, however, Diamond made many an effort to scrub her own identify from the Zimmerman case. I noticed several switches in Twitter handles. Prior to"Shesthebombb," it was "Bornstunnaaa." Soon I would notice she stripped her original Facebook page of all content. She also did not appear in the Miramar High School yearbook photos in 2013 and appears to have had a nose job that year as well. She was laying low.

The changes fooled me for a while. Eventually I found Diamond's new Facebook page under the alias, "Tiffany Eugene." This page contained hundreds of photos and a good deal of personal history. Missing from her Facebook and Instagram pages, however, were any video clips in which she could be heard speaking. I suspect she wanted to thwart any Internet sleuths who might try to match her distinctive voice to the Crump tape. Still, Diamond did not cover her tracks as well as she hoped. Thanks to Twitter, Facebook, Instagram, and some supplemental research in public records, I was able to find out quite a bit about Diamond and the largely unexplored world she inhabited.

Born on January 2, 1996, Diamond attended Norland Elementary School in Miami and then HD Perry Middle School in Miramar before moving on to Miramar High School as her older sister Virginia had. I quickly identified Diamond's mother as Eliana Sandra Eugene. Allow me to repeat the caution here that Eliana was the woman who appears to have raised Diamond as her daughter. Eliana

Eugene was one of the twelve children of Haitian immigrants, Joel and Sanvilla Eugene. Diamond was proud of her Haitian roots–she had a map of Haiti tattooed on her side–even if "These Haitians in North Miami Can't Drive for Shit!"

Diamond always lived with and among a large group of relatives, aunts and uncles and a Haitian grandmother on her mother's side. Eliana gave birth to Diamond's older sister Virginia in 1994 when she was only fourteen years old. Diamond was born two years later. She and Virginia seemingly to this point in my investigation shared the same father, Bodler Norelus, but their mother never married him.

"Never Had A Daddy In My Life," Diamond lamented in a tweet. "Mommy Played Both Parts." This absence of a loving father likely drove Diamond to seek male attention where she could find it. Bodler Norelus was just eighteen himself when Diamond's older sister Virginia was born. Norelus fathered a son out of wedlock before leaving for Haiti. The son, Jahdiah Norelus, is now a social media star who goes by the ironic twitter handle, "The Diamond Princess." He is more than a little gay.

Like teen girls everywhere, Diamond had an ambivalent relationship with her mother Eliana. She occasionally wanted her mother to "Leave Me The Fuck Alone," but they did some things together, shopping most notably. "My Mommy Paid My Bill," Diamond once tweeted, "I Love Her." Diamond was not quite as mercenary as that tweet might suggest, but she was always calculating.

In 2011, when Diamond was fifteen, Eliana married a fellow named Raymond Johnson. Together, they would have two children, the "Devil Kids" as Diamond called them. She was not fond of her stepfather either. "I Can't Stand Ray," she tweeted for public consumption. "He A Bitch Ass Nigga Dawg!!!!" Raymond drove buses for Miami-Dade County.

If eleven aunts and uncles and forty-plus cousins were not family enough, Diamond's Haitian grandmother Sainvilla, who divorced Diamond's grandfather, lived with her daughter and grandchildren as well. It was a busy home. Diamond's mother Eliana did odd jobs, mostly hair weaving, often at nights. Like several of her siblings,

Eliana found herself in trouble with the law, having been arrested in 2003 for obstructing justice and again in 2012 for providing false identification and driving with a suspended license. She was evicted from her apartments successively in 2008 and 2009 just as Diamond was coming of age.

A typical day for Diamond on Twitter started when she woke up. "Good Morning &'d Thank God For Another Day," she tweeted on February 29, 2012. This was three days after the death of Trayvon Martin, but Diamond began most days in similar fashion. Although there were more pious girls in Florida, Diamond liked to tell Twitter she was a church-going Christian and remained one even in college. "God is so good," she tweeted as a twenty-two-year-old, "and his timing is perfect." At other times she would admit, "I haven't been to church in forever." That said, from her behavior it seems unlikely that Diamond ever bothered asking herself, "What would Jesus do?"

Once out of bed, Diamond turned her attention to simple sensations that rarely failed to satisfy her. "A Hot Ass Shower Is Calling My Namee," she tweeted one morning. Showers worked at night too: "If I Don't Take A Shower Before I Go To Sleep I Wont Feel Right!"

In one quick sequence she blasted out the following four tweets: "I always take a shower before bed," "Fresh out," "Might shower again," and finally, "I'm so bored I'll take a shower." Diamond did not have OCD. She just had a relentless passion to keep herself clean, primed and ready. Nor was she reluctant to share details of her bodily functions with the world. She tweeted about "peeing" issues, "morning breath," "that time of the month," and her "titties," which "hurt" occasionally but were, of course, "So Big For My Size."

Not unusual for a sixteen-year-old girl, Diamond worried endlessly about her hair, much of which did not exactly grow on her head. She was, in her own words, "addicted to weave." She would purchase hair weaves at her local store called "Diamond Girl Beauty Supply" in Miramar, the very one I had visited, and then have her mother sew them in. Her favorites included Malaysian hair and Chinese hair of varying lengths, but almost always with bangs, "my signature look."

The weave brand she preferred was Zury, described online as "ONLY Brazilian Virgin Remy Unprocessed 100% Human hair weave." Divine intervention made the purchase possible. "Thank God," she gushed, "I was Albee to Get My Zury Hair." Ironically, the Zury hair weave image of "Bae" extracted from Trayvon's cell phone threw me off identifying Diamond early on. However, it was the photo she sent Trayvon with the Chinese wrap weave that helped me finally and easily identify her in the Miramar High School yearbook.

For all their aesthetic appeal, weaves caused problems. "Hair so tight it's giving me a headache," she tweeted on one occasion, or, "This Weave In My Face Making My Forehead Break Out." Still, Diamond liked the way they made her five-foot-three-inch frame look: "My 14 Inch Be Looking Like A 16 or 18 Inch On Me."

Diamond's hair was just one of her features she would have to fix to look the way she wanted. Skin color was another. The "black is beautiful" movement seems to have bypassed Little Haiti. "I Fucking Hate Getting Darker!" she complained one time out of many. "I Hate The Sun. I Be About To Cry When I Get Darker."

Her fairly large and distinctive nose was another issue. There was an online solution to that, the Photoshop nose filter. Having learned how to use it, she could give herself a pert little model nose at least on her social media pages. Once I figured out what Diamond was doing, it was much easier to track her from image to image. At some point, however, Diamond may have had her nose pared back surgically.

Looking good was important to Diamond, given that she was "a sucker for love." In truth, she was not that much of a sucker. Her sentiments on love and sex could have been written by Machiavelli. "In This Game of Love...There's No Rules," she observed–except there were. One rule she tweeted was that "broke boys don't deserve pussy," an expectation that must have weighed heavily on her beaus, Trayvon and Jeff. Another one dealt with "Love and Loyalty." She warned the fellows, "Never Cross The Line."

Other than love and romance, no subject grabbed Diamond's imagination more than food. "I eat like a fat girl," she tweeted on one occasion. "All I Do Is Eat All Day," she tweeted on another, "im

Getting A Gut." She admitted a preference for junk food: Doritos, Taco Bell, McDonald's, Burger King, Pizza Hut, Chinese food. There was scarcely a fast food franchise in America whose praises she did not sing at some point. As shall be seen, Diamond often used junk food as a way of coping with stress. In 2012, she would face more stress than she could possibly imagine.

As a sixteen-year-old, if her tweets are indicative, Diamond showed far more interest in junk food than she did in school and more interest in her beau, Jeff, than in either. "Talking To Jeff While Im In Class," she wrote. She used her phone to cope with the drudgery of classwork, at least when the phone was functioning: "I Hate Not Having Signal In Class, Like Really I Be So Bored."

Diamond was bored a lot. "I'm So Bored All I Can Do Is Sleep," she tweeted. It got worse, "I'm So Bored, Im About To Cry." The phone was her lifeline. When the phone was down, she was down: "I Be So Depressed When My Phone Off." Diamond was keen on sleep as well and assumed her followers would want to know whether she was getting enough shut-eye. If she woke up in the middle of the night, she would tweet what she just dreamed or explain why she couldn't get back to sleep.

If Diamond had a genuine avocation, it was fashion, and fashion was made possible by its corollary pastime, shopping. "I need new clothes, shoes, everything," she insisted. "No such thing as too much." Needing clothes, there was one institution that beckoned. "At The Mall," she wrote often, adding, "I Feel Like I Be Here Everyday." There was not a mall in greater Miami Diamond did not visit regularly. "I Was At The Mall All Day," she tweeted on one occasion, "I Never Been So Tired In My Life."

As to where this sixteen-year-old got the money to shop endlessly, I can only guess. She did not see the need to work, to wit: "Doing Better Than Most Bitches With Jobs." That she was. One down side of shopping, however, was the inevitable interaction with white people. "These white hoes be so rude, they never say excuse me," she tweeted, "rude" white people being a recurring theme.

Although her personality was distinctive, culturally Diamond fit right into the South Florida scene. Her concerns closely matched those of the characters in Diamond Johnson's novels. In the novella *Little Miami Girl*, for instance, there are twenty-three references to shopping, twenty-eight to showering, twenty-three to pussy, forty-eight to money, thirty-nine to eating, and, not surprisingly, seventy-four references to hair.

To be sure, girls of all races and classes shared Diamond's interests, but her self-absorption was considerably deeper than average. The slogan posted on her original Facebook page banner was "LOVE YORUSELF" and a tweet–"Before you love somebody, you gotta love yourself"–spoke to Diamond's relentless quest to assure herself she was worth loving. One tweet after another revealed a fatherless girl desperate to convince herself of her desirability: "Good Morning From The Queen," "The Queen Has Awaken," "I Deserve The World," I'm Not An Option, I'm A Priority," and my favorite, "My Only Competition Is In The Mirror." Hundreds of others came across as raging narcissism:

I Be Tripping For A Minute Then I Realize Who The Fuck I Am
I Need To Just Step Back And Kiss Myself
I'm About To Fuck Around And Marry Myself
Everybody Love Me, Its Hard Not To
I'm Cool As Fuck. Anybody That Don't Like Me A Hater And Sucks To Be You
If You Don't Benefit Me, What Do I Need You In My Life For?
I'm A Big Boss Bitch, I Do Not Come In Your Size!
I Become Super Emotional When I'm Not Getting The Attention I Need
Imma Worry About Me, (Ion) Give A Fucka Bout You
I Think Highly Of Myself And Nobody Can Take Me Off My High Horse

"The hallmarks of Narcissistic Personality Disorder (NPD) are grandiosity, a lack of empathy for other people, and a need for admiration," reports *Psychology Today*. "People with this condition are frequently described as arrogant, self-centered, manipulative, and demanding." This was Diamond in a nutshell, at least at sixteen.

Although she did not like all her features, Diamond saw herself as a fox. Insecure to the core, she needed others to see what she claimed to see in the mirror. Unfortunately, her boyfriend Jeff Watler's work schedule was preventing her from getting the attention she craved. It did not give him time enough to pay the queen her due. Diamond looked to fill the void with food, shopping, hair care and, yes, Trayvon Martin.

Diamond's life might have passed unnoticed if Trayvon had not wandered into it. Insecure and at dangerously loose ends, Trayvon was struggling to gain and preserve her affection. It would prove to be a fatal attraction. I suspect that on the night of February 26, 2012, Trayvon was trying very hard to show her the stuff he was made of.

The story that Trayvon's phone told had the potential to alert parents across all America, black and white, to the threats and temptations their sons face on a daily basis. By choosing not to look for that information, let alone share it, Trayvon's parents betrayed his memory, and the media betrayed their own profession.

I hired a renowned court certified forensic handwriting expert, Bart Baggett, to examine Diamond's handwriting samples and her traffic citation. I also provided him with copies of handwriting from Francine Serve found in numerous court documents from her many brushes with the law, as well as a traffic citation that Rachel Jeantel had inscribed with her signature.

Of course, the State of Florida should have done the investigation that I was doing years ago. They were obligated to do so. But the prosecutors' goal seemed to be part of a larger agenda, Lady Justice be damned. My goal was much simpler: to learn the truth.

Photos of Diamond from Travyons Cell Phone (left and right), Center Brittany Diamond Eugene from 2012 Miramar HS yearbook

Prosecutor Bernie de la Rionda displays Skittles and Arizona Watermelon Fruit Juice Cocktail in closing arguments

Eliana Johnson
July 24, 2012

Princess Brittany always in front of a mirror my baby Know she's PRETTY

Brittany Diamond Eugene 2012 photo from Eliana Eugene's facebook page

Size (Bytes):	127326	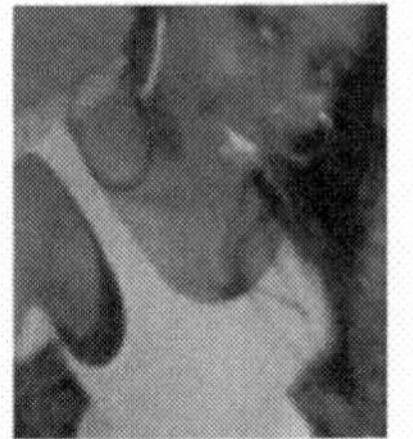
Created:	2/19/2012 4:53:29 PM(UTC-5)	
Modified:	2/19/2012 4:53:29 PM(UTC-5)	
Accessed:	2/19/2012 4:53:29 PM(UTC-5)	
Size (Bytes):	66970	
Created:	2/19/2012 6:02:06 PM(UTC-5)	
Modified:	2/19/2012 6:02:06 PM(UTC-5)	
Accessed:	2/19/2012 6:02:06 PM(UTC-5)	

Cell phone photo library shows "Lil Cuz JJ" (Alexis Jacquet) above and Diamond below that led to identification of Brittany Diamond Eugene

Benjamin Crump at March 19, 2012 press conference introducing Diamond

Brittany Diamond Eugene with author Joel Gilbert, receiving Lady Justice gift

Florida Department of Law Enforcement
Orlando Regional Operations Center
Cyber / High - Tech Crime Squad
500 West Robinson Street
Orlando, FL 32801

Cover of 750-page FDLE Extraction Report of Trayvon Martin's cell phone

Felicia Cineas

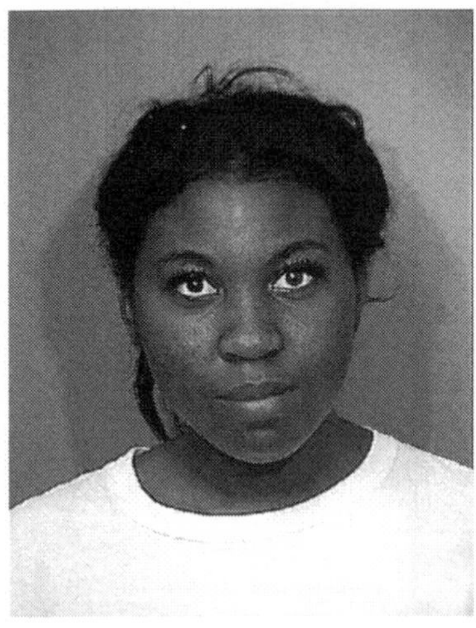

Francine Serve

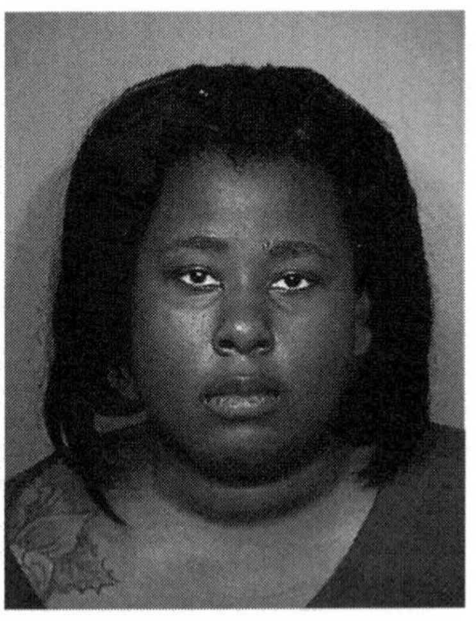

Mug shots of Diamond's best friend Felicia Cineas and her sister Francine Serve

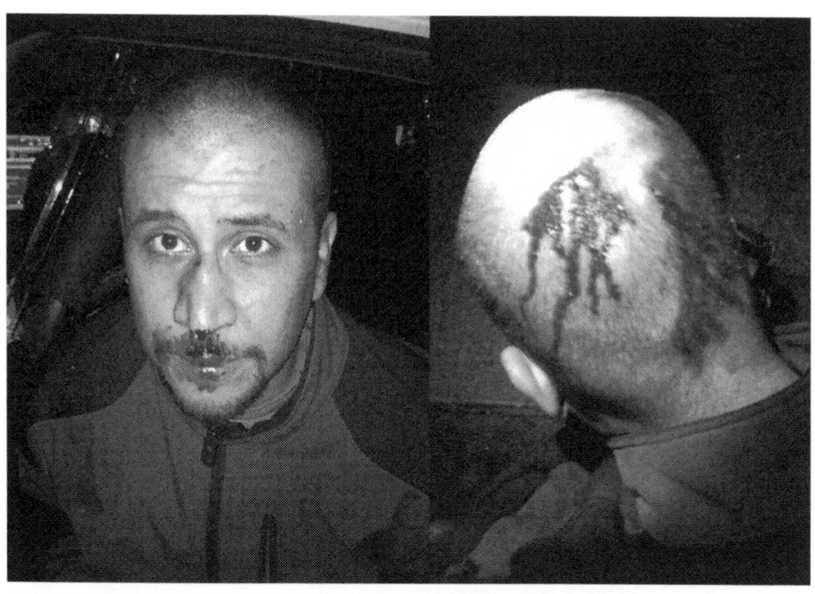

George Zimmerman's broken nose and bloody head on the night of the incident

Author/Director Joel Gilbert at the Florida Supreme Court with Lady Justice

Rachel Jeantel at a deposition trying to disguise herself as Diamond with an identical Chinese weave, but it didn't fit!

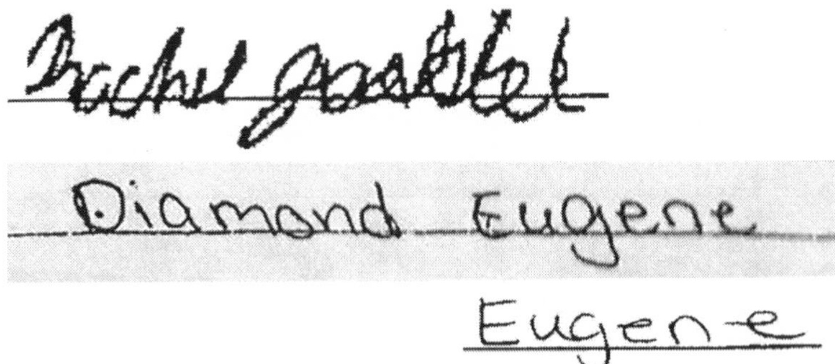

Comparison signatures of Rachel Jeantel, Diamond Eugene from the Sybrina letter, and "Eugene" from Brittany Diamond Eugene's traffic citation

Sybrina Fulton removing the letter from her Bible at her deposition

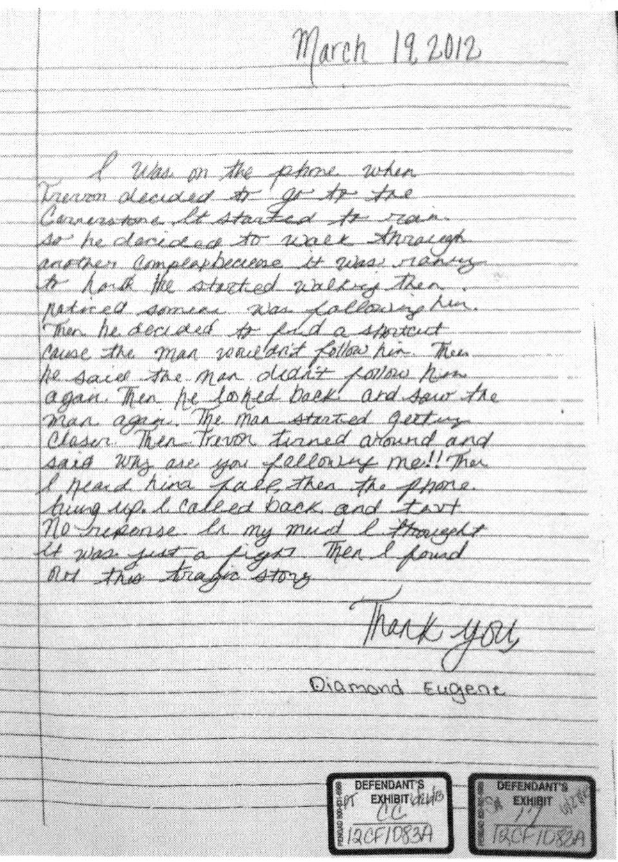

March 19, 2012

I Was on the phone when
Trevon decided to go to the
Cornerstone. It started to rain.
so he decided to walk through
another complex because it was raining
to hard. He started walking then
noticed someone was following him.
Then he decided to find a shortcut
cause the man wouldn't follow him. Then
he said the man didn't follow him
again. Then he looked back and saw the
man again. The man started getting
closer. Then Trevon turned around and
said Why are you following me!! Then
I heard him fall, then the phone
hung up. I called back and text
No response. In my mind I thought
it was just a fight. Then I found
out this tragic story

Thank you

Diamond Eugene

DEFENDANT'S EXHIBIT CC 12CF1083A

DEFENDANT'S EXHIBIT 12CF1083A

The "Sybrina" letter given to Sybrina Fulton by Diamond Eugene

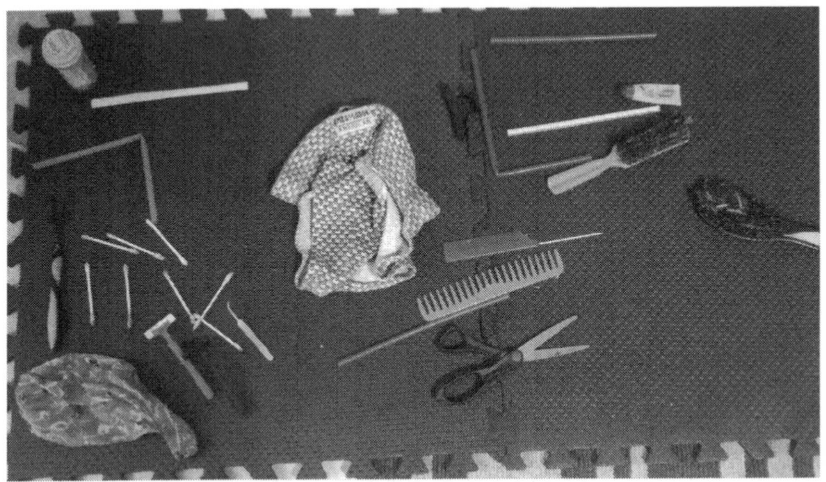

Items collected for DNA testing from Rachel Jeantel's trash outside her house

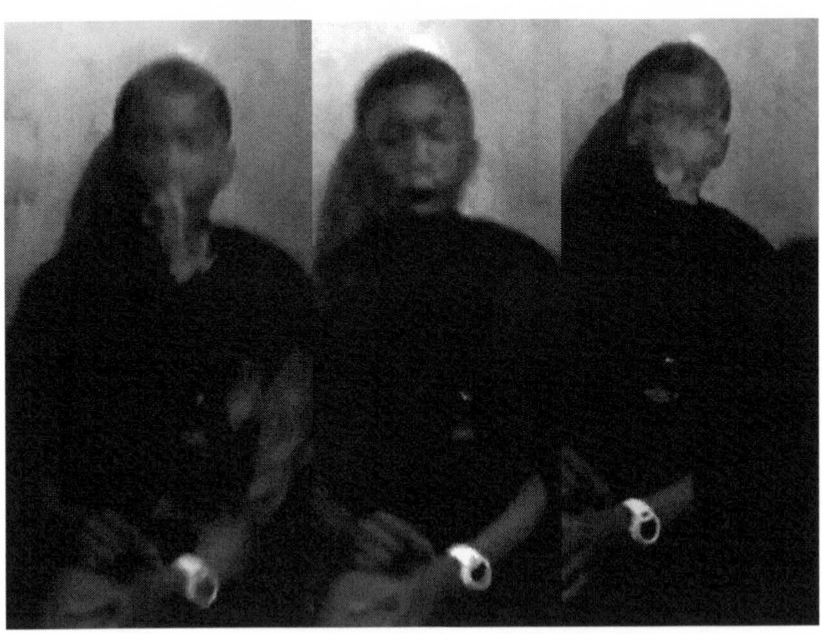

Trayvon Martin getting high in a 2012 video posted by Stephan Bramble

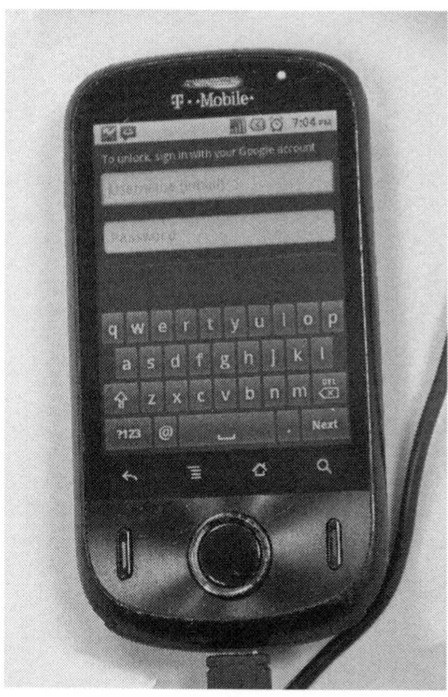

Trayvon Martin's T-Mobile Huawei U8150 Comet cell phone

Comparison of Marie Eugene, Diamond Eugene and Daniel Eugene

Author/Director Joel Gilbert comparing yearbook photos

Author/Director Joel Gilbert buying items in Little Haiti

Brittany Diamond Eugene modeling clothes for her online boutique

Mug shots of Travyon's best friends Stephan Bramble and Mario Carridice

Author/Director Joel Gilbert inspecting weaves at Diamond Girl Beauty Supply in Miramar, Florida and standing next to an Andrew Gillum for Governor poster

Author/Director Joel Gilbert reading Trayvon's text messages

Author/Director Joel Gilbert in his office researching Diamond Eugene

Brittaney Diamond Eugene posing in her many clothes and disguises

Diamond's boyfriend Van Jefferson Watler, who went by Jeff

Rachel Jeantel at a deposition descending into a whirlpool of deceit.

17

30 DAYS TO LIVE

THANKS to her prolific texting and tweeting, I understood much more about Brittany Diamond Eugene than I ever thought imaginable. Fortunately for me, her boyfriend Jeff Watler's tweets from 2012 were in plain sight as well. Given the evidentiary value of all this information, I decided to reconstruct the month leading up to Trayvon's death. From the end of January into the month of February there was much turbulence in Diamond's relationship with her steady beau of seven months, Jeff Watler. Only male attention could stave off Diamond's boredom, and she wasn't getting enough of it from Jeff.

This was hardly Jeff's fault. The industrious eighteen-year-old was working full time at two retail jobs. He sold shoes at Simon's Sporting Goods in a Miami Gardens strip mall and sold clothes at Abercrombie & Fitch in the Aventura Mall in Miami. It is possible he had a third job as well. On top of this, he played on a basketball team that practiced a few times during the week and often played games on weekends.

Complicating matters was that Jeff had no car. He would often close shop at one job, clean up, hop on a bus to the next job, and arrive home by bus after midnight. In her tweets, Diamond would often complain that she had not seen Jeff for a week or even two.

For all its difficulties, Diamond and Jeff's relationship was not unusual for Miami teens. Many young lovers went to separate high schools and could not yet drive, let alone afford their own cars. Their families, sometimes large, were typically headed by a single parent, almost always the mother. Social media helped compensate for the fact that couples could not meet up on a daily, or sometimes even weekly, basis.

By 2012, almost every Miami teen, no matter how poor, had at least one cell phone, often more than one. Diamond had two that I know of. Relationships were maintained through phone calls, emails, seemingly non-stop text messages, Twitter exchanges, Facebook posts, and by shared video chats on Oovoo, Facetime, or Voxer. Many teens, Diamond and Trayvon included, employed four or more of these media platforms on a daily basis.

Young couples engaged in a common phenomenon known as "Tweet Watching." They set up special alerts to know when their loved one had just sent out a tweet. Unlike texts, tweets were public. Anyone could read them if they knew where to look. So tweets often conveyed more than might appear on the surface. They could misdirect the audience or intentionally mislead. Diamond often did both.

We pick up this tale of fatal intrigue in late January 2012. Trayvon had only a little more than 30 days left to live.

Sunday, January 22

Diamond tweeted, "I Miss My Baby :/ When He At Work I Be Sooo Bored With Nobody To Talk To!" The "baby" in question was eighteen-year-old Van Jefferson Watler, who went by "Jeff." Diamond had been citing a host of disappointments and demands for more attention from Jeff. She often complained openly on Twitter that "I haevn't seen my boyfriend in two weeks" and "he call and wake me up and then fall asleep while we on the phone." She often complained that Jeff's friend Gary was getting more attention than she was. After midnight she tweeted, "I Walk To Get Some Juice And He Already Hung Up. SMH!" In text argot, "SMH" means "shaking my head." Jeff often fell asleep while speaking with Diamond.

Monday, January 23

Diamond tweeted, "Baby I'll Ride For You Baby I'll Die You, You Are The Only One, The Only One That Im Loving." Here the concept of "Ride to Die" was meant for Jeff. She added later, "Loyalty NEVER Cross The Line."

Tuesday, January 24

At 11:49 p.m. Diamond tweeted, "I Been Waitinq To Get On Oovoo With This Niqqa For Like 30 Minutes Now!!!" Oovoo is an app not unlike Facetime or Skype that allows for direct video conferencing. Jeff was on the way home from work, and Diamond was staying up to try to talk with him and feed her attention jones.

Wednesday, January 25

Diamond's frustration was beginning to show. She began the morning with "When You Pretty You Get Away With Alot Of Shit" and "Imma Stop Gettinq Mad And Just Get Even." When Diamond used the words, "just get even," she meant them, and this decision would prove to be a disastrous one. At 9:35 p.m. she tweeted. "All A Girl Wants Is A Niqqa Thats There For Her," followed instantly by, "A Real Women Holds Her Man Down & A Real Man Won't Let His Women Down." Minutes later she added, "I can be A GOOD GIRLFRIEND Just TREAT ME RIGHT, Do Me Right & I Promise I'll Do You Better." At 10:32 p.m. she tweeted, "Ok Im Gettinq Bored Now -_-".

At 12:04 a.m., Jeff tweeted passively, "My Phone Died." Emotionally, Diamond was going off the rails. She was pleading, praying, and threatening for attention, but her overworked boyfriend was having phone problems. "Ion do DISRESPECT," she once tweeted.

The tweets opened a window into her soul. Diamond was a "real woman" and could be "a good girlfriend," but Jeff needed to "treat me right," give her more attention. She would deliver for him, if he delivered for her. Diamond took as a personal affront Jeff's work schedule, phone problems, and lack of a car. For Jeff, all this had to hurt. His girlfriend was broadcasting to the world that he was not "A Real Man."

Thursday, January 26

Diamond was coming undone. "Never Let Your Girl Feel Like She's Unappreciated," she tweeted early in this tempestuous day. "I'll

Ride For My Niqqas," she tweeted later, promising loyalty if it were reciprocated. But she was not at all sure it would be.

"Im Not Always The Jealous Type But Whats Mine Is Mine . . . End Of Story!" she blasted and followed with a threat, "If I Ever Find Out My Niqqa Fuckinq Wit Another Bitch On Me I Hope God Wit Him."

Friday, January 27

On this Friday morning, the religious Jeff was letting his insecurities fly. "My biggest fear besides god and god not lettin me in heavin is losin Brittany [Diamond]," he tweeted, adding the condition, "When me and my gf get married she better not have no gay niggas in her family." He was likely unaware of Diamond's flaming gay half-brother, Jahdiah Norelus, who went by the ironic twitter handle, "The Diamond Princess."

"Dont Worry About Me, God Got Me Im Doinq Fine!" Diamond tweeted again later. "Don't You Be Holdinq Back Yo Love."

Saturday, January 28

The relationship with Jeff was intimate, which added both intensity and insecurity. "Woke Up With My Baby By My Side," she tweeted proudly. "I Just Noticed I Didn't Give Him A Kiss When He Left This Morning." Ever demanding, the sleepover was not enough for Diamond. "I Need Somebody To Entertain Me Since Somebody Not Doinq They Job Right," she tweeted in mid-afternoon to unnerve Jeff who recently had read her tweeted threat to "just get even." Later that evening, Diamond upped the wattage of her discontent, "Im Mad Yall ' He Went To A Party!"

Sunday, January 29

As indicated by his tweets, Jeff seemed to rouse himself about noon and head off to work at about 2:30 pm. Meanwhile Diamond was having the inevitable "sex talk with my Mom." She added, "The Stuff She Be Tellinq Me Be For My Own Good Tho." Diamond posed a good question later that day, "Where Im Going?" She would have liked to ask Jeff, but around 4 p.m. she tweeted, "I Called This Boy Twice And Didnt Get No Answer." On this day she again fell asleep waiting for Jeff's call.

Monday, January 30

Jeff actively tweeted all through the early morning hours how much he missed Diamond and how much he was looking forward to his first "real valentines."

Having started the day with breakfast at Burger King, Diamond too was getting into the "The Valentines Day Spirit." Or so she said. Her tweets suggested otherwise. Jeff was speaking so much to his friend Gary that Diamond compared the two friends to "Some Bitches." Late that night, she added, "When This Niqqa Be Out I Dont Hear From Him Until He Get In Unhuh Thats Not Gon Fly Wit Me!"

Tuesday, January 31

Jeff started his day at 11:15 a.m. by tweeting, "No energy." Diamond's messaging with Jeff today was much more positive–"I Miss You," "I'm High on You"–but she was still demanding more and more attention.

Wednesday, February 1

Again, despite Jeff's best efforts, Diamond expressed her need for more. "I Be Wanting All His Attention," she tweeted, "Gary Took My Man From Me Lol." Despite her claim to be "Laughing Out Loud," Diamond really wasn't. "Something Don't Feel Right," she added. For Jeff, the constant public pressure from Diamond had to be exhausting. At 12:53 a.m. Diamond tweeted, "His Phone Died While We Was Falling Asleep Ear To Ear."

Thursday, February 2

Although she was still expecting to spend Valentine's Day with Jeff, Diamond started making contingency plans. Filling in the void for the hard-working Jeff was a boy three days shy of his seventeenth birthday named Trayvon Martin.

Although they had exchanged a few texts with a common friend named Sean Johnson in December 2011, today February 2, 2012, was the day Diamond and Trayvon Martin started communicating on a regular basis. They appear to have met at a church youth related activity back in December. In addition to multiple texts and phone calls, Diamond sent Trayvon two photos. Diamond was now making good on her threat to get even with Jeff and find someone to entertain her because he was failing to accommodate her needs.

Friday, February 3

Diamond had clearly moved to the next level of frustration and anger over Jeff's lack of attention. Several tweets expressed how much she missed him, not having seen him in a week. But she mixed in among them a declaration of intent: "If My Niqqa Ever Feel Like He Dont Want To Be With Me Nomore I Rather Him Be Straight Up With Me Then To Sugarcoat Shit!" As a fallback, she now had Trayvon. Again, she and Trayvon exchanged multiple texts and phone calls, all short.

Saturday, February 4

Diamond expressed her excitement that Jeff was coming to see her, but the wait aggravated her, "Im Gettinq Aggravated AF !!!!," she tweeted. After Jeff arrived, things did not go well. She shared her discontent with the world. "He Just Said Something That Made Me Wanna Punch Him In His Fuckinq Mouth !!!," she tweeted. "He Just Dont Understand." She called Trayvon three times that day.

Sunday, February 5

Diamond's relationship with Jeff had bottomed out. "Baby It Breaks My Heart To Know That Lovinq Me Is Not Easy To Do," she tweeted. "You Should've Known Better I Was Safe By Your Side You Should've Known Your Girl Was Gonna Ride Or Die!" In her inimitable style, Diamond was laying the blame on Jeff for the strain in their relationship. She was also justifying the possibility of stepping out.

Diamond exchanged no texts or phone calls with Trayvon that Sunday. She may have talked to him through some alternate media like Oovoo or Voxer. Trayvon did send about thirty anonymous texts through an online texting service, perhaps with Diamond. This, after all, was his seventeenth–and last–birthday.

Monday, February 6

The drama was not doing much for Diamond's grades. "I Got An F in This Class...Lord Help Me!" she tweeted in the morning. As compensation there was always junk food. "They Sellinq Krispy Cream Donuts , Oh YESS :)".

Jeff, who was not particularly active on Twitter, tweeted, "God blesses me everyday." Trayvon made no phone calls that day and sent only seven texts. Given his propensity to talk and text, he was likely having phone problems.

Tuesday, February 7

"Im Bored &'d He Sleep *Sigh*" Diamond tweeted. She seemed to have resigned herself to a cooling off in her relationship with Jeff. She apparently found comfort again in fast food though, tweeting, "Them Donuts Got My Stomach Hurtinq !!!" She called Trayvon three times that day.

Wednesday, February 8

Diamond spent nearly three hours on the phone with Trayvon and exchanged forty-two texts with him. A certain desperation marked Diamond's tweets. "If It Wasn't For Jeff I Wouldn't Even Care To Have A Phone," she tweeted at one point, "He the Only That I Talk To All Day!" Diamond was misdirecting here. She likely aimed this barb at Jeff who would have been questioning why she did not answer the phone. This was kind of an anticipatory rebound flirtation. She was still openly yearning for Jeff–"Baby Come Closer ' Im Ready For You ;)"–but seemed to be preparing herself for a possible break-up: "Where Is My Boyfriend? He Just Sent Me A Sad Face." She finished off the day with, "I Bet He Done Fell Asleep," and, "Love Could Feel GOOD But it Could Also HURT!"

Thursday, February 9

Jeff was unusually active on Twitter. At 11:01 a.m. he started with, "I get tired Jus thinkin about goin to work." If Jeff had two jobs, Diamond now had two beaus to keep her busy. Jeff could not get ahold of Diamond on this day because she spent nearly five hours on the phone with Trayvon and exchanged 138 texts with him. She also sent Trayvon three more photos. This included an image of the KFC "Double Down Sandwich" poster she captured in still another venture to seek quick comfort in fast food.

That afternoon Jeff tweeted, "Why my gf [girlfriend] never Tex me bck," and later, "Idk [I don't know] why im so mad." At 11:37 p.m., he left his job and headed for the bus in the rain. Still on the way home, Jeff tweeted, "Dam where my baby at." In fact, his baby was on the phone with Trayvon Martin. Between Jeff's demanding work schedule and his even more demanding girlfriend, Jeff was coming unglued. Diamond used misdirection again on the subject of who was stepping out on whom, "Is Jeff On Twitter Flirting? Or Its Just My Eyes."

For his part, Trayvon assured Diamond he would honor her request not say anything about her to anyone, though he did not keep that promise. Soon enough, he would tell his friends Mario, Steve-O, and others about his new girlfriend. To preserve her double life, Brittany Diamond Eugene had Trayvon call her by her middle name, "Diamond." Jeff and her other friends and family all had been calling her "Brittany," the name she was known by in school as well.

Friday, February 10

Jeff and his friend Gary came by to visit Diamond. "They Just Left," she tweeted after the visit. "I Miss My Baby Already." She didn't miss him that much. She exchanged seventy-three texts with Trayvon and spent two-and-a-half hours on the phone with him on this day.

Given the stress of managing two relationships, Diamond gorged on donuts and cupcakes. She tweeted, "Imma Have Diabetes By The Time Im Done Eatinq These Shits." The relationship with Trayvon was junk food for her ego, something that could keep her distracted until she figured out a way to force Jeff to give her all his attention. She tweeted about Jeff, "My Niqqa, My Bestfriend, My Clostie, My Trustie, My MainMan All That In One Thats Why I Got So Much Love For The Kid!"

Saturday, February 11

At 10:59 p.m. Jeff tweeted he was standing out in the "cold" waiting for the city bus. At the same time, Diamond was tweeting, "Its 11 and still no call yet!" Jeff had no idea how cold it really was. To fill the attention deficit, Diamond had spent nearly five hours on the phone with Trayvon and exchanged forty-eight texts with him on this day.

Sunday, February 12

"Goinq To The Mall Tommarow To Do Some Last Minute Valentines Day Shoppinq," Diamond tweeted on this relatively quiet Sunday. She was shopping for Jeff, hoping he would change his ways and pay her the attention she thought she deserved. Although she exchanged twenty-six texts with Trayvon on this Sunday, she talked to him for only thirteen minutes. The initial text to him was provocative. It was just one word, "sweetheart."

Monday, February 13

Diamond was not doing well handling two beaus. "Today Happens To Be On Of My Worst Days *Shugs* Everybody Have One," she tweeted, then added sarcastically, "Im So Glad Gary Coming Back Tommarow."

Jeff meanwhile had begun to get the sense he was being played and tweeted about his nightmare. "It's a dream I be havin alot about my baby, I Hope it never come true," he tweeted, adding, "Jealously is love and hate at the same time." It wasn't just a dream. Diamond spent more than four hours on the phone with Trayvon on this day.

Diamond dangled before Trayvon the very same offer she had recently proffered to Jeff, "do u want be my ride to die nigga?" Given what the "ride to die" commitment implied, only one of the two beaus merited that designation. Trayvon cannot be faulted for thinking he was the guy. He texted back a smile, his acceptance, and Trayvon promptly labeled Diamond's second phone number in his cell phone contact list as "RIDE OR DIE."

Just a few days into the relationship, though, Trayvon was feeling Diamond's sting. She told him he was "acting like a ass lst night." He responded, "Cuz u b confusn me." He had good reason to be confused. "Smh u think i only fuck nd show off u pretty," he texted her that evening, "ion even tell nobody bout yo green ass caus u ask me not 2..... im happy dats how u fuckn feel."

Tuesday, February 14

It was not easy to play her two beaus off against one another on Valentine's Day. Jeff still had the upper hand. From her tweets, we know Diamond gave Jeff his gift and spent the afternoon with him. "Spendinq Time With The Boy I Love The Most," she tweeted. "Thats

What Today Suppose To Be About Not The Material Things." Better still, Diamond's mother let Jeff drive her car for the Valentine's date.

Given the openness of her comments about Jeff, Trayvon must not have known Diamond's Twitter handle. He exchanged 101 texts with her this day. Early in the day, Diamond implied via text that she and Trayvon might have engaged in phone or actual sex the night before. "Last night me u have a good time I like making u mad now I like the make up sex."

Diamond deceived Trayvon about how she spent Valentine's afternoon (with Jeff). In her texts, she alternately claimed she was at school, at a dance practice, at "North Miami Park," "at Fitness," and more non-locations. At one point, she claimed in a text to Trayvon that she could not talk on the phone because she was "wit my Daddy."

Diamond's deceptions were reckless. In checking, I discovered there was no "North Miami Park" and there were no dance classes offered off campus. At one point, to put Trayvon off, she even claimed she was at a park forty miles north of Miami. We know from her tweets this wasn't true, and we know too she did not spend the afternoon with her father given that he was in Haiti. She was with Jeff all afternoon and evening.

If Trayvon was unhappy Diamond was not answering her phone, Jeff was fuming. Something Diamond said or did obviously set him off. The hundred text messages she exchanged with someone else while they were together likely contributed. "Today," Jeff tweeted after arriving home from the Valentine's date, "was the first time I almost hit a girl." He took the bus home and left his gift behind in Eliana's car. Diamond was playing with fire.

Wednesday, Feb 15

Still simmering from a calamitous Valentine's Day, neither Jeff nor Diamond tweeted anything of note. Diamond did, however, find some solace in her 113 texts and three hours of phone calls with Trayvon. Trayvon found little solace anywhere, including his relationship with Diamond. Still upset over his missing Valentine, he texted Diamond, "Man stop playn w/ m emotions." He followed that seven minutes later with, "Uggghhhhh i hate yo fuck ass i hope u choke." Eight minutes later, he told her, "Die."

"No hoes u never had better than me OK," Diamond responded.

"Dumb ass," Trayvon shot back.

"U Dumb shit drop me just drop me."

"I hate u."

"Have fun with ur next hoe," texted Diamond, wrapping up the conversation. Trayvon was in love, Miami-style.

Thursday, Feb 16

Jeff tweeted, "I need a car." He needed it not just to get and to and from work but to keep his girlfriend satisfied.

"I mean I'm winning," Diamond tweeted cryptically, "but I'm still bored." She added, "I was such a sinner but the lord is a forgiver." For immediate relief from all this drama, there was always, "My Wendys Milkshake," that and three hours on the phone with Trayvon into the early morning hours.

Friday, February 17

A down-to-earth guy, Jeff tweeted again that he was tired and needed a car. The much more calculating Diamond had all sorts of unmet needs, such as a "Jamican Patty With Coco Bread NOW" or a late night talk with Jeff.

To begin the day, Diamond, who fell asleep talking to Trayvon, taunted Jeff with the worry that he might be the one who was cheating. As she often did, Diamond put the blame on Jeff. "I Remember A Year And Some Months Ago When Me And Jeff Use To Talk On The Phone Every Morning While I Was Omw To School," she tweeted. "That Been My Niqqa Since 2010, Wats Up?"

What was up on this day was that Diamond spent an incredible eight-and-a-half hours on the phone with Trayvon. In the early morning hours, Trayvon began the text exchanges with a smiley face. There were phone calls in between the texts, but an hour after Trayvon's initial text, Diamond texted him back, "I said I need someone sleep with by me now," and later she asked Trayvon, "how u want me." He answered, "I want in everyway."

To throw Jeff off the scent as to why she was not responding to him, she tweeted at 10:31 p.m. "Just Wakinq Up." followed by "Annoyed" and "Goodnight."

Saturday, February 18

Aimed at Jeff, Diamond fired off a tweet, "Unappreciated" on one of her "worst days ever." Although she did get a "nice massage from bath and body work," not much else went well, especially with Jeff's phone dying. "I Never Been So Fuckinq Aggravated Like This In My Life," she tweeted. To ease the pain, there was always junk food and Trayvon. She spent more than two hours on the phone with her new "Ride to Die."

Diamond taunted Trayvon with texts about having a gun that her mother bought her, "bae I'm Zoe we crazy she got her guns." By "Zoe" she was referring to her Haitian roots and possibly to the violent Haitian gang, "Zoe Pound," to which her father had pledged his allegiance with the "Zoe 4 Life" tattoo on his forearm. Trayvon took the bait. He cautioned Diamond, "Nd b safe bae ion need ntn hapn 2 u." Translated, Trayvon wanted nothing bad to happen to the girl he pined for. He continued to warn her, ironically texting, "Bae bullets dnt hav eyes."

Sunday, February 19

Jeff tweeted in the wee small hours, "My gf said she feel unappreciated and she want a break for a week."

This was a major step for Diamond. The week-long break she asked Jeff for just happened to correspond with Trayvon's latest suspension from school. As a sign of her seriousness, she sent Trayvon four pictures in a row, including the two photos of her cousin Alexis Jacquet (Lil Cuz JJ), and of course two of her gorgeous self. Diamond also spent more than five hours on the phone with Trayvon on this day. "Only God can judge me," she tweeted, and "I ain't been to church in forever." How convenient was this arrangement!

Following what must have been a contentious phone call, in Diamond's last text of the day to Trayvon she exploded, "fuck u then fuck nigga never my number again P.S. bye bitch." She likely just learned that Trayvon was exiled by Sybrina to Sanford and not going to be in Miami to keep her entertained after she had put Jeff on official hold while Trayvon was suspended.

Monday, February 20

Now out of school, Trayvon was giving Diamond all the phone time in the world–eight hours of phone chatter on this, the President's Day holiday. Trayvon was supposed to leave Miami for Sanford, texting Diamond his "weed" was safely stashed "in m dick." He claimed this was the "safest" place to hide it in case he was screened on the bus. "LOL," joked Diamond, "but bae my dick u can fuck up when I jump on it." Trayvon assured Diamond, "Ima b OK."

Despite the length and nature of her exchanges with Trayvon, Diamond was pining for Jeff on Twitter. "I Be Wantinq All His Attention," she tweeted. Not getting it, she warned Jeff he was "Playing with a real bitch."

Diamond was playing with Trayvon too. She sent him another provocative photo of herself, and he was clearly smitten. Trayvon labeled the photo "February 20" and marked it with four hearts in his contact list. Diamond was not nearly as intrigued. She tweeted, "Am I The Only One Bored," and turned once again to junk food to fill the void: "Waitinq On My Pizza Rolls To Be Done"

Tuesday, February 21

On this day, the love-struck Trayvon took the bus to Orlando. When he texted Diamond from the bus, she teased him, "shit bae I miss some s#x." He answered, "U shuda been on da bus ;)." Throughout the day, the two engaged in increasingly explicit talk about sex. Texted Trayvon, "Dis dick is urs."

For all the sex talk with Trayvon, Diamond was still fixating on Jeff, tweeting happily, "When He Say 'I Love You ' Out Of Nowhere >>>>." By the end of the day, the tone had changed, "I Be Wantinq To Punch @fly_dreamchaser [Jeff] In His Mouth Sometimes !!"

Diamond did not spare Trayvon either. He had texted her late in the day, "If yo ass dnt wanna b wit me nd leav den bye hoe hav fun." She snapped back, "nigga fuck u call ur mama or sis a hoe dnt call me a hoe."

Wednesday, February 22

In addition to her usual daily complaints, Diamond continued to shift the burden of advancing their relationship to Jeff. "Baby When You Give Me Love, Dont Hold Back," she had the nerve to tweet to Jeff on the same day she spent seven hours on the phone with Trayvon. She then promptly complained about *Jeff's* "attitude." The stress of deceiving both beaus was getting to her: "I Need A Vacation!" she tweeted.

Thursday, February 23

"I Really Dont Feel Good," Diamond tweeted to start the day. Diamond was coming undone. She was spending more time speaking to Trayvon than sleeping. At one point, she tweeted, "Im Gettinq Bags Under My Eyes," and then, "taking my ass back to sleep." This was her alibi for not taking Jeff's calls, but she was still thinking about him and complaining about the lack of attention: "I Swear If I Was Dien Jeff Wouldn't Be Nowhere To Be Found!"

Friday, February 24

Diamond descended into junk food hell as she tweeted, "I Got Food Poisoned !!!," and, "I Knew I Shouldnt' Have Ate That Shit!" Junk food and Trayvon were the two ways she knew how to cope with her anxiety over Jeff's lack of attention. In his possessiveness and insecurity, Trayvon had begun to irritate Diamond almost as much as junk food.

Knowing of her plans to go clubbing in Little Haiti, Trayvon texted, "if u go...u only danc wit her [Ariana]... NO NIGGAS." Throughout the evening, he repeated this concern several times. To appease her, he promised her jewelry, "2 chains.....1 I s a owl nd da otha 1 a key." Trayvon had been caught earlier in the year in possession of stolen jewelry.

On this day, two days before his death, Faith Miller, the preacher's daughter, texted Trayvon from her sister's phone, telling him she loved him. Trayvon did bother to respond. His obsession with Diamond was total.

Saturday, February 25

In anticipation of going clubbing that night, Diamond tweeted rap lyrics throughout the day, especially ones that spoke to her relationship with Jeff, "Even When I Broke Yo Heart It Was My Sins That Tore Us Apart! But Im Standing Right Here In The Mist Of My Tears."

Jeff visited Diamond in the early evening, then left to go to work. A friend of Diamond's came to the house to get some advice on what to wear to the club in Little Haiti called "Bluster's." Anxious about Diamond going to this club, Trayvon texted repeated concern about her dancing with "niggas." He texted repeatedly, "NO TOUCHN." Despite the five hours he spent with Diamond on the phone, Trayvon texted her in the early morning hours, "im so serious i feel lik u playn wit m emotion."

At this point in his increasingly wayward young life, Trayvon offered little to Diamond other than junk food for her ego–another five hours' worth that final Saturday. A break would come soon enough, but it would come much more dramatically than either could have anticipated.

18

THE LAST DAY

CONSIDER for a moment the state of Trayvon Martin's emotions at the end of February 2012. His school had suspended him for the third time that school year, and he was on the verge of expulsion. He had lost his home base at stepmother Alicia Stanley's house and the loving guidance of "Mama 'Licia" herself. Trayvon's mother Sybrina had thrown him out of her house yet again. Without a car and without income, he was dispatched two hundred fifty miles away from his girlfriend, Diamond, to the home of "My ol boi chick" in Sanford. That is, his father's girlfriend, Brandy Green.

Meanwhile, the girl who enchanted him, Diamond, had been taunting him with tales of guns, dances, and "niggas" hitting on her hot self in nightclubs. Trayvon had to know how little he had to offer her. Their exchanges on the night of February 25 ended on a sour note. "u really jus hurt a nigga feelns," Trayvon texted her. "OK," Diamond responded, "dat how you feel den lost [lose] my numba."

Sunday, February 26, started off no better for Trayvon. He could not have gotten much sleep, if any. Brandy Green's son, Chad, called him at 2 a.m. He had apparently not yet returned to the house. With his mother Brandy and Tracy staying over at an Orlando hotel, Chad was probably a little anxious about being home alone. Chad would testify that Trayvon spent the night in Green's living room while cousin, Stephen "Boobie" Martin, slept in the garage, but that "night" had to have been a very short one.

Boobie would testify that early Sunday morning he bought a "blunt," a "Black and Mild" cigar from the nearby 7-11. According to Boobie, Trayvon remained in the car during the transaction. He was too young to buy one himself. The idea was to empty the Black and Mild of tobacco and replace the tobacco with marijuana.

By 7:40 a.m. Trayvon was texting Diamond, "Was u high las nit." Diamond ducked a direct answer, and Trayvon repeated the question. When she finally admitted she was high, Trayvon's despair bled through. He texted her at 7:55 a.m., "guess yo friend was right. lemme stop wastn yo x [time], u need sumbody worth yo x [time]."

To back Trayvon off, Diamond tweeted, "Man im in church praying." The thing is Diamond wasn't at church. The "church girl" was just another act to put Trayvon on. Much of what she told Trayvon about herself wasn't true. Had she told him the truth about her relationship with Jeff, it would have devastated him. That relationship almost assuredly affected her decision making in the weeks to come, and her decisions would throw a wrench into the plans of the Martin family lawyers and the prosecution.

At 8:20 a.m., after a half hour of texting with Trayvon, Diamond tweeted, "Why am I Up So Early?" and followed minutes later with, "Thank God For Another Day!" Unlike texts, which were private, tweets were public. These were intended for her true love, Jeff, and for other friends and family as well. For Diamond tweets were a tool. She would use them strategically, often to convince Jeff of one thing or another.

At 8:27 a.m. Diamond sent a tweet about Jeff, likely for his consumption. "Yesterday He Brung Out A Side Of Him I Aint Never See Before." She added a rare note of regret and self-awareness, "I Deserved That Tho." She also resumed texting with Trayvon and would continue on and off for the next three hours. The last three texts between them demonstrated Trayvon's growing sense of futility. "wat up with u man how u feel bout me cuz u not say cuz bout to hung up ur ass," Trayvon texted, frustrated at Diamond's unwillingness to express any real affection.

She responded, "lemme say dis im not gon hang up but if uon wanna b on da phon wit m hang up den." Diamond was in no mood for Trayvon's implied threats. If he did not like the way she treated him, she was telling him, he was free to leave. She always had Jeff at the ready.

Trayvon pushed back, "dats not m nam nd im shown u how u treat me..... dont feel gud do it??" This was his final text message to Diamond.

Diamond's tweets that final day of Trayvon's life showed her going from one shopping mall to another and then to the nail salon. Perhaps as a way of keeping Diamond tethered, Trayvon held her on the line for hours that afternoon. The calls started at 12:23 p.m. Trayvon called her nine times that final day. One call lasted eighty minutes, another forty-four minutes, another forty-two, another forty. Diamond would call back when she got cut off, though it appeared they were taking turns hanging up on each other as well. The two would spend more than five hours on the line that final day.

In between calls with Trayvon, Diamond was also talking to Jeff and bragging about it on Twitter, something she did not do in regard to Trayvon. "On The Phone With My Big Head," she tweeted at 5:54 p.m. Fifteen minutes later, she tweeted, "I Just Spoke To His Mom." Trayvon's mother did not yet know Diamond, but Jeff's mom did.

This was a competition Trayvon was destined to lose, and he must have sensed it. Before the day was through, he would speak to at least three of his ex-girlfriends–Faith, Ashley, and Daisha. Given his insecurity of his relationship with Diamond, Trayvon may have wanted reassurance, needed reassurance. This anxiety may explain why Trayvon spoke on the phone to so many others that final day as well: his half-brother Derrick, his smoking buddy Jay Black, his best friend Mario, his cousin "Boobie," and his father Tracy.

At 5:09 p.m. Trayvon called Diamond once more. Although anxious, he could not have sensed that he had only two hours left to live. At about 6:05 p.m., still on the phone with Diamond, Trayvon left

Brandy Green's place for the 7-11, about a fifteen-minute walk away. At 6:21 p.m., a 7-11 security camera picked him up outside the store moving east to west.

Inside the store, Trayvon grabbed an Arizona Watermelon Fruit Juice Cocktail and a bag of Skittles and placed some bills and coins on the counter to pay for the snacks. He then pulled out a few more bills and appeared to negotiate with the clerk for some object on the racks behind the clerk. The clerk shook him off. Although he towered over the clerk, Trayvon was not old enough to buy tobacco products. He still had the bills in his hand when he left the store at 6:25 p.m.

Ninety seconds later, at 6:26 p.m., three young men, two black and one white or Hispanic, entered the store. All three wore hats, wraps, sunglasses, and/or hoodies so as to deceive the security camera. The white kid was holding a couple of bills when he entered, likely the bills Trayvon had exited with. He handed those bills to the clerk and bought two blunts.

While his buddies stayed inside, the white kid left the store at 6:28 p.m. Trayvon was still outside the store. At 6:29 p.m. the security camera picked up Trayvon walking back east towards The Retreat at Twin Lakes. The eighty-minute call with Diamond ended just at the time he made the likely transaction.

At 6:30 p.m. Trayvon called Diamond back. He stayed on the phone with her on and off for the next twenty minutes. He could have easily walked back to Green's townhouse where her son Chad was waiting for him, but he did not go there. After disconnecting from Trayvon at 6:45 p.m., Diamond called Rachel Jeantel's landline from her phone, but was interrupted after one minute by Trayvon's incoming call. She disconnected from Rachel and picked up Trayvon's call. Diamond likely asked Trayvon to put Rachel on a three-way call because at 6:46 p.m., while still on the phone with Diamond, Trayvon called Rachel Jeantel's landline for a brief three-way call. That three-way lasted only one minute when Rachel hung up, and then Trayvon and Diamond's call disconnected 3 minutes later at 6:50 p.m.

At 6:53 p.m. and again at 6:54 p.m., Trayvon called Diamond but did not get through either time. At 6:54 p.m., Diamond called back and they remained on the phone for 17 minutes. Chad called at 7:04 p.m., wondering where Trayvon was. He had been gone nearly an hour on an errand that should have taken half that time.

At 7:09 p.m., George Zimmerman spotted Trayvon standing in the rain in between two rows of townhouses and called the Sanford Police non-emergency number. This was roughly forty minutes after Trayvon had left the 7-11, which was only fifteen minutes away by foot. Diamond may very well have known how Trayvon spent those missing forty minutes. If so, she did not tell. In that Trayvon was found to have THC–the active ingredient of marijuana–in his system, he was likely smoking a blunt while talking to Diamond. At this stage in his life, Trayvon was not a casual smoker. He was a major user.

"Hey, we've had some break-ins in my neighborhood and there's a real suspicious guy, uh [near] Retreat View Circle. The best address I can give you is 111 Retreat View Circle," George told the dispatcher. "This guy looks like he's up to no good or he's on drugs or something. It's raining and he's just walking around, looking about."

For the first time that evening, but not the last, Trayvon disregarded all warning signs. Trayvon had to think the pickup truck that slowed down had something to do with the townhouse complex security. Most kids his age who were high and holding weed would disappear into the shadows and head home. Not Trayvon. For reasons only Diamond might know, Trayvon made an intimidation move on an unknown adult male, sitting in a truck no less, and approached.

George got the message. At 7:10 p.m., he said anxiously into his phone, "Yeah, now he's coming towards me. He's got his hand in his waistband. Yup, he's coming to check me out." Trayvon was on the line with Diamond when he approached George's truck, his hand in his waistband to possibly suggest a gun. Trayvon circled the vehicle slowly, boldly staring at George. The man staring back was on the phone. He looked soft and small, white or Hispanic, and he wore no uniform. This was clearly not a security guard or police officer.

After staring down George and proving his mettle, logic somehow got the best of Trayvon. Maybe he heard Mama 'Licia's voice saying, "Stay out of trouble. Don't get into fights. I love you." Maybe Diamond told him to wise up. Whatever motivated him, Trayvon left the scene suddenly and in a hurry. He disconnected his call with Diamond.

"Shit, he's running," George told the dispatcher.

"He's running? Which way is he running?" asked the dispatcher, a question with fatal implications.

"Down toward the other entrance of the neighborhood."

"Okay, which entrance is that he's headed towards?"

Feeling obligated to provide an answer to the dispatcher's repeated questions about where the man went, George got out of his vehicle. He told me the very idea that he was "following" Trayvon was a miscommunication. He should have explained to the dispatcher he was walking in the direction he last saw Trayvon, not actually following him. In fact, George had not seen Trayvon at all since the teen circled his car and took off. George's short answer "yeah" to the dispatcher's "are you following him" question would form a foundation of the prosecution case for second-degree murder.

Just as George exited his truck, Diamond called Trayvon again. It was now 7:12 p.m. The distance from where Zimmerman last saw Trayvon to Brandy Green's townhouse was roughly one hundred yards. Running, Trayvon could easily have made it to Green's townhouse in the twenty seconds before Diamond called back.

Trayvon's final conversation with Diamond lasted nearly four minutes. Angry, frustrated, high, and heartsick, Trayvon would soon get a second chance to show the stuff he was made of for an intended audience of just one. He had just five minutes left to live.

While he waited for the arrival of the police, George walked along a cut-through perpendicular to the long dog walk that led to Brandy's townhouse. While he walked, Diamond and Trayvon talked. What they spoke about during those four long minutes we do not know. Diamond never testified under oath. She told Crump that she encouraged Trayvon to run to Brandy's and that somehow George followed him there. Diamond's proxy, Rachel Jeantel, would make the same claim in her deposition and at trial. They were both lying.

Diamond had told Trayvon she came from a tough family. She bragged about her access to guns. For his part, Trayvon may well have wanted to make an impression. High at the time, his senses impaired, going only on a few hours of sleep if any the night before, feeling like a loser at school, far from home, and insecure about Diamond, Trayvon had not shown her much of anything. Yes, he had just tried to intimidate George by circling his car but then had run away.

Trayvon and Diamond had nearly four minutes to discuss his next step. If Diamond knew Trayvon planned to turn back and attack George, it would explain much of what happened in the subsequent hours and days, including her frantic phone calls, her avoidance of the police, and her reluctance to go public.

For whatever reason, Trayvon came back to confront George for the second time. This time George was vulnerable. He was outside of the vehicle and exposed. Trayvon saw him walking *away* from him toward his truck, and he sensed the man would be no match for him. Trayvon had half a foot on George and the element of surprise.

After much leading and massaging, Diamond told Crump during her phone interview, "He said this man was watching him so he put his hoodie on. Trayvon said, 'What you following me for?' The man said, 'What you doin' around here?' Then somebody pushed Trayvon because the headset like fell." Although none of this can be taken at face value, Diamond may have overheard the first part of the encounter.

In reality, after a brief verbal exchange, Trayvon surprised George by sucker punching him, breaking his nose, then began straddling him and raining down punches while George screamed for help. Seconds later neighbor Johnathan Good called out from the sliding glass entry of his townhouse just feet away, "Stop. I'm calling the police!" And again, for the second time in four minutes, Trayvon blew off any potential threat from authorities. He did not stop, nor did he slow down.

Johnathan Good disappeared back into his townhouse and

George had run out of options. His head smashed repeatedly against the sidewalk, his nose broken, the blood from the nose running down his throat choking him, and fearing he would lose consciousness, George reached for his gun and fired one shot. The shot came more than forty seconds after his first screams were picked up on the 911 call.

We know what happened from George's perspective. He saw a man hanging around in the rain in between townhomes at night for no apparent reason. Given the rash of crime in the neighborhood, he called the non-emergency number as instructed by Sanford police. He then got out of his car to assist the dispatcher and was brutally attacked.

Team Trayvon's perspective, if you can call it that, was that Trayvon was a child just trying to get home to make a candy delivery to his little brother. Then, a white racist followed and shot him in cold blood because of his skin color–The Trayvon Hoax.

What about Trayvon's perspective? Knowing Trayvon as I think I do, here is what I believe was likely his perspective that night. Trayvon was a serious marijuana user. He had gone to some effort to bring marijuana from Miami to Sanford. At the 7-11, he made a big effort to obtain a Black and Mild so he could smoke his pot. After being rejected by the clerk, he found some fool old enough to purchase it for him. Finally, Trayvon walked back to The Retreat at Twin Lakes hoping to light up en route, but the rain literally dampened his plans. On the phone with Diamond off and on, he found some refuge from the rain by standing in between two townhouses, and finally lit up.

Then a man in a vehicle spotted him and slowed down and Trayvon noticed he was being watched. Thinking it might be a security guard, he discarded his joint and took off. When he saw the vehicle pull over however, Trayvon realized it was just a regular pickup truck, no security decals of any kind. Was this just some "nigga" from the neighborhood who messed up his high after all the trouble he had gone to? What was the man's problem? Why didn't he mind his business? Trayvon was pissed and swaggered over to check out the jerk. He circled George's car and, looking inside, saw the man had no uniform. He was not a security person, and worse, the man was staring at him and making a phone call. He was snitching! What the fuck? A snitch! Trayvon split again and kept talking to Diamond. Trayvon would have bitterly complained about the snitch to her. A few minutes later, Trayvon was surprised to see the snitch out of his vehicle and walking across the cut-through. Now able to size him up, Trayvon realized he had a half a foot on the snitch as he turned to walk back toward his truck.

"You gotta problem?" Trayvon called out advancing rapidly on the man. He did not wait for an answer. Trayvon punched him in the nose as he had done the snitch a few months earlier. Once again, a bloody nose was not punishment enough for a snitch. In that his recent interactions with police resulted only in suspensions from school, Trayvon was unimpressed with Johnathon Good's threat to call the police. He was already suspended. What could they do to him? So he kept on punching. Snitches get stiches.

As George told me, Trayvon sat upright after the shot. At first George was unsure whether Trayvon had been hit and thought perhaps only the sound of the errant shot shocked him into stopping the assault. George's instinctive worry was that the bullet might have penetrated one of the nearby townhouse walls. When he slumped over, Trayvon's prophetic warning to Diamond came true: "Bae bullets dnt hav eyes."

In a moment of clarity before slipping into unconsciousness, the fallen Trayvon requested of his shooter, George, "Tell Mama 'Licia I'm sorry." On the battlefield it is said that with their last breaths dying boys call out not for their wives or for their girlfriends, but for their mothers. So it was with Trayvon. He called out for the mother he loved best, Alicia Stanley, the stepmother who raised him from ages three to fifteen. Though the world would soon canonize Trayvon Martin, Trayvon knew it was he who was at fault. With his dying words, he begged forgiveness.

The first 911 call came in at 7:16:11, seconds after Diamond's call to Trayvon ended. This is the call that recorded George's screams for help. At 7:16:24 Diamond called Trayvon back, and her call went straight to voice mail. In her phone interview with Crump, Diamond concluded by saying, "He didn't call back, so I was like okay he might have lost his phone in the grass cuz I thought it was a fight."

Less than a minute after the fatal shot, responding to George's initial call, Officer Tim Smith entered The Retreat at Twin Lakes. He found his way to the scene of the incident three minutes after the shot was fired. While George was being interrogated at the Sanford police station, Diamond made a series of calls to Trayvon's phone that went unanswered.

At 7:27 p.m., Diamond called her best friend Felicia who did not pick up. Then Diamond called Trayvon's phone two more times in succession, then Felicia again. She spoke with Felicia for about five minutes before trying Trayvon again, then one more try to Trayvon's phone. Each time it went to voice mail. At 7:41 p.m., Diamond tweeted, "My Eyes Hurt." Was she about to cry knowing Trayvon had planned to attack an adult and was no longer picking up his phone?

However vain and manipulative Diamond may have been, she had a heart. She was worried something bad had happened. At 8:08 p.m., while on the phone with Felicia, she tweeted her concern, "Might look light but I'm heavy." Likely Felicia had been assuring her that it was probably no big deal, but despite Felicia's reassurance Diamond was "heavy." She was *very* worried that Trayvon was not picking up or calling her back. She called him again at 8:10 p.m. to no avail and then called Felicia again. In the letter she delivered to Sybrina, Diamond claimed nonchalantly, "In my mind I thought it was just a fight. Then I found out this tragic story." No, Diamond had to know more based on her frantic reactions.

At 8:12 p.m. while still on the phone with Felicia, Diamond turned to her ultimate source of comfort and tweeted, "Prayers Changes Things, I Got Hope!" Prayers to change what? Diamond was on the phone with Trayvon when he decided to confront George, not just once, but twice: first when he saw George and chose to circle his truck and the second time when he spotted George walking back to it.

Only Diamond knows exactly what Trayvon was doing and saying at both times he chose to confront George Zimmerman. She also knew how high he was, how little he had slept in the past 24 hours, how upset he was over their relationship, whether he felt George was a snitch, and if he planned to "beat his ass up." It would have been much better had Diamond come forward and told authorities what drove Trayvon to act so recklessly. But given her desire to keep Jeff from finding out about Trayvon, her father's criminal history with the Haitian Zoe Pound gang, and the rap sheets of some of her aunts and uncles, coming forward to speak with law enforcement was not an option for Diamond.

In the weeks ahead, as the canonization of Trayvon gathered steam, telling the truth about the real reasons for the young martyr's violent encounter became an even less appealing prospect. The only good option Diamond had was to lay low, and that is what she tried to do. Diamond's attempt to disappear, however, was disrupted by Benjamin Crump and his Team Trayvon allies who were increasingly desperate to give life to their spurious, race-based "Skittles and iced tea" tall tale. I had little doubt that Diamond would feel enormous pressure to echo Crump's "innocent boy in a hoodie just trying to get home with candy" nonsense. No doubt too that Diamond did everything she could to resist, for a while at least.

19

BEARING FALSE WITNESS

DIAMOND'S TWEET less than an hour after Trayvon's death, "Prayers changes things, I got hope" got me thinking about the unusual role Christianity played in the lives of virtually every person mentioned in this book, from Trayvon to Diamond to Rachel to Sybrina to George.

Although I am Jewish, I came to an appreciation of the passions of followers of Christianity from the research and interviews I did for my 2010 film, *Inside Bob Dylan's Jesus Years*. Dylan sought out Jesus for spiritual salvation and as a way to save himself from heroin addiction. He righted the course by finding the Lord through the Vineyard Christian Fellowship Church and made three incredible religious albums that stand up to this day, including the Grammy Award-winning "Slow Train Coming."

For years I sang Dylan's Gospel songs with my Bob Dylan Tribute Band, "Highway 61 Revisited." On hundreds of occasions we performed classics such as "Shot of Love," "Gotta Serve Somebody," "In the Garden," "Man Gave Names to the Animals," "Slow Train," and "Every Grain of Sand." Through Dylan, I absorbed a strong sense of the fervor of the faithful who found comfort and redemption in the Lord.

Many of the people involved in this story often turned to Jesus for comfort and redemption, but their Christianity, as practiced, did not extend to honoring the most fundamental tenets of the faith. If a less than pious churchgoer, Diamond prayed sincerely and often. "I wake up & pray every morning," Diamond wrote in one tweet. "I just pray God show me who's really for me and who's not. These days you never know," she wrote in another. She had prayed for Trayvon before his death and offered public prayers on three of the four days afterwards.

What Diamond did not pray for, however, was the courage to be a good Christian. Of the seven deadly sins–pride, greed, lust, envy, sloth, gluttony, wrath–there was not a one that she failed to commit regularly and tweet about. These routine sins, however, were not the most troublesome. All of us commit some of them, and many of us commit all of them.

The violation of the commandment, "Thou shalt not bear false witness against thy neighbor," had massive consequences. Churchgoer Rachel Jeantel swore an oath to tell the truth three times in depositions and twice during the trial, then lied boldly all five times.

To justify her behavior, Rachel had crafted a spiritual exemption. In each of the five official times she was sworn in, Rachel had responded to the question, "Do you swear to tell the truth, the whole truth, and nothing but the truth, so help you God?," Rachel did not answer," I do," but simply stated, "So help me God," each time. No doubt, Rachel wanted God's help to comfort her as she lied her way through each inquiry.

Even today on her Facebook page, Rachel posts sermons from pastors that she admires. "I'm not going to give up my blessing so I fit in with you," says the Rev. T.D. Jakes in one sermon. "If you can't handle it. Take your best shot because I am blessed." Unfortunately, Rachel did give up her blessing to fit in. Although she was uncomfortable with the lie from the moment she agreed to tell it, admonishing prosecutor Bernie de la Rionda six times that she felt "guilty" and twice that "I ain't know about it," Rachel continued the lie anyway.

Trayvon's mother Sybrina Fulton was a member of Antioch Christian Baptist Church in Miami Gardens. She prayed often and openly for her son and told Trayvon as much in her texts. In her book, *Rest in Power,* Sybrina speaks eloquently of turning to God for help upon first learning of Trayvon's death.

"Finally, my questions to God about *why* turned into asking God for help in getting through it," she relates. "*Please give me strength, God. Please help me, God. Please, please, please, please, please.*" Throughout the time leading up to trial, Sybrina invoked the name of "Jesus" on a regular basis to "cover me and my family." She took her Christian Life Bible to her deposition and to court and prayed throughout the trial.

In the days and years following the trial, Sybrina has continued to invoke God at every turn. At the Democratic National Convention, for instance, she assured the audience that Trayvon was in heaven and closed on the note, "We leave you what God has given us, strength and peace."

One can understand how a mother's grief could challenge her commitment to honesty and mercy, but isn't that where faith should come to the rescue? The same might be said for the grief of Trayvon's father, Tracy Martin. Attorney Benjamin Crump was another story. He knew his team was leading the effort to "railroad" Zimmerman, but that did not stop him from praying with Trayvon's parents. When Tracy told Crump all he could think about was destroying George Zimmerman, Crump laid that task off on God: "God is going to make sure that this wrong is made right; we don't have to do anything more at this point." State Attorney Angela Cory joined in the counterfeit revival meeting. When announcing George's arrest, she stated, "The first thing my team did when we met with Trayvon's parents was open the meeting in prayer."

In all my research on Bob Dylan's journeys in evangelical Christianity, I came across no instance in which Jesus urged his followers to join a lynch mob. The only near match I found was a reference to the fact that Jesus himself was sacrificed to appease the mob and hung on the cross by the Romans. Even from the outside I could see that mob justice flies in the face of Christian tradition.

Indeed, Christianity is rooted in the concepts of justice and mercy for the individual, concepts derived from the faith's Jewish heritage, concepts at that time all but unknown to the rest of the world. "Refrain from anger and turn from wrath: it leads only to evil," wrote David in Psalm 37. For those lawmakers who focused on legalisms, Jesus reminded them of their higher obligation, "You have side-stepped justice, mercy and the love of God. You should have done these, without missing out the others."

Jesus's famed Sermon on the Mount is, of course, a tribute to mercy and justice. "Blessed are the merciful, for they will be shown mercy," and yes, "Blessed are the peacemakers, for they will be called children of God." The Sermon on the Mount is something every real Christian has heard and heeded. To a large degree, the civil rights movement was founded on these principles. The Rev. Martin Luther King took his faith seriously. He called his organization the "Southern Christian Leadership Conference." He never yielded to the temptation to provoke violence or seek revenge.

"In the story of Jesus's life, death, resurrection and historical impact rests a people who managed to take the most tragic event to occur in their collective imagination and use it to change the course of human history," wrote Rahiel Tesfamarian in a *Washington Post* article headlined, "Trayvon Martin and Christian Faith."

Writing six weeks after the shooting, Tesfamarian was not in a position to know whether the facts surrounding Trayvon's death would support a call to "change the course of history." She offered the additional caution, "Christian faith demands that those who believe do so regardless of the outcome–be it just or unjust, reasonable or unfair, victorious or devastating." In South Florida that caution was thrown to the wind.

Unlike Trayvon's parents, the two "Reverends" leading the march to injustice, Jesse Jackson and Al Sharpton, had no excuse for so stoking the mob. Their dissembling and demagoguery surprised no one who had followed their misadventures. Jackson's whole career was launched with a dubious claim, namely that he was the first person to tend to Martin Luther King after King was assassinated. It was reported instead that Jackson hid in the bushes nearby at the sound of gunshots. He recovered his senses quickly enough to dab his shirt in King's blood–or at least he said he did. Jackson then high-tailed it back to Chicago, wearing the shirt and claiming he was the natural heir to King's movement.

The Rev. Hosea Williams, who was with King at the time of his death, told the *Washington Post,* "I thought it was horrible. Why would he keep a bloody shirt on all night? The blood did not come from the body of Dr. King." The Rev. Ralph D. Abernathy, who succeeded King as head of the Southern Christian Leadership Conference, was, in fact, the first person to reach King after he was shot. He confirmed Williams's account. Abernathy, however, lacked Jackson's youthful charisma. The moment Jackson assumed the leadership of the civil rights movement, it ceased to be a civil rights movement.

Al Sharpton wrested that leadership away from Jackson and corrupted the movement even further. In the way of background, Sharpton's ascent began when Jackson appointed him as youth director of Jackson's Operation Breadbasket. Soon thereafter, Sharpton launched his own organization, the National Youth Movement.

The media strategy that made Sharpton the face of this spurious movement paralleled that of the Trayvon Martin case. In 1987, fifteen-year-old Tawana Brawley claimed to have been kidnapped, raped, and sodomized by six white men who took the time to write "KKK" and "nigger" on her body in charcoal. Sharpton emerged as her advisor and spokesman, and the media took him seriously. As he would repeatedly do, Sharpton overplayed his hand, going so far as to accuse a local prosecutor of being among the six men who raped Brawley, with Brawley claiming another attacker was a police officer, "It was a cop".

Preposterous on its face, the story fell apart when according to *Slate*, "a security guard for Brawley's lawyers testified that the lawyers and Sharpton knew Tawana Brawley was lying." The falsely accused prosecutor successfully sued Sharpton for damages and yet, amazingly, Sharpton emerged from the case all but unscathed.

Sharpton would go on to incite future racially charged disasters including the Freddie's Fashion Mart massacre and the lethal Crown Heights Riot. "If the Jews want to get it on," said Sharpton at the height of that riot, "tell them to pin their yarmulkes back and come over to my house." Always eager for a story that showed the evil of white America, real or fictional, the media continued to pay homage to Al Sharpton, a veteran con artist who became a regular White House guest and advisor of Barack Obama.

At the time of Trayvon's death, the right "Reverend" Sharpton had a nightly show on MSNBC. In the ensuing weeks, he used his show as his pulpit to demand the arrest of George Zimmerman. Sharpton was particularly manipulative in his use of Christian imagery, at one point comparing Trayvon Martin's death to Jesus' death on the cross.

"We believe in Jesus. They crucified him and never had a charge," Sharpton told a gathering of his National Action Network in April 2012. "They never charged. There wasn't no crime on his indictment. So we've got to deal with the inequities of the criminal justice system. The fact that we [black people] are overly-incarcerated, the fact that we go to court and are treated differently, and the fact that when we're victimized there is not the same response. That's what Trayvon was about."

Here, Sharpton got caught up in his own rhetoric, unwittingly comparing Zimmerman to Jesus, not Trayvon. In fact, Zimmerman was the one being crucified without being charged, and Sharpton was the one leading the mob calling for the crucifixion–justice and mercy be damned. Although any number of Florida state officials volunteered for the role of Pontius Pilate, too many alleged, God-fearing Christians joined the lynch mob for Zimmerman's head. In their grief, their greed, and/or their race hatred, they ignored the tenets of their faith and rushed madly to judgment. Sybrina Fulton went so far as to say, "I know and I believe that God is using me." Yes, Sybrina was being used, but unfortunately it wasn't the Lord almighty doing the using.

In his song "Gotta Serve Somebody," Bob Dylan gave us only two choices as to whom we serve: the devil or the Lord. There is no excusing those Christians who made the wrong choice, exploiting the tenets of their faith to advance a falsehood. As a pastor, Sharpton had even less excuse than the others. No matter. He shoved aside the Prince of Peace and swore his allegiance to the Prince of Lies. "Better to reign in Hell than serve in Heaven," said Milton's Lucifer. For Sharpton, those were words to live by.

20

THE DAYS AFTER

IN THE DAYS and weeks after Trayvon's death, the lives of those he knew and loved took turns they could never have anticipated. Circumstances would force several of those people–Diamond, Rachel, Tracy, Sybrina, and others–to make decisions that would test their character. I will leave it to the reader to judge their choices.

Monday, February 27

This had to be the worst day in the lives of Tracy Martin and Sybrina Fulton. When Trayvon had still not returned by the morning of the 27th, Tracy started calling Trayvon's friends and cousin Boobie. Having no success, he had Brandy Green call Juvenile Justice and the Seminole County Sheriff's Department, a sign of Tracy's concern about the direction his son's life had taken. Again, they struck out. Tracy then called the Sanford Police Department and shared the details of Trayvon's absence.

The Sanford PD sent a police car to Green's townhouse. In that Trayvon had no ID on him when shot the night before, the Sanford PD's Chris Serino asked Tracy for a photo of his son and compared it to a photo of Trayvon taken at the scene of the shooting. There was no question as to who died. Tracy called Sybrina soon afterwards. Understandably, she did not want to believe what she heard. Her guilt must have been overwhelming knowing it was she who had exiled Trayvon to Sanford rather than supervise his school suspension at home.

That same day, key eyewitness Johnathan Good spoke to a local TV news crew and told the reporter what he had seen, namely that Trayvon had straddled George Zimmerman and was pounding away before he heard the shot. Unreported in the media, Tracy talked to Good that same day, and Good told Tracy what he had seen. "You can't imagine how uncomfortable it is to know that you can't give someone that is in that much pain some semblance of relief," wrote Good in his e-book, *The Reluctant Witness.*

Still rattled, Diamond texted with her best friend Felicia in the 5 a.m. hour. At 8:40 a.m. she placed a call to Trayvon and got his voicemail. She hung up without leaving a message. Throughout the day, as was her habit, Diamond tweeted about the random imperfections of her life. In the morning she tweeted, "I Hate Mondays !!!" and "Lol My Boyfriend Funny He Texted Me 'Bae I Sneezed' Just So I Can Say Bless You!" If there was any doubt before, there was none now that the young man she called her "boyfriend" was not Trayvon Martin. About Trayvon's fate, others closer to the family would have known before she did.

Steve-O certainly did. At 12:12 p.m. the self-described "average neighborhood pothead" tweeted, "R.I.P @NO_LIMIT_NIGGA Tha real die young." Memorializing Trayvon later that day, Steve-O tweeted, "Tha last time me an my dawg tray blow, we hotboxed that shit." In street parlance, "hot box" means to share marijuana with friends in a confined space, like a car, and suck in all the second-hand smoke.

Felicia Cineas, who attended Trayvon's high school, Michael Krop, likely informed Diamond of the shooting. The two girls exchanged texts fifty times throughout the school day and into the evening and made several phone calls to each other as well. By the evening there was much to talk about.

Former Trayvon girlfriend Daisha Mitchell attended Miramar High School with Diamond. She was a regular tweet exchange friend with Diamond and remains so to this day. Early in the evening, Daisha tweeted, "just got bad news Be Back Later!" Shortly thereafter she exchanged tweets with a friend who wrote, "aww, I knew that boy, remember you introduced me to him? He died? Omgggg." Leaving no doubt who that boy was, another friend tweeted, "damnn tht sucks. Trayvon he got shot." As a left handed testament to Trayvon's community service, Steve-O tweeted, "That nigga trayvon always got joints for tha block."

Given Diamond's non-stop interaction with Felicia, Diamond knew Trayvon was dead by Monday evening (she later told Crump the same). There had to be some element of relief. Diamond's exploration of a relationship with Trayvon as a way of keeping Jeff off balance wasn't working. Their flirtation had all but run its course in any case. Troubled and insecure, Trayvon was never going to be a replacement even for the super busy, hardworking Jeff. With Trayvon dead, there would be no embarrassing scene, no awkward break-up. There was, however, that final phone call to deal with.

Tuesday, February 28

At Sanford PD headquarters, Investigator Chris Serino played the 911 recording for Tracy Martin on which George's desperate cries of "help" were heard for roughly forty seconds until a gunshot ended the beating. Tracy told the police that the screams for help were *not* those of his son. Sybrina remained in Miami grieving, as did stepmother Alicia Stanley.

Having learned of Trayvon's death the night before, Diamond tweeted with less concern for her own troubles than usual that morning. "Said my prayers," she tweeted. "God got me." Other than that, Diamond was back to her narcissistic self by that evening. Her tweets documented the life of a self-absorbed sixteen-year-old: "I Just Ate Like A Fat Girl" and "Fuller Then Ever :/."

Diamond ended the evening by tweeting affectionately, "With My Jeff Ugly Ass." Jeff was happy to be back in her good graces. "Chillin' with my Baby," he tweeted at 10:15 p.m. Still, he had to be confused. Just ten days earlier, Diamond had asked for a week-long break in their relationship. In the ensuing days, she had been cold and rarely available to talk even on the phone. Now, here they were together again, and Diamond was acting as though nothing amiss had happened. Jeff wasn't sold. At 10:57 p.m. he tweeted, "Something don't feel right at all."

After Jeff left, Diamond tweeted, "Stayinq Up Until He Get Home Safe!" With Trayvon dead, Jeff was the one. There was no one else to give her attention. If she sensed Jeff's unease, she pretended not to notice.

Diamond was among the few of those close to Trayvon who did not call his cell phone after his death. His cell records show how much he was loved. After his friends and family knew he had passed, they continued to call repeatedly for days, either to leave goodbye messages or just to hear Trayvon's voice on his outgoing voicemail message. Callers included his mother and grandmother, all five former girlfriends, and numerous pothead friends.

Saddest of all the calls were those from Faith Miller, the preacher's daughter. She continued to call Trayvon from different phones, thinking he was alive. A student at North Miami Beach High School, she had not gotten the word. Still thinking herself to be Trayvon's girlfriend, she did not find out he had passed until her parents gave her phone back to her a week after the shooting. Finally, the day after Trayvon's funeral, Faith called Steve-O looking for Trayvon. He informed Faith that Trayvon was gone.

Wednesday, February 29

Dissatisfied with an investigation that pointed to his son being shot in an act of self-defense, Tracy heeded the advice of a lawyer friend and had her call Benjamin Crump on his behalf. Tracy then called Crump himself and explained the details of the case. "Of course, they're going to arrest him," Crump reportedly told Tracy. At Tracy's request, a Fort Lauderdale funeral parlor director took Trayvon's body back to Miami. Tracy left Sanford soon afterwards and met with Sybrina later that day. ABC's Matt Gutman would later falsely report that Trayvon's body was left unidentified for several days at the Sanford morgue.

The *Orlando Sentinel* posted online its first article about the shooting. It was headlined, "Boy, 17, shot to death in Sanford during 'altercation,' police say." The article made no reference to the race of either Trayvon Martin or George Zimmerman.

Through her tweets, Diamond continued to reinforce her relationship with Jeff: "8 Months Strong (heart emoji)" and "My Nigga For Life Tho." Jeff was lucky to have her. "I Look Good," she tweeted simply and surely. It seemed likely, however, that Jeff had begun to hear rumors that Diamond and Trayvon were tight because, that afternoon, he tweeted a shot across Diamond's bow, "I rather my gf spit in my face then cheat on me."

Thursday, March 1

The word had spread by Thursday that the shooter was white, at least white enough, and the victim a black teen. The local president of the NAACP, Turner Clayton Jr., emailed Sanford Police Chief Bill Lee asking for a meeting. Black City Commissioner Velma Williams did meet with Lee on March 1. "I told him, 'I can see a train coming down the track at 50 miles an hour, and you better get a handle on this."

Crump sent a white attorney, Jasmine Rand, to meet with Tracy and Sybrina. Later in the day, they signed with Crump and his partner Daryl Parks "to take our case." Whatever that case was, Crump had yet to figure it out.

Diamond had reason to be anxious about her role in the shooting incident. She did not want Jeff to know about her relationship with Trayvon, and she likely would not have wanted to invite the police into her life given the criminal histories of some close relatives.

By this day though, Diamond knew she was on the hot seat. At 8:30 p.m. Felicia called Diamond and had Trayvon's best friend Mario join them on a three-way call. After the call was over, Diamond tweeted, "I don't like people who run they mouth too much. Some things just shouldn't be said."

Mario was tight with Trayvon's parents and would later travel with them to Sanford for a press conference. Felicia's sister Francine Serve was close to Sybrina Fulton. She took care of her quadriplegic brother at Sybrina's home and attended both Trayvon's wake and funeral. It is very likely Mario would have told Trayvon's parents by now about Diamond. Francine would surely have spilled the beans as well.

Friday, March 2

A public viewing was held for Trayvon at the Richardson Funeral Home in Miami Gardens, Florida. Throughout the morning Diamond exchanged texts with Mario but did not attend the viewing. She tweeted more often than usual that day but made no obvious allusion to Trayvon's wake. Most of the tweets were as superficial as ever, and about seeking comfort where she did most often: "I Need To Find Somebody Who Selling Donuts!" and "At China Town Ordering Me Some Chinese Food." In a tweet aimed at Jeff, she wrote, "You Got A Past And I Do Too, We're Perfect For Each other!"

Saturday, March 3

Trayvon's funeral was held in the morning at the Antioch Missionary Baptist Church nearby. Stepmother Alicia Stanley, "Mama Licia," was exiled from the front row. There was no media attention in Miami. At this stage, Trayvon was just another statistic. While his family readied themselves for the ordeal, Diamond was tweeting gems like, "Im Hungryyyyyy !!!," and, "Why Everybody Want Ihop ? Dennys Wayyyy Better!" As the service got underway amidst a chorus of sobs, Diamond tweeted her delight at Jeff's arrival, "My Baby Here :))))." She would later agree with Crump that the shock of Trayvon's death six days earlier sent her to the hospital and caused her to miss the funeral that day.

In *Rest in Power,* Tracy claimed he called Crump after the funeral and told him the police were refusing to arrest Zimmerman because of Florida's Stand Your Ground laws. Although Tracy claimed the family signed with Crump two days earlier, it was not until Saturday, March 3, that Crump confirmed, "Mr. Martin, I'm going to help you." The entire Crump chronology is suspect.

Tracy added another wrinkle, a thoroughly disingenuous one. He claimed that Crump fully committed to the case only after Sanford Police Chief Bill Lee held a press conference announcing there were no immediate plans to arrest Zimmerman. That press conference was on March 12. As shall be seen, Team Trayvon had slipped into high gear a week before that.

Sunday, March 4

On this Sunday, a week after the shooting, Diamond turned philosophical. “God Wouldn’t Put Us In A Situation We Cant Handle,” she tweeted at one point. “Sometimes You Out Last Your Enemies,” she tweeted at another. If she had thought about the funeral, Diamond had put it out of her mind by that evening. She and Jeff went to the movies. “Project X Was GOOD!” she tweeted happily.

Monday, March 5

Eight days out, the *Orlando Sentinel* ran only its second story on the shooting. This brief article added the detail that the shooter, still unidentified, was a member of the neighborhood watch. Again, there was no mention of race. There soon would be. Working through attorney Natalie Jackson, a board member of the Orlando NAACP, Crump reached out to Ryan Julison, a white, Orlando-based media strategist. Tracy claimed not to have spoken with Julison for at least several more days.

Diamond was back at school, apparently in Biology Honors. Only a modern American would dare complain of a Miami morning, tweeting, “Its Too Fucking Cold To Be Taking The Bus.” After a variety of tweets about food, drinks, sleep and weather, Diamond tweeted, “Once My Heart In It, Im Loyal!” That’s how she saw herself in any case.

Tuesday, March 6

Diamond tweeted at length about school: bad grades, girls with ugly purses, weak cell signal in the classroom, and, most memorably, anticipating Colin Kaepernick by four years, “Man I Get Tired Of Standing For The Pledge!” Trayvon pal Steve-O did not worry much about school. At 12:58 p.m. he tweeted, “I smoked away my brain.” Steve-O did not worry about much of anything.

Wednesday, March 7

Publicist Ryan Julison was earning his keep. Reuters had picked up the story and ran shamelessly with the angle Team Trayvon had fed it. Its headline read, “Family of Florida boy killed by Neighborhood Watch seeks arrest." Beyond the headline, the article is all about race. "The family of a 17-year-old African-American boy shot to death last month in his gated Florida community by a white Neighborhood Watch captain wants to see the captain arrested, the family's lawyer said on Wednesday." To this point, the *Orlando Sentinel* had not mentioned the race of either Martin or Zimmerman. The article quoted Crump. "What do the police find in his pocket? Skittles," said Crump. "A can of Arizona Iced Tea in his jacket pocket and Skittles in his front pocket for his brother Chad."

Diamond showed no awareness that the story was breaking nationally. In mid-day, she tweeted an anthem of sorts, "I'm A Rebel, Fuck The Devil, God Got My Back!"

Thursday, March 8

For three minutes on CBS's *Good Morning* Tracy shared with America his grief over the loss of his son and his outrage that George Zimmerman had not yet been arrested. Tracy spoke of an "arrest" as if it were a constitutional right being denied his family. Crump knew better. He knew that prosecutors would authorize an arrest only if they believed they had probable cause, the evidence to convict, but he also knew that only with an arrest could he sue some responsible entity, most likely The Retreat at Twin Lakes homeowners association. He had been down this road before.

In Orlando, Crump held a press conference featuring Tracy, Brandy, and Trayvon's cousin Boobie who held up a picture of Trayvon in a football uniform taken when he was about twelve. The Orlando TV report could have been written by Julison. Sample question to Tracy: "If your son had been white do you think he would have been shot and killed that day?"

After the press conference, Crump called Al Sharpton, and Tracy taped a segment for Sharpton's show, *Politics Nation*. Crump would later say he phoned Sharpton because, "he had a track record." Think Tawana Brawley. That same day Sybrina made her first trip to Sanford. As part of Julison's strategy, the long estranged duo who rarely spoke to each other, Sybrina and Tracy, would always appear as a couple.

Current TV's the *Young Turks* also heeded Julison's siren song. Co-host Ana Kasparian claimed, "There was no self-defense in this situation." According to Kasparian, Zimmerman called 911, saying, "There was someone in the gated community who looks very suspicious, i.e. a young black man who makes me uncomfortable." As Kasparian saw things, "George Zimmerman decides to go ahead and shoot the seventeen-year-old black boy in the chest which led to his death." That simple.

"Oh, my God," said co-host Cenk Uygur. "He just shot him?"

"He just shot him," Kasparian insisted, adding, "I get so angry when people deny there is racism in this country."

Kevin Cunningham, the "super Irish" son of political activists, read about Trayvon on a Howard University e-mail list and launched a petition on Change.org called "Prosecute the killer of our son, 17-year-old Trayvon Martin." Change.org was founded in 2002 by four affluent white male Leftists. Its goal, according to CEO Ben Rattray, was to "change the balance of power between individuals and large organizations."

If any individual needed the balance of power changed it was George Zimmerman. Without a useful connection anywhere, George would face the combined power of the Obama Justice Department, the State of Florida, and *all* of the major media. Indifferent to the facts, and eager to stoke urban fires in an election year, the young activists at Change.org sided with power.

Celebrities like Spike Lee, Deepak Chopra and Mia Farrow quickly signed the Change.org petition as did more than one hundred thousand others within the first week alone. The Left liked nothing more than the story of an innocent black boy being murdered by someone who was white or at least whitish.

Diamond still seemed oblivious to the storm building around her. Her main problem, as she expressed it, was the jealousy she faced from other girls, rivals perhaps, enemies for sure, who were likely envious of her latest fashions. She sent out an angry series of tweets, including, "Know I Must Make Alot Of Yall Hoes Sick , All I Can Tell You Is Hoe GET USE TO IT BITCH!"

It seems that the girls who most disturbed Diamond were white. "Bad Bitches Every Where BERRY WHITE!" she tweeted at one point. Another tweet was more ominous, "Killing That White Bitch OJ!"

Friday, March 9

Although fully aware that Trayvon's death had become a national story, Diamond's tweets gave absolutely no indication that his death had anything to do with her. A typical tweet read, "None Of The Vending Machines Got Doritos ~_~."

Saturday, March 10

Again Diamond's tweets gave little away. In case anyone had doubts, she posted, "Jeff My Nigga For Life!" Beyond that was her typical run of concerns: food, sleep, shopping, and more food, such as "Mommy Brought Me Mcdonalds :)."

Sunday, March 11

Sybrina Fulton led a candlelight vigil for Trayvon at the Antioch Missionary Baptist Church in Miami while the Sanford Police were wrapping up their investigation. The latter included reviews of 911 tapes, witness interviews, an assessment of the physical evidence, and several interviews with George Zimmerman. The police concluded the shooting was self-defense, and there were no grounds for charges against George.

Almost assuredly, someone at the police department tipped off Team Trayvon about the unlikelihood of an arrest. At 8:19 p.m. Team Trayvon insiders began to press Diamond to come forward. Following a text from Felicia, Trayvon's friend Steve-O texted Diamond twice. This was followed by six incoming calls from Felicia in succession, each lasting about thirty seconds each. It appears that Diamond was repeatedly hanging up on her best friend, but Felicia kept calling back. The next call was from Trayvon's best friend, Mario, followed by two more incoming calls from Felicia.

At 10:11 p.m., Diamond tweeted "Aggravated!" But the aggravation continued with three more calls from Mario. The night ended with a phone call from Steve-O at 11:21 p.m. followed by a call from Diamond to Felicia two minutes later.

The pressure on Diamond was building. It appears that someone reached out to her absentee father, former Zoe Pound gangster Bodler Norelus, in hopes that he might intervene. Norelus was living in Haiti. Diamond caught on to the game being played. "My Ol Boy Requested Me On Facebook o_o Where Df Fool Came From?" Diamond tweeted at one point, quickly followed by "Deactivating My Shit!" Despite the pressure, Diamond still found time to tweet complaints about a mosquito bite, her weave, "My Hair Itchy Af [as fuck]!" and Jeff who paid her insufficient attention, "Still No Text Back ? He Better Be Sleeping."

21

FORCED OUT OF HIDING

FOR THE FIRST two weeks after Trayvon's death, Diamond was able to stay in the shadows. As the national media turned more and more light on Florida, the shadows disappeared. There was nowhere left for Diamond to hide, well almost nowhere.

Monday, March 12

As Sanford Police Chief Bill Lee knew, George Zimmerman had made an excellent case for self-defense. "Until we can establish probable cause to dispute that," he said at a morning press conference, "we don't have the grounds to arrest Zimmerman." Unfortunately for George, the word "until" was an opening for Team Trayvon. If they could find a way to contradict the self-defense finding, there might be grounds for an arrest. That afternoon Chief Bill Lee turned the case over to the Seminole-Brevard State Attorney's Office.

With the chance of an arrest slipping away, Team Trayvon turned up the pressure on Diamond. Trayvon friend Steve-O hammered her with text messages all Monday morning at school. That evening, Trayvon best friend Mario called Diamond twice. Diamond responded as she often did when under stress: she called out for fast food, Pizza Hut on this occasion. Mario called twice more that evening, but Diamond refused to pick up. After the second call, she immediately called her best friend Felicia. Diamond's tweets, written for public consumption, gave away nothing: "On Facetime With My Boyfriend," "We Having Fun," "Thank God For Another Day."

Tuesday, March 13

Norm Wolfinger, head of the state attorney's office, announced his receipt of the case package on the shooting from the Sanford PD. He could not have been happy to receive it.

With Team Trayvon desperate for Diamond's testimony in hopes it might jump-start the case, Mario began sending text messages to Diamond at noon. Diamond turned off her primary phone for much of the rest of the day and likely relied on her second cell phone to make calls as needed. She appeared to be avoiding Trayvon's supporters. Once again, Diamond's tweets showed her in full-scale avoidance mode: "I'm In The Mood For Some Noodles," "My Tittes So Big For My Size -_-," "Going To The Water Park."

Wednesday, March 14

A crowd of supporters and media overflowed Sanford's Allen Chapel to hear rising young evangelist Jamal Bryant of Baltimore tell the crowd, "We call for an immediate arrest. We want him behind bars." So much for mercy and justice. Bryant was the first of many pastors to make the pilgrimage to Sanford.

Diamond appears to have shut down her primary phone to avoid Mario, Steve-O, and even her BFF Felicia who had been serving as an intermediary. Again, Diamond's tweets gave away nothing: "Mall In A Hour Or Two," "Got My Outfit For The Fair All That Need To Be Done Now Is My Hair," "Imma Look Good ^_^."

Thursday, March 15

Emails from citizens demanding the arrest and prosecution of "the killer" overwhelmed the computer servers at State Attorney Norman Wolfinger's offices. These were not spontaneous.

Diamond's usually busy phone was very nearly silent. She had closed herself off from the trouble and sought shelter in her world of hair, food, and Jeff: "My Mama Take So Long To Sew In Hair ~_~,"

"Mcdonald's Breakfast :)," and "Jeff The Only Reason My Night Wasn't Bad."

Friday, March 16

Team Trayvon held a press conference on the front porch of Attorney Natalie Jackson's Orlando office. Unable to recruit Diamond, Crump produced two female roommates from The Retreat at Twin Lakes who were allegedly eyewitnesses to the shooting. This was to be Crump's big moment, the "big reveal" to force an arrest of George Zimmerman. The women made various unfounded claims that Zimmerman did not shoot in self-defense and falsely stated that the police had refused to take their statements, even though the police had already done so. Unfortunately for Team Trayvon, the police quickly debunked the more outspoken of the two, Mary Cutcher, by releasing the contradictory interviews she had given earlier.

The afternoon press conference was held too late in the day to make the evening news anyway. Of greater PR value, however, was Team Trayvon's trip to the mayor's office that evening. Sanford City Manager Norton Bonaparte Jr., an African American, played the 911 calls for the Martin family. In reporting on what followed, ABC's Matt Gutman posted a piece with the headline, "Trayvon Martin Neighborhood Watch Shooting: 9-1-1 Tapes Send Mom Crying From Room."

Gutman was not on the scene. He relied fully on the word of Team Trayvon as to what happened. When Tracy first listened to the tape two weeks earlier, it should be noted again, he denied the voice was his son's. Gutman overlooked that. He would prove a useful mouthpiece for Team Trayvon in the weeks ahead. His reporting would become even more reckless and defamatory as his role with Team Trayvon and Diamond herself grew more intimate.

The *New York Times* published its first article on the case. Miami bureau chief Lizette Alvarez made several inexcusable errors for a story that was nearly three weeks old. It was in this first article that Alvarez introduced the idea that Zimmerman was "white and

Hispanic." In a later article she would compress that into the now infamous "white Hispanic."

Again, Diamond had her phone shut off most of the day and made only a few calls to Felicia and Rachel Jeantel. Tweets of note were: "Hungryyyy," "That Time Of The Month >.<," and "Chilling With My Boyfriend." For Diamond, these were the eternals.

22

THE PLOT UNFOLDS

If Diamond managed to spend the three weeks after the shooting in limbo, she would not be allowed to remain there much longer. Despite her constant need for attention, she knew enough not to seek the kind of attention that her phone witness to Trayvon's final minutes would surely bring.

Saturday, March 17

Perhaps thinking Crump's Friday press conference had taken the pressure off her to come forward, Diamond returned to her main phone on Saturday afternoon and resumed her normal pattern of calling and texting. She did, however, abstain from tweeting for a veritable lifetime. For Diamond, this abstinence was worth noting, "Damn, it's been six hours since tweeted," she observed in a 8:34 p.m. tweet.

At 9:50 p.m. Diamond tweeted that she was at the movie theater with Jeff and his parents. This was almost assuredly her way of disguising the fact that she had gone clubbing again. Three minutes later she tweeted, "This is the packest I ever seen this shit." She was not referring to the movie theater.

After speaking with Felicia for about fifteen minutes, Diamond got a call at 10:25 p.m. Although the call lasted only 2.2 minutes, it had to rock Diamond's world. The call came from Trayvon's father, Tracy Martin. Felicia likely served as go-between. She knew Trayvon. In fact, GPS coordinates show that Trayvon was at Felicia's house on the afternoon of Sept 29, 2011.

Sunday, March 18

Diamond's friend with whom she went clubbing, Ariana, began texting Diamond at 10:33 a.m. and continued with thirty text exchanges in the next hour or so. She may have been the newest girlfriend recruited to help prod Diamond into action since Felicia had not succeeded. Felicia got back into the act at 2:50 p.m., followed by another one-minute-plus phone call from Tracy Martin at 3:14 p.m. Tracy was likely asking nicely, and letting the peer pressure do the rest. Steve-O took up the cause immediately after Tracy and then tagged teamed phone calls to Diamond with Mario, calling her again and again into the evening until Diamond appears to have turned off her phone.

Given the unwanted pressure, this would have been the perfect time for Diamond to finally let Tracy and Trayvon's friends know she was not the one who spoke with Trayvon for hours upon hours, that his real heartthrob was the plus-sized Rachel Jeantel. It would have been the perfect time, that is, if any of that scenario were true. None of it was. Instead, Diamond finally yielded to the pressure and agreed to report to Sybrina's house the next day after school. The pressure must have been enormous and may have included threats to turn her name over to the police and to the public, and even inform her boyfriend, if she did not cooperate. If she did cooperate, if she talked to Crump, Team Trayvon promised to keep her identify secret based on her being a sixteen-year old and a minor, at least according to what Crump would soon report. He later told Court TV, "We pushed her making a statement."

For the first time publicly, Diamond let on that she was under siege. "This Can't Be Happening To Me :'(" she tweeted that Sunday evening. The symbol was for crying. She followed soon afterwards with, "Going For A Walk, Need To Ease My Mind." An hour later, back from the walk, Diamond turned to her traditional form of relief in times of stress, junk food, in this case "Snicker Icecream >>>."

Monday, March 19

After being dropped off after school at Sybrina Fulton's house by Francine Serve at around 4 PM, Diamond seems to have spent some time at Sybrina's house listening to a proposal from Benjamin Crump. The request was to have Diamond return that evening and tape an on-camera interview with Matt Gutman of ABC News. Sybrina later told authorities she then drove Diamond home and spoke to her mother who said she wanted Diamond's identity kept secret. As mentioned in detail earlier, Diamond backed out of Crump's plan, allowing only for an over-the-phone interview, which was recorded by Crump with ABC's Gutman listening in. The call was over by 10:04 p.m. Minutes later, the ever resilient Diamond tweeted, "Watching Shrek," and at 11:02 p.m. was "Falling Asleep To [Jeff's] Voice." That same evening, Al Sharpton dedicated the entire run of his show *Politics Nation* to the shooting. His half-hour of race-baiting was only marginally less reckless than what Matt Gutman had been doing on ABC. Meanwhile, Trayvon's friend Steve-O tweeted, "My nigga tray worldwide. #RipTray we miss you dawg."

Tuesday, March 20

On this day, Diamond's voice went out over the national airwaves, courtesy of Benjamin Crump's press conference and later ABC News. ABC's Diane Sawyer introduced Matt Gutman's piece by calling Zimmerman the "neighborhood *watchdog*." The piece focused on the many failings of the Sanford PD and closed with a photo of a young Trayvon actually hugging a baby. The media pressure emanating from Crump's press conference was hastening Zimmerman's arrest.

At the time, no one in the major media asked why Diamond had failed to contact anyone for three weeks, including Trayvon's parents, about him supposedly being chased down, beaten, and then shot by an unknown man while yelling for help. CNN's legal analyst Sunny Hostin, like most reporters, had no interest in such questions. She just wanted to see Zimmerman arrested. Diamond's phone testimony, Hostin claimed right after the press conference, "dispels the notion of self-defense." The railroading of George Zimmerman and the exploitation of Trayvon Martin were well under way on the national level.

Wednesday, March 21

Sybrina was not too grief-stricken to file applications with the US Patent and Trademark Office to trademark the phrases, "I Am Trayvon" –# 4,580,571 and "Justice for Trayvon"– #85575974. That same morning on the *Today Show*, referring to Diamond, Benjamin Crump told Matt Lauer, "She is a sixteen-year-old teenager who just lost a friend very special to her." His partner Daryl Parks would later tell HLN's Nancy Grace, "She's a minor. So it's a very delicate situation."

Declining to text on her main phone, Diamond spoke non-stop with Felicia after school and into the evening. Felicia, recall, was Francine Serve's younger sister. Diamond had to be concerned how this was all unfolding now that her voice was out on the airwaves and might be heard and recognized by her boyfriend Jeff. Her tweets, however, revealed little other than her obsession with food, her gripes about school, and her affection for Jeff "Going In The Shower And Might Take A Nap Until My Baby Come."

Meanwhile Steve-O continued to mourn the friend he lost. "That man used to ride the bike all the way from krop to our side," he tweeted, "just to chill." By "chill" he meant smoke weed. Trayvon was such a pothead that Steve-O and other friends would pay tribute to him by smoking joints next to his grave for months to come.

Thursday, March 22

Indifferent to the fact that Zimmerman was Hispanic, La Raza president Janet Murguía sided with Team Trayvon and called for "a real investigation for this grievous failure of justice." Whipped to a mindless frenzy by the media, students at Miami Carol City High School, which Trayvon had attended for two years, staged a seemingly impromptu walkout outside the Miami Gardens high school I had visited.

In Sanford, Al Sharpton led a large, angry crowd in a chant of "No justice, no peace." On that same day, a shaken Bill Lee withdrew from his job as Sanford Police Chief after less than a year in that position.

That day too, Seminole County State Attorney Norm Wolfinger took himself off the case. The potato was that hot, and the Zimmerman family was feeling the heat too. George's parents would soon have to go into hiding when celebrity Rosanne Barr tweeted out their home address.

In Tallahassee, Governor Rick Scott appointed state attorney Angela Corey to take over the investigation. A Republican and an Arab-American, Corey was up for re-election in 2012. She promptly appointed assistant state attorney Bernie de la Rionda as lead prosecutor. The wheels of injustice were grinding forward like a hell-bound freight train.

Diamond again spent much of this day on the phone with Felicia. Mario called her as well. The stress was catching up with her. She could not have been sleeping well. "I'm Soooo Tired !!!!," she tweeted in the morning and later, "I Was Knocked The Fuck Out In Class, I Needed That Lil Nap!"

23

THE ROSE GARDEN

ALTHOUGH TOO YOUNG TO vote in 2012, and largely indifferent to politics, Diamond and her friends swore their allegiance to Barack Obama. Little did Diamond suspect that she would play a major role in Obama's reelection.

Friday, March 23

Students from a dozen more Miami-Dade high schools and a couple of middle schools joined the walkout movement. Students in neighboring Broward County walked out as well.

Abandoning texts in favor of phone calls, Diamond spent much of this day on the cell phone speaking with Felicia. As yet unaware it was Diamond's voice that Crump broadcast during the press conference, Jeff tweeted to her, "I love you." Many of Diamond's tweets dealt with the school walkouts, which struck her as mindless. "I Got Alot Of Work To Make Up, I Can't Afford To Walk Out," she tweeted. "This All Just Starting To Seem Like A Competition Between The Schools!!!" She was publicly and consciously distancing herself from the issue. In none of her tweets did Diamond reveal her closeness to the biggest news story of the day.

. . .

In Detroit, LeBron James and several other members of the NBA's Miami Heat wrote messages on their sneakers, such as "We want justice" and "RIP Trayvon Martin," but the real action that day took place in Washington, D.C. In a Rose Garden press conference, President Obama showed what side he was on, and it was not the side of justice. Said he after some meaningless boilerplate: "But my main message is to the parents of Trayvon Martin. If I had a son, he'd look like Trayvon."

At the time, I remember not being surprised at all by Obama's willingness to side with the cultural Marxists. The most influential person in young Barry's life, as I reported in my 2012 documentary, *Dreams from My Real Father*, was a native Kansan and Communist Party USA propagandist who had raised Obama in Hawaii named Frank Marshall Davis, CPUSA card No. 47544. I also provided a mountain of evidence that Davis was Obama's likely real biological father, whom Obama had memorialized in a poem entitled "Pop", and not the Kenyan student.

During the late 1940's and early 1950's when Frank Marshall Davis was most active in CPUSA, the Soviet Union under Stalin had designated the United States as its main enemy. To ally oneself with the Soviets was to look to Stalin for leadership and to betray one's own country. This is exactly what Davis did when in 1948 he accepted the orders of COMINTERN to leave Chicago for Hawaii to organize a dock workers strike in Honolulu. There Davis served as chief propagandist for the communist controlled International Longshoreman and Warehouse Union, or ILWU. The ILWU's goal at the time was to cripple Hawaii by shutting down its ports, with the ultimate goal of taking over the island and expelling US naval forces which Russia considered to be an obstacle to Soviet expansion in Southeast Asia. After a six-month strike, Davis' treasonous efforts eventually failed. He landed on "Security Index A" and was put under FBI surveillance for the next 15 years, meaning he would be immediately arrested in the event of a conflict with the Soviet Union.

Of course, Davis's biggest claim to historical significance was in his role as mentor and "father figure" to a boy coming of age in

Hawaii, then known as Barry Obama. Davis had a profound impact on the young man. Obama acknowledges as much in his 1995 memoir *Dreams from My Father.* It was Davis who introduced the young Obama to the simple joys of victimhood. Although Obama was raised by his white grandparents, Davis taught him to think of them as "the other," a race apart, his potential oppressor. Rather than encourage Obama to embrace his Americanism, Davis taught him the logic and art of racial division. "She understands that black people have a reason to hate," Davis said of Obama's grandmother. "That's just how it is. For your sake, I wish it were otherwise. But it's not. So you might as well get used to it."

Obama would not only "get used to it," he would exploit race for the rest of his career. Despite a bourgeois background at an exclusive prep school and an Ivy League education, Obama never forgot his radical mentor's indoctrination. Once he moved to the mainland, he continued to reinforce Frank Marshall Davis' rantings.

"To avoid being mistaken for a sellout, I chose my friends carefully," he wrote in *Dreams* of his college days in Los Angeles. "The more politically active black students. The foreign students. The Chicanos. The Marxist professors and structural feminists and punk-rock performance poets." Barry didn't see much use for everyday Americans in his life. Obama's literary influences were the radical colleagues and comrades of Frank Marshall Davis: anti-imperialists such as Franz Fanon and Malcolm X, communists Langston Hughes and Richard Wright, and Stalin-loving fellow traveler W.E.B. DuBois. In *Dreams,* written when in his early thirties, Obama cites these influences lovingly.

Obama's best friends in Chicago–Bernardine Dohrn, Bill Ayers, Rashid Khalidi, Alice Palmer–were even more radical than his literary influences. In Chicago, Obama worked for the radical group ACORN and joined the hard-leftist New Party. Just as Obama was finding his place in Chicago as a community organizer in the Saul Alinsky school, the Soviet Union was coming undone. In 1983, while a senior at Columbia University, Obama wrote an essay, "Breaking the War Mentality," echoing the theory of the worldwide, KGB-inspired, anti-nuke protest movement. Obama argued just as the KGB had, that America's "War Mentality" was the only obstacle to peace. This concept mirrored Obama's distain for Americans whom he saw as "clinging to their guns and religion" and were in dire need of a "fundamental transformation." As the Soviet Union imploded at decade's end, Obama, like other progressives, had to stake out his own territory. Many on the Left chose "anti-racism" as their cause. Among the most notable victims of this territorial shift was one casually betrayed Obama supporter, George Zimmerman.

24

ARREST ZIMMERMAN NOW!

In a rare honest moment after the trial of George Zimmerman concluded in July 2013, Al Sharpton admitted, "We had to march to even get a trial." That is exactly how it worked. In Sanford, in March 2012, Sharpton led the mob demanding "Arrest Zimmerman now!" The mob pressed, and the State of Florida folded. The girl on the phone was the key. Without that testimony, counterfeit as it was, prosecutors would have had no rationale for the injustice that was to follow.

Saturday, March 24

Please allow me here to speculate. This is the day I believe that Diamond actually delivered the storied "letter" to Sybrina's house. Although the letter is dated March 19, and all parties claim March 19 as the day it was delivered, the timing and logic do not work well for that as the delivery date.

March 19 was a Monday. Diamond was at school all that day. Yes, she and Francine and possibly Felicia went to Sybrina's house after school. There Diamond was dropped off and met with Sybrina for the first time and quite possibly Benjamin Crump. Given her reticence to this point, it seems highly unlikely that Diamond would have arrived with letter in hand, especially a letter she herself did not write. If you recall, Rachel Jeantel claimed Francine had written the letter, and that she, Rachel, had merely signed it. As shall be seen later, Francine did write the body of the letter.

Francine worked for Sybrina. I can imagine that after the recorded phone interview that evening, Crump pressured Diamond to write an affidavit of sorts to confirm in writing what she had said over the phone. In this scenario, Diamond refused and Francine was told to write it up and just get Diamond to sign it. On Saturday March 24, after numerous texts and calls with Felicia and Rachel, Diamond texted Sybrina at 11:19 a.m. Diamond's phone records do not contain the content of the text, but we do know that Sybrina texted Diamond back at 11:23 a.m.

At 1:28 p.m. Diamond texted Sybrina. I imagine the text said something like, "We're here. I am outside with the letter." Sybrina did not text back. I believe she went outside and retrieved the letter. These two separate encounters five days apart would help explain Sybrina's shifting accounts of how she first met Diamond, who was in the car with Diamond, and how Diamond got home. I believe too that once Rachel emerged in the place of Diamond, it was clear that the signature on the letter could damn them all, which is why Sybrina concealed it until Rachel unwittingly revealed its existence in her March 2013 deposition. This forced Sybrina to produce the letter at her deposition two days later and offer up weak excuses under oath as to why she had withheld the critical evidence.

In an interview immediately after the trial, HLN's Vinnie Politan asked Bernie de la Rionda incredulously: "Why is it that this crucial witness had to be discovered by Tracy Martin and Ben Crump?" Said de la Rionda, "The only means of communication we had with her was Sybrina Fulton." The very idea that state prosecutors would allow the victim's mother to be the only conduit to communicate with a key witness was misconduct to say the least. Further, there was no excuse for the prosecutors' failure to confirm signatures once the letter surfaced. I hired a forensic handwriting expert. There was no reason for the State of Florida not to do the same.

The pressure was building on Diamond to speak to the authorities, but she resisted. Diamond had good reason to resist. She knew she had lied to Crump, simply repeating back to him the official Crump narrative and answering his questions in the affirmative. Why should she risk lying to authorities? Team Trayvon was destroying the life she knew. Her carefully constructed world was collapsing around her. She had a boyfriend and alot of shopping to do!

Unfortunately for Diamond, that afternoon on March 24, while working at Abercrombie and Fitch at the Aventura Mall, her boyfriend Jeff Watler learned that it was Diamond whose voice was broadcast during the Crump press conference. His girlfriend was, in fact, Trayvon's girlfriend! It was his sweetheart whose "puppy love" with Trayvon was now a national news story. Jeff had to feel foolish. "Dam I can't believe it," he tweeted, followed in succession by, "Dam I'm mad." "I love God," wrote Jeff, and "I hate a liar."

Diamond did not have to read Jeff's his tweets to get the message. "Why Df He Not Answering My Calls???" she tweeted anxiously. "Where Is My Boyfriend??," she continued. "I'm So Fucking Worried!!!" Diamond was self-absorbed even by the standards of sixteen-year-old Florida girls, but she didn't deserve the torment and likely threats Team Trayvon had inflicted on her to make a statement.

As to Jeff, he was a fully innocent party in this march to injustice. He did nothing to deserve the humiliation.

Trayvon friend Steve-O seemed to have overcome his grief by getting back to the basics. "Weed, Pizza, an Wings," he tweeted, "Saturday was ah great day."

Sunday, March 25

After a stressful week, Diamond was looking for some spiritual peace. "I Havent Been To Church In So Long!" she tweeted. "I Need To Get Right With God!!" The tranquility did not last long. "Something Just Pissed Me The Fuck Off!!!" she tweeted after church. That something likely had to do with boyfriend Jeff. He had a rough week too, learning through the grapevine that his girlfriend had been two-timing him with the newly sainted Trayvon Martin.

Diamond, however, saw the problem as, "My Boyfriend Love

Debating." The shortcoming was his, not hers. The fights did have a plus side: "The Best Part Of Arguing Is When We Make Up <3."

Monday, March 26

In addition to her usual calls to Felicia, Diamond and Rachel Jeantel engaged in a flurry of texts beginning at 7:49 a.m., long before Rachel was accustomed to getting up.

On this day at 9:40 a.m., Tracy and Sybrina met together with assistant state attorney Bernie de la Rionda and the investigator T.C. O'Steen. What jumped out at me in the police report was their willingness to be untruthful in this, their first meeting with the prosecution. To promote the image of responsible parenting, Tracy claimed he drove Trayvon halfway to Sanford on the Wednesday before the shooting where he met Brandy who drove Trayvon the other half. On the Tuesday before the shooting, the reader may recall, Sybrina texted Trayvon, "R u comfortable on the bus??" She added, "Go to sleep n u will be there soon." On that same Tuesday, Diamond texted Trayvon, "shit bae I miss some s#x." Trayvon answered, "U shuda been on da bus ;)." Later, Brandy would testify she picked Trayvon up at the Orlando Greyhound bus station, and Tracy admitted the same in his 2013 deposition.

During this same brief interview, Tracy and Sybrina stuck religiously to the public relations script Team Trayvon had settled on. Wrote O'Steen, "The parents advised that the Victim was a very good son and was very affectionate and had a baby face. The Victim had taken an interest in Aviation in the 9th grade." Tracy added, as reported by O'Steen, that Trayvon helped him "cook, clean, and setup the field" for the Little League football team he coached.

The parents' testimony conflicted with a story the same morning in the *Miami Herald* that detailed much of Martin's worsening behavior including his suspension from school after being caught with stolen jewelry and a burglary tool. The national media preferred the "very good son" story to the wayward and frequently suspended delinquent story. So, unfortunately for George, did the prosecution.

George Zimmerman's brother Robert sent a letter to NAACP honcho Turner Clayton reminding him of George's role in the

Sherman Ware case and asking him to "call off the dogs. Period. Publicly and swiftly." At this point, Clayton could not have called the dogs off even if he wanted to.

Late that afternoon, more than a thousand protestors marched on the Sanford Civic Center to watch Jesse Jackson, Al Sharpton and NFL great Ray Lewis among others confront the Sanford city commissioners. With two million signatures in hand, Sharpton demanded "the immediate arrest of the killer of Trayvon Martin." Sharpton added, "We do not need a trial and a jury to make an arrest." He and the others in the mob did not need evidence either.

At school that day, Diamond tweeted, "A Two Page Essay On Why We Walked Out, Where We Went, And Did We Accomplish Something By Doing That." She did not take the walk-outs too seriously. At 6:57 p.m. on Twitter, Diamond weighed in with her first public pronouncements on the shooting, but she gave absolutely no hint of having any inside information. She was once again channeling Benjamin Crump:

I Don't Get What's The Fucking Hold Up, Put His Big Ass In Jail!
Whether Or Not It Was Defense He Still Fucking Killed The Boy!
They Need To Let Me Be His Lawyer!
To Them It's Just Another Black Boy Off The Streets.
The System Fucked Up!!!!!

Projecting race into the case, Diamond tweeted, "That White Hoe Got Away With Killing Her Own Daughter." Here, she was referring to Floridian Casey Anthony, whose 2011 trial for the murder of her daughter had been the talk of Florida and the nation. "Now Zimmerman About To Get Away With This . . That's Some Fucked Up Shit Man!" Diamond tweeted.

More important to Diamond than the Zimmerman case, of course, was her now shaky relationship with Jeff. "Where My Baby At??? I Miss Him :/," she tweeted. Jeff was now sending his own tweets across her bow, "I hate when ppl ssay a jealous gf [girlfriend] a faithful one, that don't mean shit."

Tuesday, March 27

Starting at 7 a.m. Diamond began exchanging text messages with ABC's Matt Gutman. There would be fifty-two texts in all that day and four phone calls with the correspondent, including a twelve-minute call from Diamond to Gutman at 10:51 p.m. She appeared to be holding him off all day while he sought an interview, but it seems she agreed to cooperate late in the evening.

Gutman may have been talking to Diamond Eugene, but state authorities were not. They still did not who she was, only Sybrina did. On this Tuesday, in fact, the Florida Department of Law Enforcement, as defense attorney Don West later testified, filed an affidavit "to compel records...to find out who Witness Eight was." West described Diamond "as maybe the most important witness in this case."

On the home front, Diamond's mother Eliana liked Jeff. She took Jeff and Diamond out for Chinese food after school that day. Diamond must surely have spun some excellent tale to assure Jeff that she was just playing a role in this whole saga and was not Trayvon's girlfriend as Crump had claimed. In fact, this may have been when and where the "Rachel is Trayvon girlfriend" fable was born. Her later tweets include, "Today Was The Longest I Was Mad At My Baby And We With Each Other Lol," followed by "Kissed And Made Up" and "Cuddling <3." Diamond must have gotten Jeff's blessing to talk to Gutman the next day. Other friends of Trayvon were talking to the media as well. According to a tweet from Steve-O, "Mario said he told the media people he gotta .38 for Mr. Zimmerman, lol this man."

Diamond was now emotionally invested in punishing George Zimmerman as were so many others. This may explain her commitment to Gutman to do a second phone interview for ABC News. Understandably naïve, Diamond may not have realized the legal consequences of going public.

In Washington meanwhile, Florida Rep. Frederica Wilson claimed Trayvon was "hunted down like a rabid dog. He was shot in the street. He was racially profiled. Mr. Zimmerman should be arrested immediately for his own safety." Thanks to Diamond, and with a major boost from the media, this scenario was now accepted wisdom.

Wednesday, March 28

Diamond started texting with Felicia at 5:48 a.m. Soon after, Sybrina exchanged a series of texts with Diamond. This planning culminated in a 3 p.m. phone call with Matt Gutman that was recorded for use later in the evening on ABC News with Diane Sawyer. Diamond continued to text with Sybrina even *during* her interview with Gutman. In his report that evening, Gutman broadcast his new audio excerpts from Diamond to reinforce the lie he had been selling for more than a week, namely that George had chased Trayvon down and shot him in cold blood after Trayvon screamed for help for forty seconds. To sell this fiction, Gutman had to cut out George's "okay" response to the dispatcher's request not to follow Trayvon, "Zimmerman continues to pursue," said Gutman on air. "Martin runs, then slows down just seventy feet from his back door. They fight. Then the black hole–no eyewitnesses, no videos." Of course, there was an eyewitness, a very good one (named Jonathan Good no less), and the altercation took place *much* closer to Zimmerman's vehicle than to Green's townhouse.

People ran a cover story titled "An American Tragedy." Here was *People*, in violation of all journalistic standards, putting a picture of an innocent, clean-cut Trayvon, aged about thirteen, on the cover. The momentum was still building for an arrest, but Diamond's tweets such as "Everytime I Eat Hot Fries My Nose Start Running!" revealed nothing.

Thursday, March 29

"Up By The Grace Of God!," Diamond tweeted, happy to have survived the day before. "My Boyfriend Need To Wake Up!!!! and she tweeted to Jeff, "Today Makes 9 Monthss." At 2:12 p.m., Gutman sent Diamond a text, but she did not answer. That night ABC ran another clip from Diamond's interview on Diane Sawyer's show and another one on *Nightline*. All together only about sixty seconds of Diamond's forty-nine-minute call with Gutman made the air. Diamond, like

Tracy Martin, refused to allow her phone records to be turned over to the police. Prosecutors obtained a subpoena for Diamond's phone records by the end of the day.

Friday, March 30

Diamond's phone was off most of the day. She appears to have turned it on only to check voice mail or call the water company. She clearly sensed trouble. She was eating a lot, praying a lot, and fretting about Jeff. "Where Is He?" she tweeted. "Waiting On My Call," she tweeted later and then, "Still Aint Call Me ? Oh Now He Got Me Fucked Up!" The subpoena for her phone records had to have added to Diamond's anxiety.

Saturday, March 31

Protestors swarmed the American embassy in London demanding justice for Trayvon, much as communists had swarmed the embassy nearly a century prior demanding justice for Sacco and Vanzetti. Protestors rallied in Sanford as well. While Tracy Martin and Sybrina Fulton were swept up in another star-studded march led by Al Sharpton, Jesse Jackson, and NAACP president Benjamin Jealous, Diamond was back in Miami watching her semi-fictitious life come undone.

Sybrina Fulton texted Diamond at 8:17 a.m., but Diamond did not respond. Instead, she called Felicia, and they spoke for thirty minutes. At 11:18 a.m. Diamond called Crump. Although there is no record of what they talked about, one could imagine Diamond may have been seeking a way out of the mess she had been led into. If she told authorities what she had told both Crump and Matt Gutman, a narrative that ran counter to all the evidence, she would be committing perjury.

Worse, every public comment about her relationship with Trayvon was jeopardizing her relationship with Jeff. Plus, her tight knit Haitian-American family could not have wanted its secrets aired, and secrets were the one thing the family had plenty of. Later in the evening Diamond exchanged three texts with Rachel Jeantel and talked to her twice. She followed that up with a call to Felicia. The substitution strategy was falling into place.

In recruiting her, Diamond may have reminded Rachel, that on Trayvon's last night, less than an hour before he died, she did speak to Trayvon on a three-way call. This call lasted about a minute, but maybe it gave Rachel a little wiggle room in her mind. She could honestly say she had spoken with Trayvon that fateful night.

Likely others were participating in this plan, but Diamond was hardly innocent. With the state attorneys scheduled to interview her in just two days, it appears Diamond coached Rachel on what to say and soon passed off to Rachel her pre-paid cell phone number. She also arranged for someone to redirect the authorities to Francine's house after Sybrina directed them to Diamond's home on April 2. It had to have been a long and nervous Saturday. "TGFAD," Diamond tweeted at day's end. "Thank God for another day."

Sunday, April 1

The national media refused to see the evidence of Trayvon's downward spiral in the last year of his life. The *New York Times* conceded in a Sunday article that Trayvon had been suspended three times, but the suspensions were for "tardiness, for graffiti and, most recently, for having a baggie with a trace of marijuana in his backpack." The *Miami Herald* would report about the fighting and the stolen jewelry but not the *Times.*

Rachel called Diamond at midnight, but otherwise there were no calls out of the ordinary. Diamond's tweets fell into a familiar pattern: hair, phone, weather, money, and, of course, Jeff: "He Called Me 3 In The Morning Cause He Missed Me ^_^."

25

SYBRINA'S DIAMOND DILEMMA

MONDAY, April 2, proved to be an eventful day. It was the day that the corruption of this already corrupted case would become official, the day that would lead inexorably to the arrest and murder trial of an innocent man. This arrest, Team Trayvon members anticipated. What they did not anticipate were the lethal long-term consequences for the black community. For this was the day that set America on the road to division and needless racial strife for years to come.

In reconstructing the events of this day, I had access not only to Assistant State Attorney Bernie de la Rionda's interviews with Sybrina, Tracy, and Rachel, but also to an unredacted investigative report from the Florida Department of Law Enforcement. I had gotten antsy waiting for it to arrive, but the wait proved worth my while.

At about 12:30 pm, de la Rionda and investigator T.C. O'Steen arrived at the Miami airport, having flown in from Jacksonville. Accompanied by local state attorneys, de la Rionda and O'Steen were taken to Sybrina's home in northeast Miami-Dade County to interview Tracy and Sybrina. The whole Team Trayvon legal team was there as well–Crump, Parks, and Natalie Jackson. At the completion of the interviews around 5 p.m. the prosecutors attempted to locate Diamond.

Until Rachel Jeantel showed up later that day on April 2, all parties knew the girl on the phone only as "Diamond," and their only means of contact with her was solely through Sybrina Fulton. T.C. O'Steen confirmed the identity of only "Diamond" in summarizing his and Bernie de la Rionda's interview with Sybrina on April 2, 2012, a few hours before "Rachel Jeantel" entered the scene.

Wrote O'Steen of the 3:20 PM interview with Sybrina on this day, "Fulton was asked about Diamond, the girl who was talking to the Victim on the date of the incident. Fulton advised that she started hearing her name sometime around this past Christmas." Speaking about Sybrina's first meeting with the girl two weeks prior, O'Steen wrote, "Diamond arrived with another unknown black female and may have been dropped off by her." And also, "After talking with Diamond, Fulton took her home."

The FDLE report proved explosive to me in that now the addresses were not redacted: "An attempt was made to locate Rachel Jeantel at 2648 Flamingo Drive, Miramar, FL which met with negative results" (Rachel's name is used here only because the report was written after the fact). This, I knew, was not Rachel's home. It was the home of Brittany Diamond Eugene. Diamond had lived there with her mother Eliana Eugene and sister Virginia Eugene for several years. Sybrina, the person who had driven the real Diamond Eugene to this home two weeks prior, would have provided the address.

The FDLE report continued, "A secondary attempt was made at 3958 Southwest 52 Avenue #2, in the Pembroke Part area of Broward County where Jeantel was located at approximately 1830 hours." This was not even Rachel Jeantel's house, it was conveniently the home of Francine Serve, the sister of Diamond's best friend Felicia. Two cars arrived at Francine's home. There, Sybrina and the authorities expected to meet Diamond, the girl who last spoke with Trayvon. The girl they met instead was Rachel Jeantel. In those cars, were de la Rionda, Sybrina, Crump, a police officer, and possibly others.

For certain, Sybrina had met Diamond when she was dropped at

Sybrina's house on March 19. Diamond spoke with her and likely Crump about her final exchanges with Trayvon. Sybrina even drove Diamond back to her home on Flamingo Drive (and spoke to her mother), which is how Sybrina knew the address to provide to police. Sybrina later said in her deposition of the arrival at Francine's house, "I knocked on the door and axed for Diamond." Rachel Jeantel was still not yet in the picture.

Sybrina had to have been in shock when Rachel Jeantel appeared at the door claiming to be Diamond. Rachel could not be confused with Diamond under any circumstances. The anodyne FDLE report missed the turbulence of the moment: "Jeantel volunteered to be escorted to Sybrina's residence (at Northeast 210 Terrace) where she gave a statement to DCSA6 members."

Sybrina managed to break away to call the real Diamond Eugene. We know this because Sybrina told Zimmerman's attorneys that she left "Diamond" alone in the police car for a few minutes to speak with investigators, and because of Brittany Diamond Eugene's tweets. At almost exactly the time that prosecutors found Rachel, "approximately 1830," Diamond posted several tweets. The first, at 6:27 p.m., read, "Trayvon Martin Mom Just Called Me." Diamond followed five minutes later with, "She Thought I Was Trayvon Girlfriend , Asking Me Hella Questions O_o." She punctuated this latter tweet with an emoticon suggesting confusion. Diamond severed herself from the case forever a few minutes later, tweeting, "But Anywayss."

If these tweets had an intended audience, it was Jeff. The question remains as to who orchestrated the switch. Sybrina's directing the prosecutors to Diamond Eugene's address at 2648 Flamingo Drive, and her no doubt frantic call to Diamond, suggests she had no idea Rachel would be substituted as a fake witness.

Now back at Sybrina's house, the interview began at 6:55 p.m. The person interviewed was "Rachel Jeantel." This is not disputable. It is clearly her voice on the recording. According to Rachel, Sybrina sat on one side of her and de la Rionda on the other. Most of Team Trayvon was present during this interview including attorneys Daryl Parks and Natalie Jackson. That de la Rionda allowed all these people, especially the mother of the victim, to sit in for the interview attests to the State's fear of the mob and its total indifference to justice.

This was a seminal moment for Sybrina. Her son's legacy was at stake. This she knew. What she did not know is that by perpetuating The Trayvon Hoax she would help launch Black Lives Matter. Nor could she know that BLM would inflame black America at Ferguson with disastrous consequences for African American teenagers in the years ahead.

But don't let me get ahead of myself. At this moment, Sybrina Fulton, by all accounts a righteous and religious person, could have turned to de la Rionda and said, "Excuse me, we've got a problem here. This is *not* the girl that I met, the girl from whom I got a letter, the girl with whom I've been talking and texting with for the past two weeks, whose mother I spoke with. Y'all need to just hold off on everything, go back to 2648 Flamingo Drive and pick up the real Diamond, get her under oath and sort this out." Sybrina could have said all of this but chose not to.

One can imagine the pressure Sybrina was under. Much of America, the President included, had rallied to her side. Millions of petitions had been gathered. Tens of thousands had marched in the streets. Celebrities from all walks of life had taken up her cause, and now she knew that the "star witness" was a fraud. If Sybrina spoke out, there would be no payoff from the homeowners association, no more television appearances. Her "I AM TRAYVON" trademark would be worthless, and George Zimmerman might never be arrested. More chilling, "Trayvon Martin" would not be whispered in the same breath as Emmett Till. No, his name would be whispered in the same breath as Tawana Brawley's, as just another Al Sharpton race hoax.

What did Sybrina Fulton choose to do? Nothing. She simply sat on the couch next to Rachel Jeantel and cried throughout the interview. Meanwhile Diamond, the burden lifted, went back to tweeting that evening: "Fresh Out Feeling Like A Millon Bucks ^_^," "Got My Noodles And Juice, Im Tuned!." In the *Urban Dictionary*, "juice" means alcohol and "tuned" means drunk. And finally, Diamond tweeted "Im Dien Laughing Man That Was Tooo Funny!"

Two days later, on April 4, the forty-fourth anniversary of Martin Luther King's assassination, Felicia may well have asked God's mercy for her own role in the witness switch, posting on Facebook, "only god could judge me.... #cant trust nobody."

26

RACHEL'S FIRST PERJURY

On April 2, 2012, Rachel Jeantel, then 18, perjured herself in claiming under oath to have been the girl on the phone with Trayvon at the time of his death.

In 2012, when enlisted in this farce, Rachel was still a ninth grader, an *eighteen-year-old* ninth grader, but legally an adult. According to the *Washington Post*, Rachel was reading at a fourth grade level at the time of the trial. CNN said third grade. From watching her struggle in videos of depositions when presented with text to review, I doubt she could read at all.

Those who countenanced Rachel's participation and allowed her to testify, I believe, were cruel and exploitative of someone with disabilities to serve their personal and political agendas. Rachel was ripe for recruitment precisely because of her limitations. Diamond was savvy enough to know she was being asked to commit perjury. Rachel probably was not. Diamond did not need this kind of attention. Rachel initially relished it–at least it was something to do–and she eventually profited from it. To compensate for the embarrassment of the trial, a variety of good-deed doers have worked together ever since then to make Rachel's life special.

As regards Diamond Eugene, from March 19, the day she

recorded the phone interview with Benjamin Crump, through March 28, the day of her interview with ABC's Matt Gutman, Diamond was on board with Team Trayvon. Sometime between March 28 and April 2, the day of Rachel's interview with de la Rionda, Diamond bailed out, and Rachel committed the story Diamond provided to Mr. Crump to memory as best she could. We know from Diamond's phone records that Rachel and Diamond Eugene spoke with each other several times daily throughout March and this critical period. Given that they were two years apart in age, had almost nothing in common, and went to different schools, I wondered if they were related through Rachel's Haitian mother, Marie Eugene. I had not found a connection to date, perhaps because family background research in Haiti is near impossible. No online background databases like Instant Checkmate exist for Haiti.

Before the investigation was through I would find out what the connection was. By that stage I thought I was shockproof. I would soon learn I was not.

The role playing got off to a rocky start for Rachel. At the beginning of the April 2 interview, de la Rionda asked, "Could you state your name for the record, Ma'am?" In the transcript Rachel's answer is redacted, but I was able to get hold of an unedited audio of the interview. Under oath, Rachel responded to the question by asking, "real name?" Given the go ahead, she answered, "Rachel Jeantel." From the tone in which he asked the next question, de la Rionda had to know he would get the answer he wanted: "And do you have a nickname you go by?" Rachel answered, "Diamond or Dee Dee or Black." The hastily remembered nickname was good enough to please the eager de la Rionda.

As the interview progressed, it became clear that Rachel was not at all comfortable playing the role she was somehow persuaded to play, and the seriousness was now sinking in. An exchange with de la Rionda at the end of the April 2 interview reveals much about Rachel's state of mind. After de la Rionda thanked her for her time, out of nowhere Rachel's suppressed good conscience broke out, saying she felt guilty over and over. This took de la Rionda by surprise. "Huh?" he responded.

RACHEL: I got guilt.
BDLR: You've got guilt?
RACHEL: Mmm-hmm [Yes].
BDLR: Why do you feel guilt?
RACHEL: Real guilty.
BDLR: Huh?
RACHEL: Real guilty.
BDLR: Why do you feel real guilty?
RACHEL: REAL GUILTY.
BDLR: Because you were talking onto the phone and you couldn't do anything about it?
RACHEL: I ain't know about it.
BDLR: Huh?
RACHEL: I AIN'T KNOW ABOUT.

Sitting next to Sybrina, being interrogated by a state prosecutor, Rachel had to have been overwhelmed. What may have started as a favor to cover for someone close to her had turned into serious business, and I suspect Rachel wanted out. "I ain't know about it," she told de la Rionda twice, the second time almost yelling. By this time, the assistant state attorney was too invested in this story to hear her and he just moved on.

This was looking like a case of suborning perjury and obstructing justice, both serious crimes, so I continued to examine the recorded deposition. On YouTube I pulled up the March 20, 2012 press conference in which Crump told the world repeatedly that the girl on the phone was "a minor child." Specifically, she was "only sixteen years old." I suspect Crump was largely telling the truth about Diamond at that stage. At his press conference, he claimed that Trayvon and the girl "were dating" and that they were in the throes of "puppy love."

To be sure, the texts between Trayvon and Diamond confirmed a "dating" relationship. Trayvon, at least, was "in love," and the girl was not discouraging him. Their conversations were both sexually explicit and often marked by terms of endearment such as "sweetheart," "boo," "bae, "I miss you," and of course, the sentimental favorite, "ride to die nigga."

On YouTube, I pulled up Crump's entire twenty-minute phone call with Diamond. Much of what she said sounded rehearsed. For instance, Diamond told Crump she was so unnerved by Trayvon's passing her mother had taken her to the hospital on the sixth day after his death. Crump claimed to have spoken with the mother and confirmed this.

Although Diamond spoke on the Crump tape as though she actually experienced Trayvon's last day, Rachel bluffed her way through her April 2 interview. When confused, she mumbled. Diamond never did. At one point, for instance, de la Rionda tried to confirm Crump's contention that Rachel and Trayvon were in throes of "puppy love," but Rachel balked. To the question of whether they were dating, she mumbled, "Hmm mmm somethin'."

Rachel's account of the incident was much sketchier than Diamond's, less logical. She knew the rain factored in, but she wasn't quite sure how. Though Diamond had told Crump enthusiastically, "It was raining hard," Rachel told prosecutors, "It wasn't raining."

In Rachel's account, Trayvon put his hoodie up only when he left "the mail area." In fact, he had it on while still inside the 7-11. In this first meeting with the prosecutors, Rachel claimed Trayvon had gone to the store to get "some food and drinks" for his "little brother" and confirmed the drink was "iced tea" at de la Rionda's prompt. In fact, the drink was an Arizona Watermelon Fruit Juice Cocktail. The initial police report got it wrong. So did Rachel.

In this April 2 interview, prosecutor de la Rionda continually coaxed the answers he wanted from Rachel. He asked, "Did Trayvon ever say, 'The guy's coming at me, he's going to hit me?'" Rachel answered, "Yeah, you could say that."

Rachel was prepared to mimic the account Crump fed Diamond, namely that Zimmerman chased a fleeing Trayvon, but Rachel was almost comically confused about one critical point: she did not know whether Zimmerman was chasing Trayvon in a car or by foot. This, the reader should recall, was the state's "star witness," the one whose account led to Zimmerman's arrest for murder just nine days after her deposition.

As usual, de la Rionda came to her rescue. He asked Rachel whether Trayvon had said to her, "Yeah, the guy, now he's out of the car, he's chasing me." He continued, "I know you said the guy, he said the guy was following him. But did he ever say the guy got out of the car?" Rachel responded as though surprised this subject matter was outside of her brief coaching, replying "You want that too?"

At this stage in the investigation, Rachel obviously felt compelled to sustain Diamond's lie that she failed to attend Trayvon's funeral for health reasons. Under Crump's much too obvious prompting two weeks prior, Diamond confirmed in her phone interview that "shock" was her diagnosis for the night she spent in the hospital. Under de la Rionda's equally obvious prompting, Rachel claimed "high blood pressure" as the cause for her hospitalization. This was one lie Rachel would later recant.

In her phone interview two weeks earlier with Crump, Diamond spoke confidently about her communication with Trayvon early on his last day. She related, for instance, how she had asked Trayvon to call her after church. Rachel, by contrast, did not have a clue about the details of that fateful Sunday. "I'm talking about that day, February 26," de la Rionda asked her at one point, "did Trayvon send you any text messages?" Rachel stumbled, "I...one...like." In fact, there had been thirty-two texts between Trayvon and Diamond. Sensing Rachel's confusion, de la Rionda finessed her out of this jam by subtly switching the conversation from "that day" to Trayvon's final hour and leading her to say "no." Rachel followed de la Rionda's lead throughout the interview. When he asked Rachel, "Did Trayvon ever say, 'The guy's coming at me, he's going to hit me?" Rachel replied, "Yeah, you could say that."

The prosecution team knew in advance the number and time of Diamond's texts and calls. They had her subpoenaed phone records. So when Rachel said she had a T-Mobile account, they knew the girl on the phone with Trayvon had a Simple Mobile account. They simply ignored the discrepancy.

To learn more about Rachel I pulled up an interview she did with Piers Morgan after the trial. Morgan introduced her uncritically as "the young woman who was on the phone with Trayvon Martin just before he died." At one point, Morgan asked Rachel about her slow and labored way of speaking. Rachel attributed it to a physical condition–she called it an "under bite"– that had been affecting her speech since childhood. She acknowledged needing corrective surgery but had been putting it off. The fluid speaking Diamond had no such problem.

27

FRAMED FOR THE AGENDA

THIS SWITCH of witnesses was no longer a speculation on my part. I had proved six ways from Sunday that Rachel Jeantel had committed perjury. She would continue to perjure herself in two future depositions and at the trial itself. I now had to address the question of who orchestrated the switch.

The answer mattered. Rachel's perjury changed the course of race relations in the United States. On April 11, 2012, nine days after her interview with de la Rionda, the State of Florida charged George Zimmerman with second-degree murder. There would have been no charge of murder and no arrest without Rachel's lies being entered as sworn testimony. At this stage, the State was unaware of the letter Diamond had given to Sybrina, and Benjamin Crump was withholding the taped interview with Diamond from state authorities. Rachel's testimony to de la Rionda was *it*. The authors of the affidavit of probable cause against Zimmerman accepted Rachel's bogus story as gospel.

Without Rachel's testimony, there would have been no arrest, no trial. "During this time," the affidavit claimed of the minutes before Trayvon's death, "Martin was on the phone with a friend and described to her what was happening. The witness advised that

Martin was scared because he was being followed through the complex and didn't know why." The affidavit discounted George's account of events in favor of Rachel's. In the State's version, Trayvon "attempted to run home," but George "disregarded" the police dispatcher, "followed" Trayvon, and "confronted" him. At the time the State drafted this affidavit, prosecutors knew it flew in the face of all gathered evidence. Only Rachel's recent interview with de la Rionda made the charge seem credible.

One more outrageous feature of the affidavit had nothing do with Rachel. The claim read as follows: "During this time period witnesses heard numerous calls for help and some of these were recorded in 911 calls to police. Trayvon's mother has reviewed the 911 calls and identified the voice crying for help as Trayvon Martin's voice." To accept the mother's word as fact, prosecutors had to discount the simple written testament by dispassionate witness Johnathan Good, "guy getting hit on ground was wearing red calling out help." They also had to discount George's claim moments after the shooting that he had been yelling and Tracy's earlier admission that the voice was not his son's, an admission heard by at least two Sanford police officers.

In her interview with de la Rionda, Rachel repeated as best she could what Diamond had told her. She also added some new detail. For instance, Rachel claimed that Trayvon took refuge in a mail shed when it started to rain. In fact, Rachel shared this detail with Osteen and de la Rionda while she was still *in the police car* and not yet under oath. "The victim said he was at a covered/mail area," wrote Osteen in a memo only one paragraph long.

The letter given by Diamond to Sybrina made no such reference, and in her phone interview Diamond claimed Trayvon was hanging out "under a shade." Zimmerman too said he first saw Trayvon "in between the buildings, the rows of the townhouses, in the rain, in the cold, in no particular rush to get out of the rain or the cold." Rachel's "covered/mail area" allegation suggests additional coaching by someone other than Diamond.

If Zimmerman saw Trayvon in between the buildings, he had every reason to be suspicious. He would have had less reason to be concerned if Trayvon were sheltering himself from the rain in the "covered/mail area." Yes, there was a mailbox area. Zimmerman said as much on the call to the dispatcher: "If [the police] come in through the gate, tell them to go straight past the club house, and uh, straight past the club house and make a left, and then they go past the mailboxes." Team Trayvon had full access to Zimmerman's call, Diamond did not.

I was tempted to believe that Diamond, possibly with her friends, could have recruited Rachel and pulled off the switch on their own, but they had no way of knowing about the mail shed. Nor did George have any reason *not* to tell the dispatcher he spotted Trayvon by the mail shed if he actually had. No, the evidence suggests that someone consciously introduced the "mail shed" detail and coached Rachel to make this claim before her April 2 meeting. The fact that Rachel offered up this brand new information *in the police car* even before her sworn interview indicates someone emphasized to her its importance.

Among the many people who would have known about the mail shed were Tracy Martin and Benjamin Crump. Tracy had been staying at The Retreat at Twin Lakes with Brandy on and off for more than a year. He knew the mailbox area was covered. In his visits to The Retreat, Crump would have seen the covered mailboxes as well. Crump and Tracy both would have known that if Trayvon were ducking the rain in a public area such as a mail shed, his presence there would seem much less suspicious than if he were lurking "under a shade" as Diamond originally stated. "Shade" was likely the term Trayvon used to tell Diamond about the short ledge extending from the townhome roof where he was lighting up to avoid the rain.

Other information Rachel seems to have pulled directly from Diamond's accounts. In the letter Diamond claimed, "I was on the phone when Trevon decided to go to the Cornerstore." Trayvon had been to the 7-11 earlier in the morning of February 26, his final day, with his cousin Stephen "Boobie" Martin. "Sunday morning I got up, he help me take some boxes to my car, and then I drove to the store," Boobie said in his March 2013 deposition. "He rode with me to the store. He stayed in the car, I went to the store, the 7-11, the same 7-11." This was the trip in which Boobie bought a Black & Mild.

In his deposition, Boobie referred to the 7-11 as either the "store" or the "7-11." In their depositions Brandy Green and son Chad did the same. There was no reason to believe Trayvon said "cornerstore."

In April 2012, prosecutor Bernie de la Rionda asked Rachel, "Did he tell you what store he was going to?" "No, he was sayin' corner store." In her tweets, Diamond also used the distinctive term, tweeting on June 1, 2012, "I Go The Corner Store Everyday After School Just For A Hot Sausage." Again, Rachel was simply mimicking Diamond's account.

The State of Florida had Rachel to thank for the accusation that Zimmerman profiled Trayvon. According to the affidavit of probable cause, Trayvon was on his way back to Brandy Green's townhouse "when he was profiled by Zimmerman." This accusation was reinforced by the words allegedly uttered by each party at the moment of confrontation.

On the Crump tape, Diamond originally claimed to have heard George respond, "What are you talking about?" to Trayvon's question, "What are you following me for?" This answer did not suggest profiling. So Crump openly led the witness, Diamond, to change George's response to the incriminating, "What are you doin' aroun' here?" In her 2012 interview with de la Rionda, Rachel claimed she heard George say the exact same words to Trayvon, "What are you doin' aroun' here?"

As mentioned, Sybrina directed state prosecutors to pick up Diamond up at her 2648 Flamingo Drive home to which she had driven Diamond home two weeks earlier. When Sybrina and the prosecutors were redirected to Francine's home, there to be greeted by Rachel Jeantel, Sybrina frantically called Diamond. Almost assuredly Sybrina did *not* know Rachel was being switched for Diamond just before the sworn April 2 interview. It was no wonder Sybrina cried throughout the interview. She may have been crying for her own future.

George's defense attorneys shared some of my suspicions. Unfortunately, the court refused their request to depose the Honorable Benjamin Crump. They did, however, get ahold of the ABC tape of Crump's interview with Diamond. What they were able to ascertain was that the tape Crump eventually gave the FBI was heavily edited.

In its argument to depose Crump, the defense contended, "The recording released by ABC News contains a substantive conversation between Mr. Crump and Witness 8 (Diamond) that Mr. Crump did not record and which, according to his sworn affidavit never took place." On the ABC tape, Crump can be heard focusing Diamond's attention on certain issues and asking her to emphasize certain key points when "he turns on his recording device."

28

LIES, LIES, AND MORE LIES

On April 11, 2012, nine days after Rachel Jeantel told her tall tales to state prosecutors, George Zimmerman turned himself in to authorities in Jacksonville. An officer promptly put Zimmerman in leg irons and informed him he was under arrest for second-degree murder.

With the attention focused on George as it would be until the trial in the summer of 2013, Rachel Jeantel slipped quietly out of sight. Other than the cyber sleuths at the Conservative Treehouse website who sensed something amiss, the media remained fully oblivious. Meanwhile, Prosecutor Bernie de la Rionda proceeded as though Rachel were the real deal. However, did he know he had a problem? In August 2012, four months after her initial interview, de la Rionda flew Rachel and Francine Serve to Jacksonville for a very discreet meeting, the content of which went undocumented.

Defense attorney Mark O'Mara never raised the question of a witness switch, but he had his doubts about Rachel Jeantel from the outset. On August 23, 2012, he requested Rachel's hospital records for the night before Trayvon's funeral. Getting no response from the prosecution, he sent a letter on September 19 and was ignored again. On February 21, 2013, O'Mara filed a motion to subpoena Rachel's hospital records. This time, the prosecution buckled, conceding two weeks later, "No hospitalization records existed for Witness #8."

Days later, on March 13, 2013 in Miami, Rachel resurfaced for her formal deposition. This was the first time she would face critical interrogation. She had obviously been coached in the interim year to sustain the "Diamond Deception," but she did not coach well. The question of her hospitalization came up early in the deposition.

"So let's talk about last week, you got a call, about whether you had been in the hospital?" defense attorney Don West asked her. As Rachel explained, "I was axed, was I in the hospital. I said no." She continued. "And I already, he axed did you lie, and I said, yes, I did lie about that." Rachel also owned up to another falsehood. "I had to lie about my age too," she told West, explaining why she initially said she was sixteen when she was eighteen. After repeated questioning by West, she claimed she lied about her age for reasons of "privacy."

The video of the deposition shows Rachel wearing the exact same style Chinese weave with bangs that Diamond wore in one of the photos she had texted to Trayvon. The weave represented a futile effort and borderline comic attempt to make Rachel look at least a little bit like Diamond. If the defense lawyers had discovered the photos of the real Diamond in the Cellebrite phone records as I had, at least Rachel would have a matching weave. However, she would still have to explain how she gained more than one hundred fifty pounds in the past year and looked nothing like Diamond but for a weave that obviously did not fit her head.

The defense attorneys never got the chance. The State did not allow them time to dive into the 750 pages of Trayvon's phone records as I had. As a result, they were not able to ask Rachel about the incredible weight gain nor why she did not resemble the slim and sexy girl in the photos sent by Diamond to Trayvon, nor about her relationship to Alexis Jacquet, aka "Liz Cuz JJ."

In discussing her alleged first visit to Sybrina's house in March 2012, Rachel did her best to recount Diamond's actual experience. Inevitably, she got tangled in the lies. As Rachel told the story, Tracy first called her on Saturday, March 17. On Monday, March 19, Francine drove her to Sybrina's and dropped her off. Rachel explained that Francine knew the way given that she tended to Sybrina's quadriplegic brother. This relationship came as news to Don West.

In reciting the events of that day, Rachel casually mentioned that she brought a letter to Sybrina's house for Sybrina to read. This was the first time the defense lawyers learned of the letter's existence. "I didn't understand what you meant when you said the letter. So you had actually written a letter to Miss Fulton?" West asked Rachel after she first mentioned the letter.

Rachel had unwittingly given the game away. In fact, the real Diamond did deliver a letter to Sybrina. "I did not plan for me to go [to Sybrina's]," said Rachel, capturing Diamond's own hesitance. "I did not even wanna go there. Whatever my mom said, I just didn't wanna go. I was just gonna, tell, Francine to drop me, and I'll just drop [the letter], by there and leave. But, it ain't go that way." Rachel's mother, Marie Eugene, was visiting Haiti the entire time, from February 24 through mid-April 2012, making this story far-fetched. In fact, the several consultations with Diamond's mother cited by both Crump and Sybrina point to the mother being Diamond's mom, Eliana Eugene. I called Rachel's mother Marie Eugene myself to inquire about her house cleaning services. I spoke in English and she repeatedly responded in French-based Creole that she didn't understand what I was saying. I switched to French after I realized Marie did not seem to speak English. However, Diamond's mother Eliana Eugene was living at 2648 Flamingo Drive in Miramar during this period and spoke perfect English.

Rachel mentioned the Sybrina letter several times in her March 2013 deposition. She claimed that the letter explained why she failed to attend Trayvon's funeral. The letter, of course, mentioned no such thing, but Rachel had never read the letter. As would soon enough become clear, she could not read it.

Quite possibly the prosecutors did not know about the letter until Rachel mentioned it either. The defense quickly grasped the letter's importance. The next day, March 14, 2013, Don West asked Tracy Martin about it during his deposition. Tracy reacted very nervously,

"I have no knowledge of what was in the letter," said the fidgety Tracy. "I never read it, never had it read to me, never had it sent to me, never had it in my possession," he rattled off quickly. There was something fishy about Tracy's legalese as he scurried to distance himself from the letter. To me, he sounded like an ex-con who didn't want to go back to jail.

On the following day, March 15, Mark O'Mara asked Sybrina during her deposition, "I understand that [Rachel] had given you a letter." Although surely displeased that Rachel had mentioned the letter, Sybrina was now prepared. She had the letter with her, folded within the pages of her Christian Life Bible. The letter was not something The letter was not something Sybrina would want to share if for no other reason than it contained Diamond Eugene's signature, a signature I had submitted to a forensic handwriting expert. O'Mara's exchange with Sybrina in this deposition just weeks before the trial elicited a rather weak attempt to justify concealment by Sybrina of critical evidence, evidence that could expose the witness fraud:

O'Mara: Had you disclosed this letter to the state before yesterday?
Sybrina: No.
O'Mara: Did you discuss the existence of this letter with your attorney?
Sybrina: I did not.
O'Mara: Did you consider this letter significant?
Sybrina: I considered that letter to be personal and sentimental.
O'Mara: What did you do once you read it?
Sybrina: I received several letters, um, so I put it in a box.

Sybrina's voice wavered noticeably on "in a box." The letter held other major problems for Team Trayvon. In the letter, Diamond wrote the following: "Then Trevon turned around and said why are you following me!!" The next sentence reads, "Then I heard him fall, then the phone hung up." The letter comprised the total of sum of Diamond's knowledge about Trayvon's final minutes, at least as massaged by Crump. In the letter, George did not respond at all to

Trayvon's question, let alone say, "What are you doing around here?" Nor did the letter have Trayvon saying, "get off, get off," a flourish Rachel added out of the blue during the March 2013 deposition. Nor did the letter mention anything about Trayvon seeking shelter from the rain in the "mail shed" or anyplace else. Here again is all that the letter said. Any details added after it was written are suspect:

> *March 19, 2012*
>
> *I was on the phone when Trevon decided to go to the Cornerstore. It started to rain so he decided to walk another complex because it was raining to hard. He started walking then noticed someone was following him. Then he decided to find a shortcut cause the man wouldn't follow through him. Then he said the man didn't follow him again. Then he looked back and saw the man again. The man started getting closer. Then Trevon turned around and said why are you following me!! Then I heard him fall, then the phone hung up. I called back and text. No response. In my mind I thought it was just a fight. Then I found out this tragic story.*
>
> *Thank you,*
>
> *Diamond Eugene*

According to Rachel, the original plan was to drop off the letter and leave, but Sybrina came out and wanted to talk. Rachel insisted she did not go into the house. Instead, she gave Sybrina the letter while they were outside, and Sybrina read "some of it." In her conversation with Sybrina, Rachel explained the "details" of Trayvon's fatal encounter, including Trayvon's sense he was "being followed" and his exchange of words with Zimmerman. In the letter there was no mention of the wake or funeral as Rachel claimed, but this was one of Rachel's lesser errors.

Another red flag in Rachel's testimony was her stumbling response to what should have been a simple question, "When did you find out that [Trayvon] had been shot and killed?" As proved earlier, Diamond knew for sure by the next day, on Monday, February 27. She even told Crump this in her phone interview. Rachel had no idea how to answer the question. She first volunteered Wednesday, then switched the date to Tuesday. She wasn't sure whether Felicia told her or she heard it on the news. None of this uncertainty bothered the State.

Not surprisingly, Sybrina's account of the initial March 2012 meeting with "Diamond," the name Sybrina always used for the girl interviewed by Crump over the phone, varied considerably from Rachel's. According to Sybrina, the letter was "personal." She "did not read the letter" in Diamond's presence. "[Diamond] didn't talk specifically about the conversation she had with Trayvon," Sybrina told O'Mara. "She, was just more, verifying to me that she was on the phone with him."

Sybrina soon forgot herself. A few minutes after this exchange, Sybrina explained why she ran out of the room crying when listening in to Diamond's phone conversation with Crump. "[Diamond] was telling the, the same thing, the same story again and I just couldn't take it," said Sybrina. O'Mara caught the slip. "But had you heard it before?" he asked. Yes, Sybrina conceded, "when I met her the first time."

Sybrina then told O'Mara the details of Diamond's final conversation with Trayvon as recounted by Diamond during their first meeting: how she implored him to run; how Trayvon lost sight of his pursuer; how Trayvon saw him again; how Diamond heard the final exchange between Trayvon and George.

In *Rest in Power*, Tracy Martin told a different story altogether. Written four years after these depositions, Tracy now claimed Diamond came into the house with the letter on March 19. Sybrina read it, and Tracy heard Sybrina cry as she did. Other than Diamond visiting that day, all other details are either false or suspect.

Of note, Sybrina claimed not to know the name of the young woman who drove Diamond to Sybrina's house in March 2012. Was this was a strategic deception on Sybrina's part? Francine knew too much, including the respective roles played by both Diamond and Rachel in the identity switch. She was also the older sister of Diamond's best friend and instinctively honest. Understandably,

Sybrina might be concerned if Francine were to be exposed or deposed.

Testifying as they did within days of each other, Rachel and Sybrina could not quite get their stories straight. Rachel was trying to remember what Diamond told her. Sybrina was finessing the actual meeting or meetings with Diamond. Was it to protect herself? In Rachel's March 2013 account, Sybrina drove her home from that first imagined meeting on March 19, 2012. In Sybrina's March 2013 account, the unknown friend stayed throughout the whole conversation and drove Diamond home. Sybrina could not even keep her own accounts straight. She may have forgotten that on April 2, 2012 she told de la Rionda and his investigators that she drove Diamond home and even spoke with her mother. The likelihood that Diamond came to Sybrina's house twice, the second time with the letter, may have been used by Sybrina looking for wiggle room.

When questioned about the two-week period between Diamond's phone interview with Crump and Rachel's first interview with de la Rionda, Sybrina made an untrue statement. O'Mara asked if Sybrina had spoken to Diamond during that period. Sybrina answered crisply, "I had not spoken to her since [March 19]." From Diamond's phone records, however, I knew that Sybrina communicated frequently with Diamond during that mysterious two-week stretch. On March 20 and on March 24, they exchanged texts. On March 28, they exchanged ten texts, six of them while Diamond was being interviewed on the phone by ABC's Matt Gutman. Later on March 28, Diamond called Sybrina, and they *spoke* on the phone for more than five minutes.

On Saturday morning, March 31, Sybrina texted Diamond. Later that same morning Diamond called attorney Benjamin Crump and spoke to him for more than three minutes. Later that same day Diamond shared multiple texts and phone calls with Rachel Jeantel and Felicia Cineas, sister of Francine Serve. This would seem to be the day the plot to switch witnesses was finalized.

Sybrina, however, did not seem to be aware of the plot. As mentioned earlier, she called Diamond on April 2, 2012, immediately after meeting Rachel. "I knocked on the door," Sybrina told O'Mara in March 2013. "Francine answered the door, and I axed for Diamond. Um, Diamond came to the door, and then we came outside." This was Rachel Jeantel, and not Brittany Diamond Eugene. Understandably, in her deposition with O'Mara, Sybrina did not mention her frantic call to Diamond Eugene upon meeting Rachel, which Diamond fortunately memorialized on Twitter, "Trayvon Martin Mom Just Called Me," and "She Thought I Was Trayvon Girlfriend, Asking me Hella Questions O_o."

In answering West's question about his first call to Diamond on March 17, 2012, Tracy Martin said he was met with "silence" when he explained to the girl she was the last person to speak with Trayvon. "I can recall her just being in silence. That's what I can recall," he told West. "Her conversation, I don't remember what exactly her response was to my, my pitch to her."

In *Rest in Power,* Tracy tells a different story. In this account, on picking up the phone, the girl said to Tracy, "This is Diamond."

Then, she freely volunteers a detailed account of the incident, beginning with, "A man was following Trayvon," and culminating with Trayvon's "high pitched wail," the one supposedly picked up on the 911 call. That was a lot of information to convey in a 2.2 minute introductory phone call, way too much.

In the book, Tracy described the girl on the phone as a "young woman" with a "deep, sad, somber voice." Conveniently, the "deep" voice line aligned with the voice of Rachel Jeantel. According to Tracy, "She almost sounded like she was grieving as much as I was." Tracy concluded this section in *Rest in Power*, writing, "There were other things we didn't yet know about Diamond. Like her age. She said she was sixteen, but she was actually eighteen. We would also learn that her name wasn't Diamond. It was Rachel Jeantel." Did Tracy manufacture this information to fit Rachel's testimony in her depositions and at the trial?

The Sybrina letter posed all sorts of problems for Rachel, starting with the signature. Her explanation as to why she signed the letter "Diamond Eugene" should have set off alarms throughout the state attorney's office. "I said it on the letter, 'Hi, my name is,' my name, was a lie," Rachel told West. "I was not called Diamond Eugene. Diamond is just a nickname. Eugene is just, I got from my mom last name so I had to thought of it quick." Rachel then let off a nervous laugh.

Rachel wanted the court to believe that "Diamond" was her nickname–there is no evidence it ever was–and that she thought up "Eugene" on the spot. For the prosecutors not to stop this nonsense as soon as they heard this was borderline criminal. Less than an hour into the deposition, the state's "star witness" admitted she had lied about her age, her name, and her hospitalization. West summarized, "So you said 'my name is Diamond Eugene and I'm sixteen'?". Rachel now appeared exhausted from defending the lies and demanded of West, "Don't say my name, or my fake name. Don't say my age, my fake age." It would get worse.

As in her April 2012 interview with de la Rionda, Rachel had to explain her relationship with Trayvon. "He was not serious. We're not that serious with each other," she told West. "It was getting there," Rachel said of a possible boyfriend-girlfriend relationship. "But it was not there yet." By March 2013, prosecutors had had a year to review the texts between Diamond and Trayvon that I had. They knew the two engaged frequently in explicit talk about sex. The two "just friends" were not just "getting there." They had gotten there.

West also caught Rachel repeating a falsehood from Diamond's interview with Crump in March 2012. "In the interview with Mr. Crump," West asked Rachel, "you said that he went to get an Arizona Iced Tea. How did you come up with that?" Said Rachel, "That's what [Trayvon] told me." By this time, West knew the drink was an Arizona Watermelon Fruit Juice Cocktail. "Are you sure somebody else didn't tell you he got an iced tea rather than Trayvon?" asked West. Rachel insisted Trayvon told her, but West knew she was lying, and he must have suspected who was the original source of this lie.

In addressing Trayvon's final minutes, Rachel was actually helped by her disabilities. Her account of the hoodie, which Trayvon was forever putting on and taking off, was confused to the point of comic.

West could barely follow what she was saying. Rachel's account climaxed with Trayvon running away but unable to shake the plodding 200-pound Zimmerman: "Oh shit, nigga's still behind my back." Trayvon then asked the man, "What you following me for?" He responded, "What you doing around here?" This confrontation allegedly occurred "right by the daddy girlfriend house," roughly two hundred feet from the actual site of the confrontation which was much closer to George's truck.

During her 2013 deposition, Rachel claimed she heard Trayvon repeatedly say, "Get off." Towards the end of the deposition, West played for Rachel the entire Crump tape recording with Diamond Eugene from a year earlier. Diamond's account ended with a push, not with Trayvon saying, "get off." By this time, late in the deposition, an exhausted Rachel was indifferent to such fine points and just blew him off.

When West asked how Rachel knew it was Trayvon speaking, she answered, "Trayvon do not have a manly voice. And, like you said, and like the records show, I have been talking to Trayvon for a longest." One more problem for the prosecution was that Trayvon did have a manly voice. If proof were needed, an old girlfriend posted on his memorial site, "I loved his deep voice."

Rachel cringed and fidgeted as West played for her the many excerpts of Diamond's voice from Crump's recorded interview. That voice was obviously not Rachel's. As the tape played, she buried her head in her hands, hoping against hope that West would not suddenly exclaim, "Hey, wait just one minute! You don't sound anything like Diamond! That's not you speaking to Mr. Crump, is it?"

For a year, the prosecutors had the Crump tape and the Cellebrite cell phone records in their possession. They had a year of dealing with Rachel. Is it possible they didn't realize the fluty voice on the Crump tape did not belong to the sonorous Rachel Jeantel? But from the get-go, de la Rionda and his colleagues ignored all obvious and glaring discrepancies and used their office to facilitate the railroading of George Zimmerman.

The arrest gave Crump the authority to sue The Retreat at Twin

Lakes homeowners association. He had already rejected a $1 million offer from the Travelers Casualty and Surety Company of America, the association's insurer. Three weeks after the March 2013 depositions, the cover story still not blown, Crump accepted a much larger settlement on behalf of Trayvon's parents. Tracy and Sybrina paid a high price for that settlement. The ill gotten money could not bring back their son, but it could and did cheapen his memory.

29

RACHEL ON TRIAL

THE MOST MEMORABLE moment of the trial of George Zimmerman occurred on the morning of the fourth day, Rachel Jeantel's second day on the witness stand. "She wore a ruffled bronze-colored blouse under a black blazer," wrote Sybrina Fulton in *Rest in Power*. "She sat erect in the witness chair. Her speech had slowed and she spoke more deliberately." Was Sybrina's comment about "slowed speech" an attempt to cover for the obvious? Diamond spoke in a confident fast-paced speech pattern with a broad vocal range on the Crump tape, while Rachel spoke in a slow monotonal drawl, often mumbling, and struggled to begin and end sentences.

The big moment in question involved what I had always thought of as the case's most damning evidence, namely "the Sybrina letter," the letter Diamond gave to Sybrina in March 2012. "Do you recognize that letter as being one that you said earlier was prepared to be given to Ms. Fulton?" defense attorney Don West asked Rachel in showing her a copy of the letter. Rachel claimed that she did recognize it.

"That letter was prepared with the assistance of a friend of yours named Francine Serve?" Yes, it was. "But the contents of the letter are yours." Yes, again. "Are you able to read that copy well enough that you can tell us if that is in fact the same letter?" asked West in his amiable, avuncular way.

"No," said Rachel defiantly.

"Are you unable to read that at all?" asked West, this time with a bite.

"Some of it," said Rachel.

"Can you read any of the words on it?"

"I don't understand cursive," Rachel mumbled while looking down, apparently in shame. "I don't read cursive."

Like most people who saw this exchange either while watching the trial or on news coverage, I remember feeling sorry for Rachel. This poor girl just happened to be on the phone with Trayvon at the end of his life. Suddenly she found herself in an awkward, embarrassing moment, not at all of her own choosing. Like many people too, I questioned an educational system that could produce a nineteen-year-old unable to read cursive, if at all. But I also recall the feeling that something didn't smell right.

This time I watched the exchange through fresh eyes. I still felt sorry for Rachel but for different reasons. I knew much more about her now, about her being held back two grades in school, about her struggles to get up in the morning, about her placement in the Exceptional Student Education (ESE) program, about her eagerness to find a place in a social milieu that devalued girls who were large, slow, and homely.

In *Rest in Power*, Sybrina claimed the defense had set Rachel up for the fall. West "knew what was coming next, and he must have known it would be dramatic, something that could devastate the jury's perception of Rachel," wrote Sybrina. Sybrina was right. The defense had learned about Rachel's inability to read the letter in a deposition that took place six weeks earlier. Having established West's cold heartedness, Sybrina wrote, "I kept thinking that this is someone's daughter, who has to go through this at such a young age."

Sybrina, however, was casting stones from a glass house. It was she and Team Trayvon who made Rachel "go through this at such a young age." Sybrina knew Rachel Jeantel was not Diamond Eugene.

Then too, it was Sybrina's concealment of Diamond's letter "in a box" that necessitated Rachel's second deposition with Don West on April 24, 2013. During that second deposition, Rachel desperately tried to explain why many key details surrounding Trayvon's death were missing from the letter.

West wasn't buying it. "You said that when you wrote the letter, you intentionally left out some important information?" he asked. Rachel said she had. When asked which information she left out, Rachel specified that she only shared with Sybrina the question Trayvon that asked had George–"Why you following me?"–but not George's alleged response, "What are you doing around here?" Rachel's explanation of why she included Trayvon's question but not George's answer was unconvincing to the point of absurd. Once again, Rachel's incoherent rambling eventually forced Don West to simply give up and move on.

Equally unbelievable was Rachel's insinuation that she was saving key information for the authorities. "Like I told Francine, I said, 'Sybrina ain't no cop. If she want information, let the cop come to me. Let the officer call me and then I will give them more detail what happened and I'm more calm.'"

To further cover her earlier deceptions, Rachel claimed she had shared with Francine other key details, such as her rationale for missing Trayvon's wake, and these Francine wrote up in a longer draft of the letter. That draft, alas, was no longer available. In an incriminating bit of rhetorical overkill, Rachel claimed the draft had been "ripped up" and, if that were not enough, "incinerated."

With every question West asked during the April 2013 deposition, Rachel sank deeper and deeper into a whirlpool of deceit.

As mentioned earlier, on the day after Trayvon's death, Diamond and Felicia exchanged some fifty texts and multiple phone calls. Rachel had been briefed on those phone records, and her answers reflected that. "You can look at my phone record," she said at one point to West. When questioned by West about those texts and phone calls, however, Rachel slipped up and referred to Felicia, her presumed best friend, as "what's her name."

For much of Rachel's April deposition, West explored the content of the text exchanges between Diamond and Trayvon, the conversations, that is, about drugs, sex, guns, and fighting. Here too, Rachel ducked and dodged, "I have friends that come over my house, my room, my computer, they go on my account, they go on my Facebook and go on my Twitter," said Rachel. How else was she to account for everything that had been said under Diamond's name, texts included?

Given what he had learned in the March and April depositions, West came to the June 2013 trial well prepared. He quickly made the jury aware that the State's "star witness" had lied about her age, about her hospitalization, even about her name:

"Did you sign [the letter] at the bottom?" asked West

"Yeah."

"What name did you use?"

"Diamond Eugene."

"It's not actually your name?"

"No."

"That's a name you made up."

"That's my nickname."

"But your last name isn't Eugene."

West scarcely bothered to put the last two "questions" in this sequence into question form. Although he did not want to seem like a bully, he had to show the jury that nothing Rachel said could be taken at face value, not even her name. He did a good job too in getting Rachel to admit that Crump was involved in shaping the story that Diamond and then later Rachel herself would tell. Rachel did not know enough about Crump's involvement to resist this line of questioning.

In her lengthy account of Rachel's trial testimony in *Rest in Power*, Sybrina talked repeatedly of her own nerves "fraying" or being "on edge." When the courtroom camera cut to Sybrina however, I could see her shooting nervous glances Tracy's way and he back to her. She had much to be nervous about. "I worried the prosecution had done irreparable damage, not only to our star witness, but to our entire case," Sybrina would write. But her biggest worries may have been that the defense would expose Rachel as a fraud on the witness stand, that the word "hoax" would be attached forever to her son's name, and that the good folks at Travelers Casualty and Surety Company of America might be placing a phone call to Mr. Crump, as in "Regarding that two million dollars..."

Giving credit where it is due, Rachel stayed in the "Diamond" character throughout. West never broke her. Rachel's best defense was her incomprehensibility. Her seeming honesty on details unflattering to Trayvon–for example, her admission that Trayvon referred to George as a "creepy ass cracker"–helped as well. That much said, Rachel was a terrible witness. How could she not have been? This somewhat slow, barely literate nineteen-year-old had been tasked with telling a story she had not experienced. Complicating matters was that the Crump-led story she inherited from Diamond was in large part fictional to begin with.

If there was a villain in this drama it was not Don West. It was those who knew the truth and allowed a stumbling amateur with severe disabilities to play a role that not even a skilled liar could have played, not caring a whit if she humiliated herself in the process or suffered PTSD down the road.

In the final analysis, it did not much matter how good a job Rachel did on the stand. The State lost its case when prosecutors called Johnathan Good as a witness. They called him because they knew the defense would if they did not. Good was the one eyewitness who mattered, the only one who saw what happened. Good was the reason the state avoided a grand jury. If grand jurors had listened to Good, they would have rejected all charges. At the trial, Good proved that witnesses do not come much better. The thirty-something Good was succinct, dispassionate and fully credible.

In his cross-examination, O'Mara read back Good's initial report to the Sanford PD, then asked, "And do you stand by that today, that what you saw was a Ground-and-Pound event?" Good affirmed that it was. When O'Mara, quoting Good, asked if "the guy in the top in the black hoodie [was] pretty much just throwing down blows on the guy kind of MMA-style?" Good answered, "Correct."

Just as critically, Good told of how Trayvon ignored his call for him to stop. Here, O'Mara made the point that if a threat to call the police could not deter Trayvon, nothing Zimmerman could do or say would, nothing that is short of a gunshot. Observed Andrew Branca in *Legal Insurrection,* "The testimony of State witness Jonathan (sic) Good was remarkably, almost shockingly, destructive to the State's theory of the case."

Tracy Martin did not see Good's testimony in quite the same light. In *Rest in Power,* Tracy argued that the prosecution missed numerous opportunities to challenge Good's account. One of Tracy's more disingenuous criticisms spoke to the forty seconds of screams for help picked up on a 911 call.

"Do you think that it was the person on the bottom who was screaming for help?" Tracy quoted O'Mara as asking.

"I mean, rationally thinking, I would think so," Good had answered.

"Rationally thinking?" Tracy wrote. "Wouldn't it be more rational to think the unarmed person on the wrong end of a gun would be the one screaming–regardless of who was on top and who was on the bottom?"

At the time Good testified, Tracy had no idea his original reaction to the voice on tape would help free George Zimmerman. Among the witnesses the defense called were Sanford PD Officers Chris Serino and Doris Singleton. Both testified that two days after the shooting they saw and heard Tracy listen to the 911 tape on which a voice could be heard calling for help. Both insisted they saw and heard Tracy deny that voice belonged to Trayvon. In a bold stroke, O'Mara called Tracy to testify on this very same subject. Tracy wrote about this obviously uncomfortable moment in *Rest in Power.*

"And now, the trial was turning out to be about that tape, but in a way I never would've predicted," wrote Tracy. "The tape was the evidence the defense tried so hard to use to prove that Trayvon's last moments on Earth were spent in attack instead of trying to ward off his attacker. But I wasn't budging on what I knew to be true. It was Trayvon's voice." Of course, it was not Trayvon's voice. There was nothing "he said-she said" about it, as Tracy suggested. *All* evidence confirmed that the voice belonged to George. Even the prosecutors refused to claim the voice was Trayvon's. They let Sybrina make that claim and then dropped it.

As I was learning, this was not the first time Tracy had reversed himself on what he said and what he did not say to authorities. Early in this investigation, I was inclined not to share what I had learned about Tracy's past. I thought, and still do believe, that his love for his son was real and his grief genuine. The deeper I got into the case, however, the more appalled I became at Tracy's routine deceptions. At the time of Trayvon's death, for instance, Tracy had a tattoo on his neck that may have indicated allegiance to the Crips gang, "CAT" which for the Crips meant "Crippin' All The Time." The Crips were a well-known street gang with national reach. As the case got media attention, Tracy quickly had the Crips tattoo covered with an image of praying hands. The media chose not to notice.

Much of what Tracy did was equally mendacious. It troubled me that Jay-Z made an inflammatory six-part series rooted in that mendacity. Tracy and Sybrina were putting money in the bank based on that mendacity. Having requested and received Tracy Martin's court records from the State of Missouri, here is what I learned. On February 7, 1989, two DEA agents took note of the twenty-two-year-old Tracy Benjamin Martin's arrival at the St. Louis airport. They spotted him coming off a plane from LaGuardia, a known drug courier route. He was walking quickly, looking repeatedly over his shoulder, and carrying no luggage.

The agents followed Tracy to the baggage carousel where he picked up a garment bag and headed out to a garage to look for a car. The car was under surveillance and one that a known drug dealer had recently provided his couriers to use after flying in cocaine from Central America. As Tracy reached the drug dealer's car, the officers approached him and asked if they could search his bag. According to the officers, Tracy said, "Go ahead." They did and found two kilos of almost pure cocaine, street value roughly $1 million, and arrested him. They read Tracy his Miranda rights and took him to an office in the airport for further questioning. There, Tracy ratted out his contact, Charles White, and explained that he was to receive three thousand dollars for his role as a drug courier.

A few months later, once Tracy realized the gravity of his situation, he changed his story. He claimed in sworn testimony that, when approached by the officers, he had asked to see a search warrant. They blew him off, and the one officer "just grabbed the bag." In a motion hearing to have all evidence dismissed due to coercion and improper search, the holes in Tracy's story leaped out. Yes, Tracy conceded, the officers never pulled out a weapon, touched him or tried to restrain him before the arrest. Yes, too, he did finger Charles White. The court did not buy his BS. Tracy pleaded guilty to possession with intent to distribute and was sentenced to sixty-three months in federal prison. He would spend the next several years in the "Big House" at Leavenworth. The presiding judge was none other than Stephen Limbaugh, Rush's uncle.

Tracy need not have taken the acquittal of George Zimmerman too personally. All the evidence supported George's innocence. In her ridiculous book, *Suspicion Nation*, NBC legal correspondent Lisa Bloom insisted the prosecutors' "biggest blunder" was their failure to present a comprehensive "theory" about the incident. They did not present a theory because there was none. They could not explain away George's broken nose, his bloodied head, his cries for help, Trayvon's bruised knuckles, Good's testimony, nor the location of the attack.

In his most Perry Mason-like moment, one that George himself suggested, Mark O'Mara put a clock on a podium and watched in silence as four minutes ticked away. Those four minutes represented the time Trayvon had to get away from Zimmerman if he chose to. He only had to go about a hundred yards to Brandy Green's townhouse. As O'Mara suggested, some men could run a mile in that time. Instead, after four mysterious minutes, Trayvon turned up at the cut-through seventy yards from Green's place and perhaps ten yards from

George's vehicle to confront and attack George, who was walking *away* from Trayvon and toward his truck. Fortunately, Johnathan Good was there to witness what happened.

Had she been on the phone, Rachel might have actually encouraged Trayvon to just go to Brandy's townhome, but Rachel wasn't on the phone. Diamond was. My theory of the attack is that it was largely a drug (marijuana) related event. I think Trayvon had identified George as a loathsome snitch and felt the need to show off for Diamond what a badass gangsta he was by beating the ass of the snitch. I also think he likely relayed as much to Diamond. Whatever the case, Diamond refrained from tweeting about the trial for its duration. The day Rachel struggled through her court testimony, Diamond tweeted, "I Guess I'm Vamping Again Tonight."

30

THE VERDICT

ALTHOUGH SHE COULD HAVE ENDED the trial by coming forward, Brittany Diamond Eugene saw fit to join the chorus of disbelief at trial's end. "Zimmerman Was Found Not Guilty. Wtf," tweeted Diamond on the evening of July 13, 2013, followed by "My Heart Goes Out To Trayvon Martin's Family. I Can Imagine How Their Feeling." The media had so misled their audiences that Diamond, who knew more than anyone, was but one of millions worldwide registering shock at an all but inevitable outcome. Predictably, in the middle of that night Diamond awoke and at 3:23 a.m. tweeted, "I want some Krispy Kreme doughnuts."

The verdict could not have come soon enough for George Zimmerman. "I was not necessarily surprised. I was elated. I had a resurgence of faith in the justice system, especially the jury system," George told me. The elation did not last long. Within minutes, the very same activists and media who had demanded "just an arrest" vied with each other to denounce the outcome of that trial. It turned out their agenda was much bigger than "just an arrest" as they so often had insisted early on.

"George Zimmerman skirted justice with an all-white jury of his peers which consisted of all women," announced the Left-leaning UK

Guardian. The *Guardian* was not alone in referring to the jury that acquitted George as "all white." Jesse Jackson reinforced this theme upon hearing of the verdict, complaining there was "not one black on the jury." Said Jackson, whose opinion on the trial was shared by nearly 90 percent of African Americans, "Something about it was stacked from the very beginning."

In *Rest in Power*, a low-boil stew of racial propaganda, Sybrina said of the jurors, "[N]one of them were black." She preferred to describe the jurors as "five middle-class white women and one Hispanic woman." In fact, the Hispanic woman was a Puerto Rican of obvious African descent.

In similar spirit, Sybrina referred to George only as white, never as Hispanic, never as Peruvian. Nor did Sybrina ever make any reference in her race-saturated book to the Afro-Peruvian roots of George's mother Gladys. The fact that African Americans made up only 10 percent of the Seminole County jury pool impressed neither Sybrina nor any of the race hustlers who yearned for a loaded, OJ-style jury. Only a guilty verdict would have satisfied their mob definition of "justice."

Sybrina's attorney Benjamin Crump, who played a major role in the dubious case, cheapened black history with his blasphemous assertion, "Trayvon Martin will forever remain in the annals of history next to Medgar Evers and Emmett Till, as symbols for the fight for equal justice for all." He was one of many to make the spurious allusion to the fourteen-year-old Till lynched in the Jim Crow South forty years before Trayvon was born.

Not one to mince words, Al Sharpton called the verdict an "atrocity." Sharpton blamed the all-female jurors. "What this jury has done," he said, "is establish a precedent that when you are young and fit a certain profile, you can be committing no crime...and be killed and someone can claim self-defense."

State Attorney Angela Corey proved to be as mendacious as Sharpton. In a post-verdict interview on HLN, Corey described Trayvon as "prey" and "an unarmed teen just walking home." Said Corey of Trayvon with unintended irony, "He never had a fighting chance." Asked for a one-word description of George Zimmerman, she huffed, "murderer." When asked for his one-word description of Rachel, Bernie de la Rionda said with a straight a face as he could muster, "truthful." In revisiting this clip, I spontaneously burst out laughing and could not stop for some time.

As Sybrina noted proudly in her book, the useful idiots in the entertainment world joined the mindless rush to pile on. In Ireland, Bruce Springsteen sang a song in Trayvon's honor. Justin Timberlake dedicated a song to Trayvon in Yankee Stadium. Stevie Wonder promised to boycott Florida unless the state repealed its Stand Your Ground law, which wasn't used by Zimmerman for his defense and had nothing to do with the trial. Beyoncé sang about her love for Trayvon in Nashville, then joined Jay-Z for a vigil in New York.

Much as communists welcomed the execution of Sacco and Vanzetti in 1927, hardcore leftist activists, black and white, welcomed the not-guilty verdict in 2013. What good would Zimmerman have done them in prison? For the last century, the reigning strategy has been to exploit black discontent to enhance Leftist power. By the late 1960s, however, the demand for racial injustice had outstripped the supply. The election of a black man as President in 2008 threatened that supply and the activists' very future. They feared they were about to go "out of business." In January 2009, the month of Obama's inauguration, 79 percent of whites and 63 percent of blacks held a favorable view of race relations in America. For the Left, this could not stand.

31

CSI MIAMI

ALTHOUGH I HAD STARTED REVIEWING the Trayvon Martin case as a part of a political documentary, I ended up producing what could have been an episode of CSI Miami. Along the way, I kept asking myself, 'Why did the State of Florida *not* do what I was doing?'

The conclusions I reached were startling. Before going forward with them, however, I wanted to confirm the identity switch through every relevant forensic methodology. Given the importance of the letter Diamond gave to Sybrina, I contracted with the best forensic handwriting analyst in the field. Document examiner Bart Baggett works out of Southern California. I was able to meet with him and film his interview for the documentary.

When Baggett's results came in, I gathered my film crew and headed eagerly to his office in nearby Sherman Oaks to record his findings. Although I had seen him on TV–he worked on the Zodiac and Jon Benet Ramsey cases among others–I was eager to meet the man in person. Baggett did not disappoint. He proved capable not only of identifying the samples with a high degree of probability and certainty, but also of drawing personality profiles of the three young women that tracked well with information gathered from other sources.

During the trial, the reader will remember, defense attorney Don West asked Rachel Jeantel, "Did you sign [the letter] at the bottom?"

"Yea."

"What name did you use?"

"Diamond Eugene."

Rachel made the same claim during her depositions. She claimed that Francine Serve, the young woman who worked at Sybrina Fulton's home, wrote the body of the letter, but Rachel insisted she was the one who signed it, "I signature as Diamond Eugene." Sybrina claimed she gave the letter no significance, finding it to be "personal and sentimental." Bart Baggett dismissed that out of hand. "There is nothing about this letter that is sentimental," he said flatly. "It's a clearly a witness statement of what happened." Baggett continued, "Anytime someone hides evidence or protects stuff, there's obviously some fire there, there's something we need to know about." I suspected that Sybrina may have concealed the letter out of fear that a handwriting expert could compare Rachel's illegible handwriting to the signature on the letter, and Baggett agreed this to be a possibility given the circumstances. Handwriting analysis is something the prosecutors should have done, and the defense attorneys would have done if they had more time.

I had provided Baggett with all the handwriting samples I could gather, including a copy of the Sybrina letter itself. For Diamond, these samples included the Christmas cards I had her sign and her traffic citation. For Francine, the samples consisted of her many signatures on public court documents as well as letters to judges requesting leniency for traffic violations and grand theft credit card fraud. Rachel had signed a traffic citation that I provided with her signature that looked to be scribbled by a 1st grader.

After examining the samples and completing his analysis, Baggett was careful to qualify everything he said, but on one point, the most critical, he was definitive. "The one thing that is conclusive," he said for the record, "is that Rachel Jeantel did *not* write the words 'Diamond Eugene.'" In his formal report, Baggett wrote, "The evidence available suggests that Rachel Jeantel did not sign the name 'Diamond Eugene' nor did she author the body of the letter." Baggett affirmed the accuracy of his report "under penalty of perjury" and expressed his willingness to testify in court. The messy and disorganized Rachel, he told me, "does not have the neuro-muscular habits to write (the words 'Diamond Eugene') with this kind of clarity."

Just based on her handwriting samples, Baggett envisioned Rachel as a young woman with low self-esteem and little formal education. He sensed she was deeply anxious about writing anything and was emotionally unstable. This profile reinforced everything I knew about Rachel.

As to the body of the letter and the date, Baggett attributed the handwriting to Francine Serve. "The body of the writing was absolutely Francine's," he said on camera. As to the signature, he found as "probable" that the last name "Eugene" was written by Brittany Diamond Eugene, while the first name "Diamond" looked more like Francine's handwriting. He said, "it's kind of an odd and interesting twist to this case that each girl wrote one of the names." On the report, he noted that either Diamond or Francine "could have written some or all of the name 'Diamond Eugene.'" In fact, my first impressions were confirmed. A quick glance at the signature shows that the words "Diamond" and "Eugene" have different slants, different sized letters, and an abnormally large space in between the two words.

Baggett deduced from Francine's handwriting that she had low self-esteem, a fear of change, difficult relations with men, and "some demons within her." He was much more positive about Diamond. Baggett saw her as friendly, outgoing, bubbly, and relatively mature. He imagined her to be the most emotionally stable of the three.

Based on his analysis of their handwriting, Baggett told me on camera, "All of these three individuals would be good targets for some savvy manipulative individual if they had the right bait." This much seems undeniable. In my communication with Francine (I had called her to get a recommendation on a Haitian church on her Facebook page), she struck me as pliable, loyal, and eager to please. One person she surely wanted to please was the woman at whose home she worked, Sybrina Fulton. Rachel, born prematurely and always two steps slow, might not have understood what was being asked of her. Yes, she committed perjury over and over, but I cannot imagine a prosecutor ever bringing charges against her.

Of the three, Diamond proved to be the most resistant to pressure. She resisted coming forward to tell any story for three weeks before caving in to what were likely threats of some kind. True, she did talk to Benjamin Crump and then to ABC's Matt Gutman. At that point, she likely felt she had no choice but to repeat back Crump's narrative and agree with every question he posed to her. But then Diamond shocked Team Trayvon by backing out. I have suggested any number of reasons why: to preserve her relationship with her beau, Jeff Watler; to protect herself and family from exposure; to conceal any possible role in not dissuading Trayvon from an attack on Zimmerman; or to preserve the public image of Trayvon as the victim rather than as a conscious predator looking to beat up a snitch.

To escape involvement, Diamond and possibly others did something diabolically ingenious. They recruited Rachel Jeantel to play "Diamond." One question that nagged at me as I did my research was how Rachel was convinced to sign up for the plot. Why would Rachel Jeantel agree to take Diamond Eugene's place? Two years apart in age, she and Diamond went to different schools and had absolutely nothing in common save for the shared family last name of "Eugene" between Diamond and Rachel's mother, Marie Eugene. From the get go, I felt they had to be related. Although "Eugene" was a somewhat common name among Haitians, the fact that Diamond's second phone number was registered to Rachel's Haitian half-brother, Daniel Eugene, made some kind of familial relationship all the more likely.

In full CSI mode, I decided to test the respective DNA of Diamond Eugene and Rachel Jeantel for a connection. From Diamond I was sure I had her DNA on the envelope flaps that she had licked shut for Christmas cards that she provided with clothing I had ordered.

Next, I zeroed in on Rachel Jeantel. I had collected abandoned trash from outside of Rachel's home where she lived with her mother,

Marie Eugene. This was perfectly legal according to the United States Supreme Court in *Greenwood v. United States.* It was held that (1) a person has *no* reasonable expectation of privacy for contents of garbage and (2) a person has relinquished any property interest in garbage, even when it sits in trash cans or plastic bags at a person's home awaiting collection.

Among the huge haul of discarded trash that included fast food boxes, candy wrappers, and cosmetics was a headband, likely belonging to Rachel, and underwear the size of which indicated it was likely worn by her mother, Marie Eugene.

I carefully packaged the items separately and then sent the items from Rachel's trash and Diamond's envelopes to a well-established forensic DNA lab, Speckin Forensic Laboratories in Michigan. This firm specialized in biological fluid and DNA identification. First, the lab reported that its scientists successfully obtained a DNA profile for Diamond from saliva in the envelope flaps. Next, testing the two samples from Rachel's trash, Speckin Forensic Laboratories reported with "greater than a 99 percent probability" that "Headband" (Rachel) was, as expected, the daughter of "Underwear" (Marie Eugene).

I then asked Speckin Forensic Laboratories to compare the DNA profile from Diamond (Envelopes) to the profiles from both Rachel (Headband) and her mother Marie Eugene (Underwear). If you think this has been a wild ride so far, hang on. You ain't seen nothing yet. The lab reported with "greater than a 99 percent probability" that Brittany Diamond Eugene was *also* the daughter of Marie Eugene! I was floored!

Next, Speckin Forensic Laboratories reported in its official findings letter, "The shared mother confirms a biological relationship between the samples presumed to come from Female Aged 23 [Diamond] and Daughter-25 [Rachel]. Comparison of the major donor profiles from the envelope flaps and the headband indicates that these women are half rather than full siblings." Brittany Diamond Eugene and Rachel Jeantel are half-sisters! Even though I had my suspicions from the get-go, it was a shocking revelation that explained a lot! Diamond was her half-sister! I knew I had not contaminated the samples. Still, I was so shocked that I checked with the lab just to make sure they had not mixed up the samples. I was assured they had not and had never done such a thing. In fact they said there were three distinct, though related, individuals. My head is still spinning.

Doing a little research, I learned that although upper class Haitian families favor the nuclear family model prevalent in the West, lower socioeconomic Haitian families routinely feature "plasaj," a form of common-law marriage. These relationships, often fluid, are reinforced by a strong extended-family network. Moving children from one home to another among extended families is not uncommon at all. Obviously given the large number of calls and texts between Diamond and Rachel I had observed in Diamond's phone records, they were enjoying a close relationship as half-sisters. For Rachel to assume Diamond's identity may seem outlandish to us, but in an extended Haitian Eugene family clan, it may not have been that big a deal.

32

THE TRAYVON HOAX

THE FACTS of my investigation are undeniable. A legitimate phone witness to the final minutes of Trayvon Martin's life, Brittany Diamond Eugene, was replaced with a fraudulent witness, Rachel Jeantel, her half-sister. Without this fake witness, George Zimmerman would not have been charged with, nor tried for, murder. In that Zimmerman's case resulted in the most public political and racially charged trial since O.J. Simpson's, the boldness of this witness swap takes one's breath away.

Having put all the pieces together, I came to see that "The Trayvon Hoax," although specific, served as the evil template for a larger, more general hoax being pulled on the American public every day. The hoax might have as "victim" a Muslim, a woman, an immigrant or any "marginalized" person with a "L," "B," "G," T," or "Q" assigned to them.

The most powerful of the victim narratives, however, still involves an African American. It goes like this: asking no questions, the media report a story of an innocent black person, acting normally, who is attacked out of the blue by a white person (or cop of any race) for no reason other than skin color. The media tell us the white person represents "America" or, today, "Trump's America." To protect themselves and their families against this violence and hate, African Americans are encouraged to seek shelter on the Left and vote for Democrats.

From following the social media postings of Trayvon's friends, I could see they had bought into this narrative even as kids. Trayvon's death, as the media interpreted it, reinforced their anxieties and strengthened their antipathy towards Republicans. As a case in point, Felica Cineas posted on Facebook in October 2016, "Vote Obama or Die!"

These young people were hardly alone in their naiveté. Thanks to the black vote, just about every major city in America except New York City has had a Democrat for mayor for the past fifty years or so. To prevent black voters from connecting their city's inevitably appalling schools, high crime rates, rampant drug cultures, and chronic unemployment to the Democrats they voted into power, the media regularly manage to find and massage new hate crimes, real or fictional, to keep black voters in line. The need to sustain this urban power arrangement is what caused The Trayvon Hoax to go national.

Two questions that need to be asked are: who knew about the stunning witness fraud and obstruction of justice in the Zimmerman case and who should be held responsible? Diamond knew. Rachel knew. This is beyond argument. Diamond was a *minor* at the time. I cannot imagine her being prosecuted. Rachel was arguably not mentally competent. I cannot imagine her being prosecuted either.

Of all the other likely insiders, Trayvon's mother, Sybrina Fulton, may have the most explaining to do. By all accounts, including her own, Sybrina met Diamond Eugene when Diamond came to her house on March 19, 2012. By her own account too, Sybrina drove Diamond to her 2648 Flamingo Drive home and even spoke to her mother. In her March 2013 deposition Sybrina claimed she alone met with Diamond outside the house, indicating that Tracy had not also met with Diamond when she did on March 19, 2012. In *Rest in Power*, however, Tracy blew this cover by casually observing that Diamond came into the house, allegedly with the letter in hand.

Francine Serve was clearly involved with both Diamond and

Rachel. When I spoke with Francine for the church referral, I came away with the impression that she is basically a decent and honest person, with loyalty being her downfall. Her sister, Felicia Cineas, was very involved with Diamond, but she, like Diamond, was sixteen at the time.

If I were a prosecutor, I would offer these young women, Diamond and Rachel included, immunity in exchange for testimony about any adult individual or individuals who helped orchestrate the witness switch and/or coached Diamond and Rachel. My first question would be, "What was the role, if any, of family attorney Benjamin Crump?"

If I were Crump, after an obligatory rant about Americans having racist DNA, I would disclose everything I knew about the roles of state attorneys Bernie de la Rionda, John Guy, and especially Angela Corey: "Did they know about the witness switch and, if so, when did they know it?" Corey's shockingly dishonest comments to HLN after the trial suggest that she used the trial largely as a way to troll for black votes, justice be damned.

The prosecutors had access to all the cell phone data I used to find my way to Brittany Diamond Eugene. They had that information for more than a year. They also had experienced investigators on staff and subpoena powers that I could only envy. Instead of revealing the truth, again and again they made extraordinary efforts to withhold that evidence from the defense. In fact, the defense attorneys spent two-thirds of their time in court trying to get discovery of information they had every right to have without prodding. Following *Brady* precedent, prosecutors should have volunteered any evidence that pointed to the innocence of the defendant or that enabled the defense to impeach the credibility of government witnesses. Given the credibility problem of their star witness, the Florida state attorneys resisted disclosure.

Only one example: even though they knew Rachel was eighteen at the time of Trayvon's death, they denied the defense access to her on the grounds she was a minor until just before the trial. They stonewalled the defense on Rachel's medical records as well. The prosecutors had a full year to review voice and handwriting samples from Diamond and Rachel but chose not to scrutinize any of it.

On April 2, 2012, Sybrina Fulton directed de la Rionda and company to 2648 Flamingo Drive in Miramar to pick up Diamond for her first formal police interview. On not finding her there, de la Rionda and his associates should have checked rental and property records to see who actually lived in that house. I suspect they did check who lived there on the way over as police routinely do when approaching a residence. They would have discovered, as I did, that Eliana Eugene lived there with her apparent daughter Brittany Diamond Eugene and Diamond's sister Virginia Eugene. On hearing the name "Brittany Diamond Eugene," or just the last name "Eugene," they would have understood why the letter at the center of the case was signed "Diamond Eugene," not "Rachel Jeantel." Admittedly, Sybrina withheld the letter until March 2013, but the prosecutors still had three months before the trial to run a simple address and name check as well as handwriting comparisons.

Prosecutors also chose to ignore the glaring discrepancy between Diamond's openly sexual exchanges with Trayvon and Rachel's denial of anything beyond "just friends." On appearance alone, it should have been hammer-over-the-head obvious that Rachel was not and could not have been the object of Trayvon's adolescent lust. The prosecutors chose to ignore the obvious. The desire to advance their careers, in my opinion, explains less than their fear of the mob and their desire to keep it pacified.

To get the defense's perspective on the witness swap, I called Zimmerman's attorney Mark O'Mara early on. He expressed skepticism that Rachel was a fraud. "She was such a terrible witness," he asked me rhetorically, "why would anyone use her as a substitute?" I explained to O'Mara that those who knew the depth of the evidence exonerating George–his broken nose, his recorded screams for help, Johnathan Good's testimony–never expected to get a conviction. Nothing any fake witness could say could overcome the hard evidence, I told him. But then again conviction was never the point; an arrest was what mattered. For Crump, an arrest opened the door to a civil suit. For the State of Florida, an arrest kept the mob at bay. For Barack Obama's Justice Department, an arrest meant getting out the black vote for Obama in 2012 in Florida and hopefully nationwide.

For Al Sharpton and his crowd of Leftists, an arrest and trial advanced their racially charged agenda. Just as Sacco and Vanzetti were more useful dead than alive, George Zimmerman was more useful acquitted, and loose on the streets, than convicted. For the hard Left, political expediency has always trumped justice.

33

VERY BAD CONSEQUENCES

THE EFFECTS of The Trayvon Hoax endure to this day. Among the perpetrators and victims, no one has suffered more than the man who was arrested because of it. In short order, George Zimmerman lost his job, his chance at an education, and his wife. George described to me how ill equipped he was to handle the unending public abuse especially since it came from the liberals activists that he had previously thought of as allies.

George found himself internalizing their negativity. If they were going to think of him as a loose cannon, he would show them he could be. He would live down to their expectations. In this he succeeded. No legal incident was too minor to thrust him back into the news. When a man very nearly assassinated him–and got twenty years for the failed effort–the media somehow blamed George. "I threw all caution to the wind," George confided in me. "I acted like a total knucklehead, and I'm really sorry about it." As he explained, it took him several years just to get back to who he was. "I am at peace again," he insisted.

Key witness Johnathan Good learned there was little reward for telling the truth. At the time of the shooting, Good and his wife-to-be were planning their wedding. "Add into that the media frenzy, public scrutiny, death threats, anxiety over safety, and an upcoming trial," wrote Good in his short e-book, *Reluctant Witness*. "Please picture how that would make you feel. Now picture how that would make your significant other feel." If the media ignored Good, the trolls on social media did not. As Good observed, they presumed he testified as he had only because he was white. As a final irony, he and his wife felt compelled to "become trained in firearm safety."

The one black juror endured worse. Unaware of the politics of the case before the trial, the Puerto Rican mother of eight learned about them soon afterwards. Unnerved by the hate spewed at her and her family, she begged forgiveness from the masses for her "not guilty" vote. "I literally fell on my knees and I broke down. My husband was holding me," she told ABC's Robin Roberts. "I was screaming and crying, and I kept saying to myself I feel like I killed him."

I have little doubt that Sybrina Fulton would gladly exchange all the rewards she has reaped since Trayvon's death to see her son alive again, but the rewards have been considerable and inevitably corrupting. On the financial front, she shared in the estimated two million dollar settlement from The Retreat at Twin Lakes homeowners association. Then there was a book deal and a TV series on top of that. She even recorded a Hip Hop song.

As a speaker, Sybrina is represented by APB, the same agency that represents Bob Woodward, Goldie Hawn, and Sarah Palin among others. She has spoken at numerous events around the country, none more prestigious than the 2016 Democratic National Convention. Sybrina is one of the main purveyors of The Trayvon Hoax today. Her speeches often include the warnings "people in our community don't feel safe going to the store" and "because of the color of your skin, people hate you so much that they want to kill you." She finished off her stump speeches for Hillary Clinton, saying, "Get out and vote. Your life depends on it!" That's The Trayvon Hoax in action.

Sybrina today fronts for the Trayvon Martin Foundation at its attractive offices on the campus of Florida Memorial University in Miami Gardens. She recently announced she is running for public office in 2020, seeking a seat on the Miami-Dade Board of Commissioners. When she announced, she told voters, "I am you." Tracy Martin represents the Foundation as well. Although he has benefitted much as Sybrina has, he seems less comfortable in his role as spokesman and is certainly less visible.

Not surprisingly, Benjamin Crump has profited immensely. Trayvon's death made him a national figure. Like mentor Al Sharpton, Crump has cashed in on ill-gotten notoriety, as honors have come flowing his way. Crump was named to the National Trial Lawyers Top 100 Lawyers in America. Ebony Magazine ranked him among the 100 most influential African Americans. In 2017, Crump opened a new national law firm, Ben Crump Law, PLLC. In 2018, he joined the board of the National Black Justice Coalition.

Then Crump went Hollywood. He has appeared on numerous TV shows, including a 2018 show ironically called "Evidence of Innocence." The show focused on people wrongly convicted of crimes. Were the show to include the wrongly arrested, George Zimmerman could serve as Client Zero. Late in 2018, Crump started his own production company called Brooklyn Media to "create scripted narrative content for film, TV and digital media." Of course, Crump endorsed Andrew Gillum to be governor of Florida and appeared with him on the campaign trail where Gillum frequently repeated Crump's "Skittles and iced tea" tag line.

For the prosecutors the results were mixed. In February 2013, four months before the trial, Angela Corey made the pages of the *Florida Times-Union* when it was discovered that she "spent $235,000 in taxpayer dollars to upgrade her pension and the pension of her senior prosecutor." That prosecutor was none other than Bernie de la Rionda. The media coverage was not flattering.

In 2018, de la Rionda retired after thirty-five years on the job. "He's amazing," Corey told the *Times-Union* upon de la Rionda's retirement. "He lived and breathed that job but never let it get in the way of being a man of God and a family man." There was God again thrust into the mix.

Corey left office a bit more abruptly. Although re-elected in 2012, Republican voters sent the incumbent state attorney packing in the

2016 primary by an embarrassing margin. Her grandstanding in the deeply flawed case against Zimmerman did not play well among Republican primary voters who knew the law and the facts better than did the general public. As for prosecutor John Guy, his connection to the Zimmerman case has only helped. In 2015, Guy was appointed to a judgeship in Florida's Fourth Judicial Circuit.

Rachel Jeantel has never quite recovered from the trial. She dropped out of Norland High School and apparently went through some extended trauma from her experience. The guilt she expressed early on about participating in the conspiracy had to affect her as did the subsequent humiliation from having her disabilities put on full display. Said her attorney Ron Vareen, "She was depressed. We actually had her evaluated and she was suffering from Post-Traumatic Stress Disorder as a result of this ordeal.

To compensate her for the embarrassment of the trial, some good spirited citizens–"a village of mentors," said the *Washington Post*–worked together to help Rachel get into an alternative high school. When she graduated A.C.E. High School at age twenty-one, ABC news profiled Rachel, now obviously tipping the scales at three hundred pounds or more. None of the journalists who covered Rachel dared expose the cruelty of those who allowed her to testify.

Unfortunately, Rachel seems to have learned little from her experience. In the 2018 documentary series, "Rest in Power," Rachel helped sell Jay-Z's racist propaganda, pretending once again to have been on the phone with Trayvon at the moment of his death. With the pressure off and with the luxury of repeated takes, she restated calmly and in improved English the false claims she made at her depositions and at the trial. Rachel stills lives in the same house with her Mom and recently attended a Joel Osteen revival.

Brittany Diamond Eugene has done better than many of her peers. She graduated from Miramar High School in 2014, attended Broward Community College and then transferred to Florida State University where she majored in Criminal Justice. From her FSU digs, Diamond runs her online Boutique website called "She's Bomb." I am likely her best ever customer, having purchased her entire inventory in December 2018. Diamond now tweets only once every few days, but when she does tweet she is happy to remind the world of her greatness and of her love of fast food. Diamond graduated from FSU in May 2019 with a degree in criminal justice.

Although Diamond stunningly withdrew herself from the George Zimmerman case, in part to protect her relationship with boyfriend Jeff Watler, Jeff finally left her, tweeting, "Brittany was looking so good but I had to drop her." The break up happened around the time Rachel Jeantel appeared on the witness stand in the guise of "Diamond Eugene" in the summer of 2013. By September of that year, Diamond picked up with classmate Noah Allen-Bouey and stayed "strong" with him through their 2014 senior prom. Other boyfriends kept Diamond occupied until her love life came crashing down on May 6, 2015. On that sad day, she tweeted, "Single as fuck!"

For Diamond's best friend Felicia Cineas and Felicia's sister Francine Serve, there has been trouble with the law. On July 17, 2015, the nineteen-year-old Felicia was caught shoplifting food items and a pair of sandals at a Wal-Mart in Miramar, but she caught a break and was assigned to Broward County's Misdemeanor Diversion Program.

Felicia "successfully completed" the program on February 28, 2016. The program supervisor recommended that the charges against Felicia not be pursued. This is not the same as "expunged" and just as well. Ten days before her allegedly successful completion of the program Felicia had already violated its terms. Apparently partial to the Wal-Mart product line, she, sister Francine, Francine's twin Francina, and a friend did some serious shopping with a Wal-Mart gift card. Alas, the young ladies had purchased the gift card with a credit card obtained by theft of the identity of a fellow named John Peak.

After Peak alerted the authorities, detectives reviewed Wal-Mart's surveillance video and found all four of the women loading fifteen hundred dollars' worth of goods into shopping carts and taking the stolen goods out of the store. Francine was the one who made the purchase. On March 17, 2016, detectives visited Francine at her home in Kissimmee, Florida. The pliable Francine "immediately advised she knew what was done" and quickly gave up her sisters and her friend. All four were arrested. Given Francine's fundamentally honest nature when confronted, it is understandable why Sybrina tried to minimize inquiries about Francine when deposed.

In fact, many of Diamond's friends and relatives ran previously afoul of the law for crimes like identity theft. Such was the Haitian-American milieu in which Diamond came of age. Diamond's second phone number was registered to Rachel's half-brother, Daniel Eugene, who is likely Diamond's half-brother as well. He could not have been a good influence. In February 2012, Daniel Eugene posted photos of high-end women's purses on his Facebook page in much the same sprit hunters put elk heads on their trophy walls. Other photos he posted included himself gambling in casinos and making gang signs.

In the course of my research, I had to remind myself that Diamond was only sixteen-years-old at the time. For all her issues, the more I learned about her life before and after Trayvon, I began not to judge her. In some ways, Diamond has lived a classic bootstrap American life. Her biological mother appears to have given her up at some point. She had no father in the home, the man she likely thought was her father was a former gangster who lived in Haiti. She and her family had endured any number of evictions and dislocations. When she attended family reunions, she was surrounded by uncles and aunts who had been to prison. And yet, despite her family background, she managed to will herself through high school, attending night school as well. Then she attended community college, found her way into a major state university, and launched a sophisticated side business. When I met her, I felt the voodoo priest was wrong. Diamond was a good person and she had a good heart.

In 2012, at just sixteen years of age, Diamond faced enormous pressure to come forward and tell a story, then repeat it. This included entreaties from both of Trayvon's parents, the constant cajoling of attorney Benjamin Crump, dozens of high-pressure phone calls and texts from Trayvon's scary friends, and the smooth-talking seduction of ABC's news hunk Matt Gutman. Although she accommodated Crump on one occasion with a load of bullshit and Gutman on another, she rebelled and extricated herself from the case.

To be sure, Diamond was no innocent. Given her family background, she had the wherewithal to pull off a switch in cell phones and an identity swap so bold it still makes my head spin. As to her relationship with Trayvon, it is hard to judge her from afar. Lacking a father, she had a desperate need for male affirmation, and Jeff was not around enough to provide it. In the relationship game, Trayvon, who was no saint himself, got played.

To this day, the Trayvon faithful refuse to acknowledge the direction in which his life was heading. Every February 5, Trayvon supporters flood Twitter with birthday greetings along the lines of "Trayvon Martin would be 24 years old today, but he was murdered in 2012 by a violent racist" or "Happy 24th birthday in heaven, Trayvon Martin."

Trayvon was not heading heavenward. Had he not been shot that fateful night in 2012, chances are that his first stop would have been prison–for months if George had lived, for years if George had died. The evidence against Trayvon was overwhelming. A "he snitched on me smoking weed" defense would have found little sympathy. No race hustlers would have come to his defense and certainly no rock stars. Alive, you see, Trayvon did the movement no good at all.

Even if Trayvon had avoided prison, his fate would likely have mirrored those of his best friends. Romario Carridice, "Mario," has subsequently been convicted of stealing a car and resisting arrest as well as marijuana possession. Worse, in early 2019, Mario was arrested for pimping. Stephan Bramble, "Steve-O," was convicted of burglary and grand theft. Cousin Stephen Martin, "Boobie," was arrested for possession of marijuana. Without serious intervention, Trayvon was fated to end his days as a statistic.

Other than for George Zimmerman, the cultural consequences of The Trayvon Hoax were more profound than the legal ones. Not wanting to say any more than he had to, President Barack Obama chose to go with the progressive flow. A week after the verdict Obama interrupted a White House press conference to address the Zimmerman verdict, a verdict he called the "Trayvon Martin ruling."

Obama began by sending his "thoughts and prayers" to the family of Trayvon Martin. He did not even mention the Zimmerman family nor chastise those who forced the family into hiding. As he did a year earlier, Obama identified his path through life with Trayvon's. "Trayvon Martin could have been me thirty-five years ago," said Obama, ignoring the fact that Trayvon had launched a savage and unprovoked attack on a stranger, something not even the admitted Hawaiian pothead Obama ever considered as a teen. Let's face it, as soft as Obama was, he would have gotten his ass kicked. As to the victim of Trayvon's attack, an Obama supporter and civil rights activist whose life was ruined by the trial, Obama offered not a word of consolation.

Nor did Barack Obama do the one thing he was uniquely positioned to do as the nation's first black president, namely use the verdict as a teachable moment. A useful point of reference would have been Tracy Martin's deposition in March 2013. In a series of questions, defense attorney Don West challenged Martin about the downward spiral of Trayvon's life after Tracy broke for good with "Mama 'Licia," Alicia Stanley, in November of 2011.

"In November 2011, Trayvon was kicked out of Sybrina's house," said West.

"This is my first of ever hearing that," said Tracy.

"Were you aware of his Twitter account? (No Limit Nigga gang)," asked West.

"I knew he had a Twitter account, I wasn't aware of the name," Tracy responded.

"Were you aware that he was skipping school - a lot?

"No, I wasn't.

"Were you aware that he had been disciplined for vandalism and possessing jewelry under suspicious circumstances?"

"After the fact, after he was deceased, that's when I found out about that."

"Were you aware that he was smoking marijuana?"

"I found out after the fact."

"Were you aware that he had been suspended more than once?"

"I was aware of him being suspended after his death."

"Any parent-teacher conferences?," West asked.

"I may have been invited, I didn't attend." Tracy replied.

Here in brief was the malady that plagued Trayvon and millions of young black men across America. The problem, Obama should have said, was not the presence of armed white men in the streets. The problem was the absence of strong black men in the home. When Trayvon and his friends started to go astray, there were no fathers waiting at home to corral them. Instead, the boys fed off each other's insecurities, pulling their images of masculinity less from real life Miami role models than from fictional Miamians like Tony "Scarface" Montana, an icon in hip-hop America.

Being biracial and insecure in his own identity as an African American, Obama seized every opportunity to reinforce his legitimacy. Make no mistake, Obama was just as radical as his allies, but he was the soft spoken one, the stealth radical, the one who preferred scheming behind closed doors to screaming from a soap box. Obama's radicalism was in his actions, quietly enabling The Trayvon Hoax narrative at every turn. The results were disastrous. An NBC News and *Wall Street Journal* poll taken after the trial showed the effect of the incessant racial pot stirring by Obama and his acolytes. By July 2013, only 52 percent of whites and 38 percent of blacks still held a favorable view of race relations in America, down from 79 percent and 63 percent just four years earlier when America elected a black President.

As feckless as his response was, Obama did make one point that those who would exploit Martin's death refused to accept. Said Obama, "I know that there's been commentary about the fact that the stand your ground laws in Florida were *not* used as a defense in the case." Unfortunately, Obama threw away this line, and race hustlers like Andrew Gillum felt free to ignore it.

Gillum had no more use for the facts in 2013 than he would in 2018. In Tallahassee, he seized the moment. Within two days of the

Zimmerman verdict, the city commissioner was announcing a town hall meeting to deal with fears stoked by the Zimmerman trial. "There's still a lot of unease," said Gillum at the time. "You still have a number of parents, of mothers who are saying what does this mean for my child? How does this verdict now color any future situation?" The verdict would certainly color his future.

A day after Gillum's announcement, a group of alleged student activists calling themselves the "Dream Defenders" began a sit-in at the Florida Capitol building in Tallahassee. The group had been formed in the wake of Trayvon's shooting long before the facts of the case were known. In truth, the facts were never relevant. The founding fathers of the group–Umi Selah, Ahmad Abuznaid, and Gabriel Pendas–may have left their student days behind them but not their fondness for racial agitprop.

A flattering 2016 article on Abuznaid in a publication by the Institute for Middle East Understanding (IMEU) told of how the Jerusalem-born Abuznaid was "empowering the next generation of Palestinian-American youth organizers to mobilize alongside other communities of color." The IMEU article described the Dream Defenders as a "non-profit organization that provides trainings for youth (primarily ages 13-35) around Palestine, campaign strategy, power mapping, mass incarceration, the school to prison pipeline, and more." Activists call the fusion of these movements–in this case, black and Islamic–"intersectionality," a chilling concept that inevitably works against the best interests of African Americans.

Not surprisingly, the Florida Jewish community expressed alarm at Gillum's association with Dream Defenders in general and Abuznaid in particular, given that Abuznaid, according to *Heritage: Florida Jewish News,* was "a supporter of the U.S.-designated terrorist group the Popular Front for the Liberation of Palestine (PFLP)."

In October 2018, *Heritage* took exception to Gillum's shout-out to the Dream Defenders during a primary debate. Said Gillum, "When you all slept in for 30 days on the cold, hard marble floors of the state capitol, I was pleased and proud to sneak food into you every night so you could eat." Gillum expressed solidarity with the group for "standing in the gap on behalf of marginalized communities, shaking up the political process, having politicians across this state run scared because they are afraid of your power." Gillum appreciated in particular the group's eagerness to vote for Andrew Gillum.

When I last saw Gillum on TV, he was defending the anti-Semitic Congresswoman Ilhan Omar. When I last read about him, he was boasting about his selection to the advisory board of a dark money group financed in part by George Soros and aptly titled, "The Collective." "I want to help The Collective finish this month off stronger than ever so they can invest early in the next round of progressive candidates," wrote the ever cheerful Gillum soliciting funds for his new adventure. As the field shapes up for the Democratic presidential nomination, Gillum is surely on every white candidate's short list for vice president, not because of his experience as Tallahassee mayor, but because of skin color and his willingness to exploit it. While he bides his time, Gillum works as a commentator for the allegedly "mainstream" CNN.

If the Dream Defenders were aggravating the racial divide in Florida, Black Lives Matter was causing even greater trouble nationwide. On its website, the group's radical founders traced the formation of the movement "to the acquittal of Trayvon Martin's murderer, George Zimmerman." BLM was never about racial healing. If the movement had a purpose it was to make sure blacks remained alienated from the larger culture. Says the website in its typically hyperbolic prose: "Black Lives Matter is an ideological and political intervention in a world where Black lives are systematically and intentionally targeted for demise." Its goals include "globalism," "transgenderism," "gay rights," and "black villages." This was nonsense straight out of the 1970s May 19 Communist Organization bulletins I had read in my research on Obama's Chicago friend and mentor, terrorist emeritus Bill Ayers.

Imitating the Team Trayvon public relations model, BLM took to creating racial incidents to prove the "demise" was imminent. None of its creations proved quite as catastrophic as the one spawned in Ferguson, Missouri. In August 2014 BLM activists flocked to the city soon after the shooting of "unarmed teen" Michael Brown by Ferguson Officer Darren Wilson. Relying solely on the words of Brown's partner in crime, Dorian Johnson, who insisted Brown had been trying to surrender when shot in cold blood, BLM adapted as its slogan, "Hands up, don't shoot." This rallying cry was heard around the world. In fact, no political hashtag in Twitter's history was as popular as "#Ferguson." On the scene promptly were veteran race hoax artist Al Sharpton and his new protégé Benjamin Crump. Working the successful Trayvon Hoax model, Crump told an angry crowd that the local prosecutor "has no regards for the young person of color." In this model, law enforcement never has regard for young people of color.

Six months or so after the incident, black *Washington Post* reporter Jonathan Capehart, wrote a story headlined, "'Hands up, don't shoot' was built on a lie." The lie was clear within days to anyone paying attention, but Capehart waited for the ruling by Obama's DOJ to say the obvious. In the Zimmerman case, Capehart had bought into the "bag of Skittles and iced tea" ruse, but the BLM "hands up" hoax was apparently one scam too flagrant for the high-profile columnist.

"The anti-police frenzy since the Ferguson tragedy has caused a crime disaster in the black neighborhoods of America," observed Ernest Evans, one of the few political scientists willing to speak up about the incident's aftermath. FBI statistics make Evans's case for him. From 2006 to 2014, except for one minor blip, the murder rate in the United States declined steadily year after year. After the Ferguson incident in August 2014, the murder rate shot up, the 2015 increase being the highest in a quarter century. In 2016, three thousand-plus more Americans were murdered than in 2014, the majority of them–perhaps eighteen hundred–were black.

"Cops are backing off of proactive policing in high-crime minority neighborhoods, and criminals are becoming emboldened," wrote criminologist Heather MacDonald in a September 2017 piece for *City Journal*. "Having been told incessantly by politicians, the media, and Black Lives Matter activists that they are bigoted for getting out of their cars and questioning someone loitering on a known drug corner at 2 a.m., many officers are instead just driving by." MacDonald coined the term "Ferguson effect" to describe a phenomenon that is still claiming lives in 2019.

In the years since Trayvon's death, and especially in the years since Donald Trump's election, racial hoaxes have become more common than actual hate crimes. Sanford, Florida, was something of Beta site for future hoaxes. Given the success of The Trayvon Hoax, race hustlers have been feeding on the media's eagerness to believe the worst of conservative America and now America writ large. The sheer outlandishness of the Jussie Smollett hoax in Chicago may have finally embarrassed the media into wising up, but if so, the damage has already been done.

It is not at all a stretch to think that if one of those who knew the truth had stood up before the verdict and said, "This is all a hoax," thousands of black lives might have been spared. But as history records, none of them did.

"I believe that God is using me," Sybrina says often, especially when speaking to church groups. In fact, Sybrina is being used, her grief is being exploited, but not by God. As we learn in Proverbs 6:16, "For The Lord hates a heart that devises wicked plans, a false witness who breathes out lies, and who sows discord among brothers."

It was an evil plan indeed to use a troubled black teen's tragic death to imprison an innocent Hispanic man, for no greater good than to control black voters. But this is the way the Left has sought power for a century, sowing discord among brothers. With The Trayvon Hoax, they did just that.

I know Trayvon. At heart, he was a good kid. He knew right from wrong. He never would have wanted anyone to die for a hoax in his name.

ABOUT THE AUTHOR

Joel Gilbert is a documentary film maker based in Los Angeles and President of Highway 61 Entertainment. Gilbert is also a political commentator and foreign policy analyst. He has produced documentary feature films on Barack Obama, *Dreams from My Real Father (2012)*, American politics, *There's No Place Like Utopia (2014)* and Donald Trump, *Trump The Art of the Insult (2018)*. He has also produced films on Middle East politics including *Farewell Israel (2008)* and *Atomic Jihad (2010)*. Gilbert's other films cover music icons Bob Dylan, *Inside Bob Dylan's Jesus Years (2010)* as well as comedies on Paul McCartney and Elvis Presley.

Made in the USA
Monee, IL
15 September 2019